Early Warning Mechanisms for Online Learning Behaviors Driven by Educational Big Data

The book aims to design and construct early warning mechanisms based on the dynamic temporal tracking technology for online learning behaviors, driven by educational big data.

By studying a massive amount of learning behavior instances generated in various interactive learning environments worldwide, the book explores the continuous sequences of correlated learning behaviors and characteristics. From various angles, the authors have devised a series of early warning measures that could effectively solve multiple issues in learning behaviors driven by educational big data. Additionally, the book predicts patterns and identifies risks by analyzing the temporal sequences of the entire learning process. While presenting a range of theoretical achievements and technical solutions to improve and design new online learning mode, it also provides relevant technical ideas and methodologies for research on similar problems.

The book will attract scholars and students working on learning analytics and educational big data worldwide.

Xiaona Xia is a professor and earned her PhD from Qufu Normal University. She is also a member of IEEE Computer Society and China Computer Federation (CCF). Her research interests include learning analytics, interactive learning environments, collaborative learning, educational big data, educational statistics, data mining and service computing.

Wanxue Qi is a PhD supervisor of Qufu Normal University. He is a famous education expert and has made remarkable achievements in higher education and moral education theory. His research interests include educational big data and moral education.

Early Warning Mechanisms for Online Learning Behaviors Driven by Educational Big Data

Xiaona Xia and Wanxue Qi

Routledge
Taylor & Francis Group

LONDON AND NEW YORK

This book is published with financial support from Shandong Provincial Education Summit Discipline Publishing Fund and Natural Science Foundation of Shandong Province (Grant No. ZR2023MF099)

First published 2024
by Routledge
4 Park Square, Milton Park, Abingdon, Oxon OX14 4RN

and by Routledge
605 Third Avenue, New York, NY 10158

Routledge is an imprint of the Taylor & Francis Group, an informa business

British Library Cataloguing in Publication Data
A catalogue record for this book is available from the British Library

Library of Congress Cataloging in Publication Data
Names: Xia, Xiaona, 1985– author. | Qi, Wanxue, author.
Title: Early warning mechanisms for online learning behaviors driven by educational big data / Xiaona Xia and Wanxue Qi.
Description: Abingdon, Oxon ; New York, NY : Routledge, 2024. | Includes bibliographical references and index. |
Identifiers: LCCN 2024001503 (print) | LCCN 2024001504 (ebook) | ISBN 9781032776811 (hardback) | ISBN 9781032778099 (paperback) | ISBN 9781003484905 (ebook)
Subjects: LCSH: Web-based instruction—Evaluation. | Web-based instruction—Psychological aspects. | Education—Data processing. | Big data.
Classification: LCC LB1044.87 .X53 2024 (print) | LCC LB1044.87 (ebook) | DDC 371.33/44678—dc23/eng/20240130
LC record available at https://lccn.loc.gov/2024001503
LC ebook record available at https://lccn.loc.gov/2024001504

ISBN: 978-1-032-77681-1 (hbk)
ISBN: 978-1-032-77809-9 (pbk)
ISBN: 978-1-003-48490-5 (ebk)

DOI: 10.4324/9781003484905

Typeset in Times New Roman
by codeMantra

This book is dedicated to my doctoral supervisor,
Mr. Wanxue Qi, for his detailed and careful guidance
on my academic journey.

Xiaona Xia

Contents

Figures

Tables

Acknowledgments

This book is supported by "811" Project of Shandong Province's First Class Discipline "Education", Shandong Provincial Education Summit Discipline Publishing Fund and Natural Science Foundation of Shandong Province (Grant No. ZR2023MF099).

Meanwhile, we sincerely appreciate the technical support provided by University of Oxford (UK), University of Pennsylvania (USA) and Tsinghua University (China), as well as the theoretical guidance and practical reference of University of Agder (Norway) and Qufu Normal University (China).

1 Introduction

Abstract

This chapter will briefly introduce the research significance of this book and the main work of the following chapters. The main content of this book is based on educational big data and strives to provide a series of effective early warning mechanisms based on the description and representation characteristics of online learning behaviors. The main content is divided into seven chapters that address the early warning mechanisms for different descriptions of online learning behaviors, design relevant models and methods, and use large-scale learning behavior instances for training and measurement. As a result, rule mining and decision intervention are conducted for the results of temporal sequence analysis. Numerous experiments have shown that early warning tracking and decision feedback driven by big data are feasible and reliable. This book can provide assistance in the design of early warning mechanisms for online learning processes and also compare it with similar problem research and method designs. It has strong theoretical value and practical significance.

Early warning mechanisms in online learning behaviors driven by educational big data are important mechanisms in interactive learning environments, providing crucial support for tracking learning behaviors and delivering decision feedback. This book addresses the significant drawbacks of high dropout rates and low pass rates in online learning processes. By studying a massive amount of learning behavior instances generated in various interactive learning environments worldwide, it explores the continuous sequential sequences of correlated learning behavior characteristics. From different perspectives, a series of early warning measures for online learning behaviors have been designed, effectively addressing multiple issues in educational big data-driven learning behaviors. Furthermore, the book predicts patterns and identifies risks through the analysis of temporal sequences of the whole learning process. It offers valuable guidance for the design of early warning mechanisms in interactive learning environments, presenting a range of theoretical achievements and technical solutions to improve and design new online learning mode Additionally, it provides relevant technical ideas and methodologies

DOI: 10.4324/9781003484905-1

for research on similar or related problems, demonstrating its significant theoretical value and practical significance.

The book mainly addresses the following seven key issues.

1   Multidimensional Temporal Fusion and Risk Prediction in Interactive Learning Process

This chapter will provide the feasibility and implementation methods of multidimensional time series fusion and risk prediction for online learning, as well as the importance of early warning and intervention for online learning. This is a key foundation for the work of subsequent chapters. Therefore, this chapter focuses on the significance of calculating and analyzing learner-centered data. It introduces various features in both the learning and non-learning processes and proposes a multidimensional temporal topology fusion approach for integrating multiple categories of features. The research begins by addressing the diversity of data features and the complexity of their relationships. An improved multidimensional temporal topology fusion neural network model is developed and designed accordingly. After extensive data training, the effectiveness and reliability of the model are demonstrated, showing its suitability for analyzing and correlating multiple categories of features. Furthermore, by visualizing experimental results, the study analyzes latent rules and existing issues in learning behavior across multidimensional temporal intervals. This analysis helps verify the significance and correlation of different features and relationships. Finally, we evaluate the outcomes of the data analysis and formulate a risk prediction and early warning strategy specifically tailored for the interactive learning process. The goal is to provide timely and effective interventions. Overall, this research provides valuable insights into dynamic early warning systems and decision. It is the foundation of the work in Chapter 3.

2   Learning Enthusiasm Enabled Dynamic Early Warning Sequence Model

Based on the conclusions of multidimensional temporal fusion and risk prediction in interactive learning process, the following work is to realize the tracking, prediction and decision of data-driven dynamic learning process, and improve learning enthusiasm and learning effectiveness for the application of learning analytics in interactive learning environment. This chapter integrates the learning enthusiasm in the dynamic early warning process of interactive learning. Before constructing relevant methods, we design and integrate the multi-layer Bayesian model and hidden Markov chain model, through the training and testing of massive learning data; it has been proven that the method has good robustness and reliability. With the help of learning enthusiasm enabled dynamic early warning sequence model, on the one hand, it associates, predicts and analyzes the massive data, mines the potential learning enthusiasm and laws, realizes the mapping between learning enthusiasm and the optimal early warning intervention sequence, and deduces the corresponding early warning intervention strategies. The dynamic early warning sequence model plays a good role in optimizing the learning process. It is a key business capability to achieve early warning value propagation for continuous learning behaviors. It is the foundation of the work in Chapter 4.

3   Early Warning Value Propagation Network for Continuous Learning Behaviors

Based on the conclusions of learning enthusiasm enabled dynamic early warning sequence model, the following work is to achieve the dynamic early warning value propagation. After all, the dynamic early warning propagation of interactive learning process plays an important part for improving learning behaviors, which is also the key issue to realize the relative optimal learning paths. This chapter proposes and designs a diversion inference model of learning effectiveness supported by differential evolution strategy. First, we analyze and design the definition and principle of differential evolution strategy; Second, the convolution neural network is improved and optimized based on differential evolution strategy, the multi-level inference process of convolution neural network is transformed into the task topology of learning behaviors, and the diversion inference model of learning effectiveness is realized; Third, the algorithm corresponding to the model is applied to the full training and testing of big data sets. The experimental results show that the model is reliable and feasible. Finally, based on the visualization of the experimental results, we analyze the problems and rules found in the diversion inference results and put forward the intervention measures suitable for the interactive learning environment. The whole research process of this chapter not only provides a set of feasible solutions for the dynamic early warning propagation but also demonstrates some key conclusions, which provides theoretical support and practical for early warning pivot space. It is the foundation of the work in Chapter 5.

4   Early Warning Pivot Space Model of Multi-Temporal Interactive Learning Process

Based on the conclusions of early warning value propagation network, the following work is to achieve the early warning system and realize the transformation from linear warning of learning behavior to spatial warning. The interactive learning process produces massive dynamic data and multi-complex relationships, which expands the characteristics and attributes of learning behaviors so that the research of interactive learning process needs to fully consider the dynamics, autonomy and continuity of learning behaviors, involving the correlation analysis and prediction. According to the complete pivot space theory, this chapter designs an early warning pivot space model integrating hyperplane division and spherical division, mines early warning pivots and relationships from multi-elements, constructs space topology, as well as corresponding learning rules and analysis algorithms. Fully parallel experiments show that the model is effective and reliable for multi-temporal interactive learning process, and the test conclusions are further derived. This chapter explores an early warning model of multi-element space that enriches the dimension and depth of early warning research and application in interactive learning process. It is the foundation of the work in Chapter 6.

5   Early Warning Model Design and Decision Application of Unbalanced Interactive Learning Behaviors

Based on the conclusions of Chapters 2–5, the following work is to deepen the early warning needs and decision applications brought about by imbalanced learning behavior instances. The online learning platform not only promotes the teaching objectives but also realizes the enthusiasm and autonomy of learners. However, it also breaks away from the direct supervision and tracking of instructors in the traditional classroom, so that the learning behavior presents a strong discreteness and the generated data has a strong imbalance. This chapter explores MT-BCSSCAN applied to the early warning model of unbalanced learning behavior. It divides interactive learning behavior into three types, i.e. generative, browsing, and interactive and collaboration, and introduces other online behaviors into the feature calculation, realizing unbalanced multi-source data fusion. The experimental results show that MT-BCSSCAN can effectively support the prediction of interactive learning behavior based on high performance and further draw the conclusion of relevant test problems. After fusing other online behaviors of learners, the three types of learning behavior form significant relationships, and the corresponding early warning model and decision application strategy are derived. The whole research adopts a deep learning method, creatively constructs the prediction method of massive unbalanced interactive learning behavior, realizes the fusion calculation of multi-source data and improves the quality of the early warning model; it is an important basis for implementing temporal tracking and decision intervention of unbalanced learning behaviors; it is of great significance for precipitation prediction in the early warning model, as well as the foundation of the work in Chapter 7.

6   Cost Sensitivity Analysis and Adaptive Prediction of Unbalanced Interactive Learning Behaviors

Based on the early warning model and corresponding decisions achieved in Chapter 6, the following work is to design a cost-sensitive analysis method of unbalanced interactive learning behaviors. The interactive learning behavior has obvious discreteness and autonomy, resulting in the problem of data imbalance, which poses a great obstacle to the research of interactive learning behavior; this also cannot ensure the quality and reliability of learning analytics. However, it is almost difficult to obtain balanced data from the interactive learning process, especially in the online learning environment, which brings more difficulties to the direct application of traditional learning analytics and methods. Therefore, the analysis of unbalanced interactive learning behavior cannot just rely on the existing means. It is necessary to design new applicable models and algorithms driven by data, so as to effectively reduce the interference caused by noise or outliers, and highlight the value and law contained in the data. So in this chapter, the multi-structures, multi-features and multi-relationships of interactive learning behavior are analyzed; then an unbalanced interactive learning behavior analysis strategy is designed that integrates cost-sensitive learning process and Bayesian optimal prediction theory. Through the comparison of multiple correlation methods, this novel method is suitable for the feature analysis of interactive learning behavior. The whole study realizes value mining and law tracking, and achieves the reliable classification and adaptive prediction; it also provides an effective analysis method of unbalanced interactive learning behavior; it will provide important conclusions for the work in Chapter 8.

7   Diagnostic Analysis Framework and Early Warning Mechanism of Forgettable Learning Behaviors

Based on the conclusions of Chapter 7, namely the application of the precipitation prediction model in the early warning mechanism of learning behaviors, the following work is to analyze the early warning model of forgettable learning behaviors. This chapter designs a diagnostic analysis framework for forgettable learning behaviors, constructs a set of matching data segmentation rules, and designs an adaptive data segment aggregation method. The feasibility and reliability of the technical framework are verified by sufficient comparative experiments. Furthermore, the topological relationships of forgettable learning behaviors are visually built, and the potential problems, laws and corresponding early warning strategies are discussed. The whole research process is a key attempt of applying intelligent decision technology to the diagnostic analysis of massive learning behavior, which can provide effective theoretical basis and feasible technical support for the forgettable learning behavior, and has strong practical significance. On the one hand, this chapter implements and demonstrates the feasibility of early warning for forgetting learning behaviors, and on the other hand, the early warning diagnosis framework is a comprehensive research of all the work of Chapters 2–7 mentioned above.

The main content of this book is based on educational big data and strives to provide a series of effective early warning mechanisms based on the description and representation characteristics of online learning behaviors. The main content is divided into seven chapters that address the early warning mechanisms for different descriptions of online learning behaviors, design relevant models and methods and use large-scale learning behavior instances for training and measurement. As a result, rule mining and decision intervention are conducted for the results of temporal sequence analysis. Numerous experiments have shown that early warning tracking and decision feedback driven by big data are feasible and reliable. This book can provide assistance in the design of early warning mechanisms for online learning processes, and also compare it with similar problem research and method designs. It has strong theoretical value and practical significance.

2 Multidimensional Temporal Fusion and Risk Prediction in Interactive Learning Process

Abstract

This chapter will provide the feasibility and implementation methods of multidimensional time series fusion and risk prediction for online learning, as well as the importance of early warning and intervention for online learning. This is a key foundation for the work of subsequent chapters. Therefore, this chapter focuses on the significance of calculating and analyzing learner-centered data. It introduces various features in both the learning and non-learning processes and proposes a multidimensional temporal topology fusion approach for integrating multiple categories of features. The research begins by addressing the diversity of data features and the complexity of their relationships. An improved multidimensional temporal topology fusion neural network model is developed and designed accordingly. After extensive data training, the effectiveness and reliability of the model are demonstrated, showing its suitability for analyzing and correlating multiple categories of features. Furthermore, by visualizing experimental results, the study analyzes latent rules and existing issues in learning behavior across multidimensional temporal intervals. This analysis helps verify the significance and correlation of different features and relationships. Finally, we evaluate the outcomes of the data analysis and formulate a risk prediction and early warning strategy specifically tailored for the interactive learning process. The goal is to provide timely and effective interventions. Overall, this research provides valuable insights into dynamic early warning systems and decision. It is the foundation of the work in Chapter 3.

Keywords

Multidimensional Temporal Interval; Early Warning; Fusion Neural Network Model; Interactive   Learning Environment; Learning Analytics; Risk Prediction

DOI: 10.4324/9781003484905-2

1 Introduction

Interactive learning environment collects and manages learners' data, which involves the whole process of learners' participation and other interactive activities generated around learning needs (Kabudi et al., 2021; Tuma et al., 2021). With the help of corresponding platform tools and data collection mechanism, the static data and dynamic data of interactive learning process are recorded more comprehensively (Xia, 2020a), including the relevant description attributes, such as start time, end time, participation frequency, weight and order, which have become some important factors to describe the learning behavior. Analyze these data and build a multidimensional temporal behavior in order to accurately perceive the learning state, provide key data support and process enabling, facilitate tracking and make appropriate prediction and decision (Kaplar et al., 2021; Linh & Vu, 2021).

By effectively associating the learning behavior with non-learning behavior, it can enrich the description and influencing factors, and more comprehensively understand learning, improve learning and intervention learning (López-Zambrano et al., 2021; Xia, 2021a), but the learners' other behavior will cause great interference to the analysis process. The scale of meaningless and incomplete data is large, and some data closely related to learning behavior are incomplete because of time delay or interaction interruption. This will inevitably affect the data correlation and consistency between learning process and non-learning process. In order to solve this problem, first, a feasible data processing scheme is to plan the temporal interval of the learning process and define the features of the learning behavior (Guo et al., 2021); second, according to the temporal intervals and features, other interest preferences are evaluated that may be related to learners in the learning process; a series of interaction trends of learning process or non-learning process are formed (Chaka & Nkhobo, 2021), the correlation is calculated and the applicable boundary of non-learning process is defined; third, the applicable data are mined and correlated, which runs through the whole learning process and the multi-category features; Finally, the topological relationship between non-learning process and learning process is realized, as well as the prediction of learning risk that could provide a reasonable basis for early warning and decision (Hwang et al., 2021).

This study takes the online interactive learning environment and smart campus as the data source platforms, gets learning process and non-learning process, demonstrates the multidimensional temporal topology fusion method and risk prediction strategy, designs the models and algorithms for temporal topology training and testing based on deep learning, and realizes the prediction and early warning of the learning process. Based on the analysis of the learning behavior, learning content, learners, teaching mode and learning interaction methods, the massive data will define the features of the learning process, and intercept the complete learning period, classify the assessment methods and learning results, so as to form a complete data flow of learning process. Furthermore, we evaluate the key features, and determine the effective data of non-learning processes that may affect learning behavior, so as to realize the temporal topology fusion and serve as the direct data set for the models and algorithms, then explore the effectiveness of multi-category features in multidimensional temporal topology and finally demonstrate the feasibility and accuracy of risk assessment and early warning strategy.

2   Related Work

The key technology of multidimensional temporal interval is to realize multi-source data fusion. It is necessary to comprehensively analyze the description method, process deployment, relationship characteristics and data structure of learning process, combined with learning needs and behavior preferences. It is also needed to locate as much complete relevant data as possible and realize effective integration, obtain unified multi-source data for each learner and mine more effective related features of learning process (Habib et al., 2021). Therefore, by enriching the learning process through applicable and reliable topology, the learning behavior is given more representation elements and influencing factors, more comprehensive learning interaction can be obtained, which is useful to the accurate evaluation and prediction of learning process and learning state (Xia, 2021b).

The fusion of multi-source data is a process of data recognition, correlation, use, prediction and feedback. The whole process associates many data with different structures, properties and forms, and reflects different integrity and availability, which makes it difficult to ensure the appropriate technologies and models.

According to the research sequence of corresponding references, the fusion strategy for multi-source data is mainly reflected in three aspects.

The first aspect is the direct fusion of original data. The original data is directly analyzed and the possible feature relationships are mined, in order to clean and merge the effective data. This fusion method ensures the integrity of the original data as much as possible, with less data lost, but has great constraints on the scale and complexity (Hafez et al., 2021). This method is suitable for data with the same or similar structure, nature and type. If there are large differences in data sources or large data scale, the effectiveness and accuracy of this method will be greatly reduced. The data analysis and selection will also consume a lot of computation and seriously reduce the efficiency of data training and testing (R. Yu et al., 2021).

The second aspect is model-based fusion. With the help of data standardization and cleaning model, the preprocessing of multi-source data is completed, and the intermediate features after preprocessing are obtained. Before implementing feature fusion, this method first evaluates and mines useful data, which can reduce interference data, reduce the amount of data analysis, and effectively improve the rate of feature fusion (Hameed & Stünda, 2021; Saeed et al., 2021). However, this aspect is limited to the standardization and cleaning of data. It focuses on the structure and type, and it is easy to ignore the semantics, so that the key data is regarded as noise, which will affect the accuracy and effectiveness of data analysis.

The third aspect is decision-based fusion. For different data sources, corresponding decision models are used for analysis, and fusible features and existing or potential feature relationships are found according to prediction and evaluation

(Musallam et al., 2021). This fusion effect is more practical than that of the first two aspects. The multi-decision model is used to analyze and evaluate the data, and then the prediction results are fused to realize the comprehensive decision. This method can fuse different types of data, requires less computation, and has good fault tolerance and anti-interference (Cichiwskyj et al., 2021). However, it will still cause data loss and less accuracy.

The learning process and non-learning process are particularly complex. Therefore, the most feasible data fusion strategy is to analyze the features and relationships for behavior fusion and risk prediction in multidimensional temporal topology, and then associate possible data sources to realize data mining and association (Moodi et al., 2021). In this process, it is necessary to demonstrate the needs of data fusion for the complete learning process and non-learning process. According to different sub-problems, flexibly use the above-mentioned three aspects to design efficient decision models and algorithms on the basis of ensuring accuracy and reliability. This study will define the multidimensional temporal topology between learning process and non-learning process, and design a deep neural network learning model to realize multi-category feature fusion.

3   Data Processing and Problem Description

In order to analyze the multidimensional temporal topology of learning process and non-learning process, the interactive learning process comes from one online interactive learning environment, which has been in normal operation for several years. Especially during COVID-19, the platform provides great convenience for the development of online teaching, as well as for exploring the problems existing in the online learning process. It provides massive data and continuous learning period, and produces complex learning behavior. The interactive learning environment adopts a blended mode and realizes relatively complete data through online and offline cooperation. In 2020, the online interactive learning process has been fully applied, including course selection, online listening, learning guidance and assessment. The platform has collected complete data. This study selects the learning behavior of the two periods in 2020, the whole data set includes 34,219 learners and the scale of all learning behavior is 1.34PB. Anonymous desensitization processing is completed before data analysis.

For these learners, the data corresponding to the non-learning process is mined through the smart campus. These data are also presented in the form of anonymity, with a scale of 5.47PB. Then, we realize the mapping, association and integration of learning process and non-learning process (Kew & Tasir, 2021). In order to better complete the experiment, it is defined that the data generated by the learning process is a positive sample, and the data generated by the non-learning process is a negative sample, used to demonstrate the early warning measures and risk strategy.

Table 2.1 shows the online interactive feature classification of the learning process, which is mainly divided into nine categories, including course video (CV), course page (CP), course guidance resource (CR), question (QN), answer (AN), forum exchange area (FM), download corresponding materials (DL), upload corresponding materials (UL) and other behaviors (OR). As can be seen, there is a

Table 2.1 Online Interactive Feature Classification of Learning Process

No.	Categorization Labels	Description	Scale
1	CV	Course video	3,861,003
2	CP	Course page	4,127,337
3	CR	Course guidance resource	1,930,277
4	QN	Question	798,054
5	AN	Answer	239,405
6	FM	Forum exchange area	2,370,119
7	DL	Download corresponding materials	42,106
8	UL	Upload corresponding assignments	19,311
9	OR	Other behaviors	11,044

large amount of data in CV, FM, and CR, and learners interact frequently with the platform. The data of QN and AN is different, which indicates that there are many problems that have not been answered, or the problems that have been answered continue to generate new problems. In terms of tracking the learning process, this aspect has not been well echoed and fed back.

Table 2.2 shows the online interaction feature classification of non-learning process that is mainly the statistical results of learners' behavior of smart campus network. It is mainly divided into eight categories: game (GM), shopping (SP), instant messaging (IM), entertainment (ET), common life tools (CT), information and news (IN), download some files (DL) and other behaviors (OR). Among these interactive features, IN, CT and IM are more involved, which accounts for a large proportion in the non-learning process. Learners' online participation in non-learning process far exceeds the interactive learning environment, which further shows that learners' behavior accounts for a large part of learners' online interaction.

In addition, there are other correlation features that will be related to learning process such as learners, course, teaching and learning organization. In order to improve the accuracy and reliability of the multidimensional temporal topology, and mine the effective laws of the learning process, this study introduces the key features listed in Table 2.3, directly participates in the operation with the labels of the features and deeply analyzes the interactive interest of the two periods of the learning process and non-learning process. Among the six classification features in Table 2.3, gender (GD) can divide learners into two categories. Grade (GR) is a classification of learning stages. Learners at different stages have different understanding of learning process and learning preferences. MR is a major classification for the professional trend. Many majors are divided into NS and SS. There is also a necessary correlation between PT and MR. AM is an assessment method. It is related to MR and PT, but it will be affected by the relevant features of the learning process. AR is the assessment result that is used as the observable variable in the construction of multidimensional temporal topology in the learning process.

In the processing of multidimensional temporal topology and analysis of multi-category features, the features listed in Tables 2.1–2.3 become the descriptive factors in different temporal intervals. Therefore, the two periods involved in the data set are divided into different statistical intervals. Each period includes

Table 2.2 Online Interaction Feature Classification of Non-learning Process

No.	Categorization Labels	Description	Scale
1	GM	Game	6,048,329
2	SP	Shopping	7,884,301
3	IM	Instant messaging	10,120,355
4	ET	Entertainment (Music, Film, Opera, etc.)	2,542,338
5	CT	Common life tools	12,695,077
6	IN	Information and News	13,210,325
7	DL	Download some files	994,490
8	OR	Other behaviors	411,003

Table 2.3 Other Key Features

NO.	Features	Description	Value
1	GD	Gender	(Male, Female)
2	GR	Grade	(I, II, III, IV)
3	MR	Major	(SS: Social Science, NS: Nature Science)
4	PT	Project	(Yes, No)
5	AM	Assessment mode	(CA: Computer Based, TA: Teacher Based, MA: Mixed)
6	AR	Assessment result	(Distinction, Good, Qualified, Fail, Withdrawn)

20 weeks. The restriction and association between multiple types of features are counted every week, and the topological trend of learning behavior is tracked according to the relationship indexes. Therefore, the construction of the data set is mainly divided into the following key steps:

Step 1: Take the learner list (L-List) contained in the interactive learning environment in 2020 as the retrieval clue, extract the required features and relationships of the learning process, and realize the feature classification and the correlation calculation under the condition of classification labels in Table 2.1;

Step 2: Take the learner list (L-List) as the retrieval clue, access the smart campus data, extract the features and relationships corresponding to the non-learning process, and take the classification labels in Table 2.2 as the condition to realize the feature classification and the correlation calculation;

Step 3: Take the learner list (L-List) as the retrieval clue, mine the features in Table 2.3 corresponding to learners, and realize the correlation calculation of PT and MR;

Step 4: The data obtained from Step 1, Step 2 and Step 3 are associated and merged under the condition of learner list (L-List) then to form a complete data set;

Step 5: Taking the period as the classification condition, the whole data set is divided into two parts. In each period, week and learner are used as the dual retrieval conditions to realize the association and merging of similar features then to form two standardized key data sets.

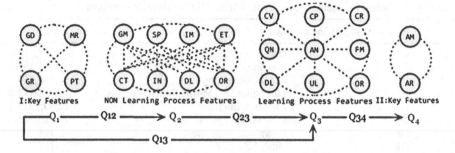

Figure 2.1 Multi-category Feature Relationship

AM and AR related to learner assessment are taken as the observable variable, and the other four key features are taken as the influencing factors. In this way, the features in Table 2.3 are divided into two groups. On this basis, the feature relationship required for multidimensional temporal topology is described in Figure 2.1, involving eight key test problems, which are mainly reflected in:

Q1: multidimensional temporal correlation of "I: key features";
Q2: multidimensional temporal correlation of non-learning process features;
Q3: multidimensional temporal correlation of learning process features;
Q4: multidimensional temporal correlation of "II: key features";
Q12: multidimensional temporal correlation of "I: key features" with non-learning process features;
Q13: multidimensional temporal correlation of "I: key features" with learning process features;
Q23: multidimensional temporal correlation of non-learning process features with learning process features;
Q34: multidimensional temporal correlation of learning process features with "II: key features";

Based on the correlation test of these eight problems, the multidimensional temporal topology is visualized to further demonstrate early warning and risk strategy.

4   Method

The multi-category feature relationship in Figure 2.1 makes the analysis and prediction no longer a single data. In this study, an improved fusion neural network based on multidimensional temporal features (iFNN) is proposed to realize the fusion analysis and correlation calculation of learning process, non-learning process and other key features. The behavior tracking in temporal intervals is applied for the prediction of learning behavior and assessment results.

iFNN is used to integrate relevant key features with learners as clues, no longer perceive learning behavior with a single learning process, but coordinate learners' generalized behavior along the learning period. In order to have a more comprehensive understanding of learning behavior, the interactive learning environment

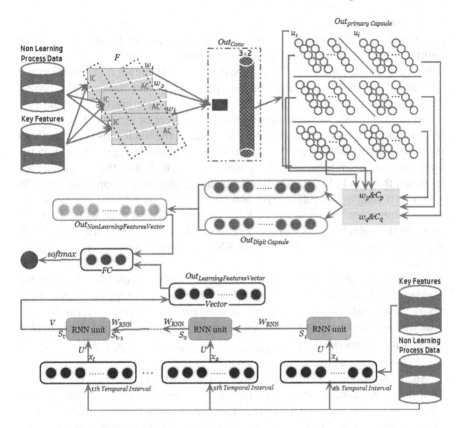

Figure 2.2 Data Analysis Process of iFNN

might make accurate prediction and fundamentally make targeted early warning and decision.

The prediction analysis of iFNN is mainly divided into three steps, as presented in Figure 2.2.

Step 1: retrieve the data set and calculate the association between learning process features and key features, so as to obtain a multi-category feature set; input the feature set into the first layer convolution network, extract low dimensional features, obtain two vectors and splice them as the input of the second layer convolution;

Step 2: retrieve the data set and calculate the correlation between the distribution of non-learning process features and key features. In this part, the decision analysis of cyclic neural network is adopted to extract the key features corresponding to temporal intervals and output a multidimensional vector;

Step 3: the output results of the first two steps are spliced and used as the unified input of a fully connected network. On this basis, the features are sufficiently trained. The final result is optimized and selected by the "SoftMax" layer so that the relatively optimal prediction result of the data is obtained.

For the fusion data of learning process and key features, in Figure 2.2, an iterative neural network training model is constructed using the feature sequence of multidimensional temporal intervals. In the training process, the state variable is introduced that can be used to ensure the historical temporal information and facilitate the correlation calculation between the previous data and the current data. The data of multiple temporal intervals jointly determine the current prediction and correlate the learning situation. x_t is the vector generated by the input layer of the tth temporal interval, S_t is the state of the hidden layer corresponding to the tth temporal interval, U is the weight matrix of the transition from the input layer to the hidden layer, W_{RNN} is the weight matrix of the current hidden layer and the next hidden layer, V is the weight matrix of the transition from the last hidden layer to the output layer and $Out_{LearningFeatures}$ is the final feature vector. In the whole iterative prediction of RNN (recurrent neural network), S_t depends on x_t and the output layer S_{t-1} of the previous hidden layer; there is a corresponding activation function f between each RNN, and the activation function of the output layer is g.

In the analysis process of each RNN, the relevant features of each temporal interval are calculated first, and then input to each RNN for prediction. Suppose the number of neurons contained in the hidden layer is m, the number of temporal intervals of RNN is defined as n and the vector dimension of the final output is $m \times n$. The calculation model can be described as $Out_{LearningFeaturesVector} = g(VS_t)$, $S_t = f(Ux_t + WS_{t-1})$, which implements an iterative calculation.

About the fusion data of non-learning process and key features, the encapsulated neural network is adopted to analyze the temporal decision. The last data processing layer is the Digital Capsule layer, that is composed of multidimensional vector neurons. The dimension means how many feature classifications the data has. The data set of this study involves four key features and eight features of non-learning process, a total of 12 features, corresponding to two 12-dimensional vectors. The maximum norm of these two vectors determines the final prediction result of non-learning process. The data analysis of encapsulated neural network can refer to our previous research results. The model might better obtain the high frequency and make effective judgment, which might help in achieving the accurate feature analysis and tracking of high frequency intervals. This study will not be introduced in detail.

The prediction vectors obtained from the learning process and non-learning process are merged and input into a fully connected neural network, in order to support the strategy of back gradient propagation and train the neural parameters. The output vector of the learning process is $Out_{LearningFeaturesVector}$, the output vector of the non-learning process is $Out_{LearningFeaturesVector}$. After splicing the two vectors to form a new vector, it receives the iterative training of the parameters of the fully connected network layer again, and the final prediction result is judged by "SoftMax". The whole prediction calculation process is relatively independent, which not only ensures that the parameters in Figure 2.2 do not participate in the weight operation but also helps realize the robustness of the training process.

5 Experiment

Based on the data set obtained in this study, sufficient experiment of iFNN is carried out, and four indexes are selected, namely Precision, Recall, F_1 Score and Accuracy. F_1 Score combines Accuracy and Recall; it is more comprehensive. Accuracy is the ratio of the correct number of samples to the total number of samples and does not distinguish between positive samples and negative samples. Accuracy is the ratio of the number of positive samples correctly predicted to the total number of positive samples, and Recall is the ratio of the number of positive samples correctly predicted to the total number of samples. These four indexes can comprehensively measure the prediction effect of learning process and non-learning process.

Since each period of the data set involves 20 weeks, in the experiment, the length of the temporal sequence is defined as 20, corresponding to 20 temporal intervals of the interactive learning environment, the number of neurons contained in the hidden layer is set as 50, the whole training process uses a single-layer RNN, the output of the fully connected network is set as a two-dimensional structure and the learning rate of the whole process is 0.0015. The positive and negative samples may be incomplete and unbalanced.

In order to better test the effectiveness and reliability of iFNN, three similar and optimal algorithms are selected for comparative experiments. (1) RNN (Recurrent Neural Network) is a part of iFNN. RNN is used as a comparison algorithm. In the algorithm design, a single-layer RNN prediction process is adopted to analyze all data. Similarly, the output of the prediction process adopts the fully connected network. The algorithm mainly tests the non-learning process; (2) LST-DNN (Long and Short Term Temporal Patterns with Deep Neural Networks) is a long- and short-term prediction algorithm based on deep neural networks. Because the algorithm mainly analyzes the feature labels, when designing the algorithm, the features with different labels are spliced with temporal sequences to form a two-dimensional matrix that is used as the input data. The algorithm uses eight convolution kernels. In the prediction process, the step of temporal sequence is set to seven. The algorithm is mainly used to test non-learning process; (3) LST-TPA (Long and Short Term Temporal Patterns with Temporal Pattern Attention) is consistent with the input data of RNN and is used to obtain implicit states in different temporal intervals. Convolution is realized with the help of CNN (Convolutional Neural Network). The dimension of convolution kernel is consistent with that of hidden layer, and the convolution results are weighted and summed. The features obtained at the end of training are fused with the implicit state, and then the linear transformation is performed to determine the optimal prediction. The algorithm mainly tests the learning process. In the process of algorithm design, this study verifies the indexes of some machine learning algorithms (such as logistic regression algorithm, K-neighbor algorithm, support vector machine and decision tree), and the experimental results are very unsatisfactory. Therefore, it is considered to introduce the fusion idea of deep learning model to support the prediction. Some machine learning algorithms are no longer used for comparison.

After sufficient experiments, the prediction indexes of different algorithms are obtained, as shown in Table 2.4. Since Accuracy, Recall and F_1 Score are the

Table 2.4 Indexes of Comparison Algorithms

Algorithm	Positive Sample			Negative Sample			Accuracy
	Precision	Recall	F_1 Score	Precision	Recall	F_1 Score	
RNN	0.403	0.354	0.377	0.891	0.902	0.896	0.885
LST-DNN	0.512	0.466	0.488	0.887	0.895	0.891	0.863
LST-TPA	0.720	0.592	0.650	0.914	0.929	0.921	0.908
iFNN	0.877	0.705	0.782	0.933	0.954	0.943	0.922

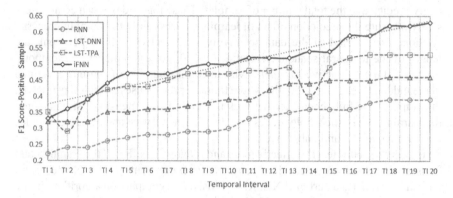

Figure 2.3 F_1 Score of Positive Samples in Temporal Intervals in the First Period

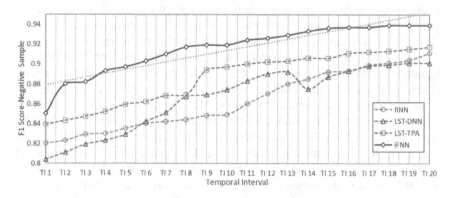

Figure 2.4 F_1 Score of Negative Samples in Temporal Intervals in the First Period

indexes to evaluate positive samples and negative samples, learning process and non-learning process are divided in the analysis. It can be seen from Table 2.4 that the indexes of iFNN are the best, especially in terms of Accuracy.

On this basis, all algorithms are applied to the prediction and evaluation of the temporal intervals. Since this data set involves two periods, positive samples and negative samples are classified for each period to form two data subsets. Each period is divided into 20 temporal intervals. F_1 Score realizes more comprehensive data test of positive samples and negative samples. After sufficient data training, the calculation results of F_1 Score are shown in Figures 2.3–2.6.

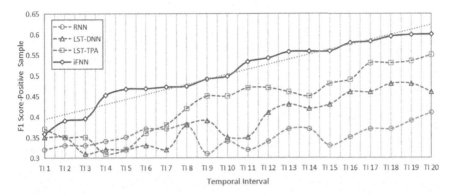

Figure 2.5 F_1 Score of Positive Samples in Temporal Intervals in the Second Period

Figures 2.3 and 2.4 show the F_1 Score distribution for positive samples and negative samples in different temporal intervals in the first period, respectively. As can be seen from Figure 2.3, the range of F_1 Score is (0.2, 0.65), and LST-TPA shows a large decline in the second and the fourteenth interval, which is directly related to the change of feature participation in the learning process, indicating that the algorithm is easy to be affected by data changes and has general stability. The F_1 Score by the other three algorithms shows a fluctuating upward in different temporal intervals. With the increase of temporal intervals and the amount of data analysis, the F_1 Score of iFNN basically rises steadily, and is higher than the other three comparison algorithms. As can be seen from Figure 2.4, the range of F_1 Score is (0.8, 0.94). The F_1 Score of negative samples predicted by the four algorithms is large. Compared with the other three comparison algorithms, the prediction results of iFNN are more reliable and stable.

Figures 2.5 and 2.6 show the F_1 Score distribution for positive samples and negative samples in different temporal intervals in the second period, respectively. From the comparison between Figures 2.5 and 2.3, Figures 2.6 and 2.4, it can be seen that the F_1 Score of the temporal intervals in the second period is slightly higher than that in the first period, which is directly related to the more diversified behavior features and high participation in the learning process. As can be seen from Figure 2.5, the range of F_1 Score is (0.3, 0.65), RNN, LST-DNN and LST-TPA have very significant fluctuations in the whole temporal intervals, and the instability of prediction results is obvious. With the increase of temporal intervals and the amount of data analysis, F_1 Score of iFNN is basically in a steady upward trend, which is higher than the other three comparison algorithms. As can be seen from Figure 2.6, the range of F_1 Score is (0.81, 0.96). Similarly, in terms of the stability and reliability of the prediction results, the distribution topology of F_1 Score obtained by iFNN tends to be more stable, and the performance and function of the algorithm are relatively optimal.

Through iterative training, testing and verification of multiple dimensions of the data set, iFNN is suitable for temporal interval analysis of multi-category features and has good performance. iFNN fully considers the key feature traction of learning interaction environment, integrates learning process and non-learning process,

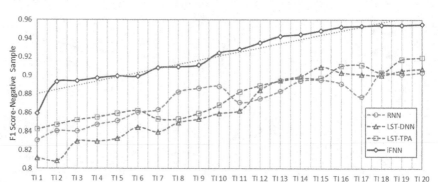

Figure 2.6 F_1 Score of Negative Samples in Temporal Intervals in the Second Period

and obtains reliable data analysis results. It is useful for multidimensional temporal topology fusion and risk prediction.

6 Result

According to the analysis results of iFNN on learners' multi-category features, taking the period assessment results as the observable variable, the temporal interval correlation is analyzed for the multi-category features of the two periods, and the eight problems Q1, Q2, Q3, Q4, Q12, Q13, Q23 and Q24 proposed in the third part are demonstrated. After a lot of iterative feature calculation, the correlation between different features related to these eight problems is obtained, and the topology of strong correlation ($|r| > 0.8$) is visualized. The whole visualization process is divided into two steps. The first step is to mine all the data corresponding to the multi-category features in Figure 2.1 to obtain the key path. The second step is to calculate the key features and correlation of 20 temporal intervals in two periods and construct the topology with strong correlation.

After visualizing the data analysis results in the first step, Figure 2.7 is obtained. As can be seen, the topology realized by correlation is divided into two obvious key paths; there are some similarities and differences between learners of Natural Science and Social Science in learning process and non-learning process.

1 I: key features. The strong feature correlation occurs in grade II and grade III. Among the learners majoring in Natural Science, the participation of male learners is significant, while the learning behavior of female learners majoring in Social Science is more significant.
2 Non-learning process features. SP, IM, IN and DL all have strong correlation, indicating that learners' participation in these four aspects tends to be very concentrated after class. At the same time, Natural Science learners have a strong trend in GM, while Social Science learners prefer ET. Therefore, there are significant differences in amateur interests between Natural Science and Social Science learners, which is also directly related to the whole learners who have

interest preferences. There are more boys in Natural Science and more girls in Social Science.

3 Learning process features. Learners participate in CV, CP, CR and FM. On the one hand, these features reflect the resources related to learning content such as videos and resources. On the other hand, FM has a high participation, which reflects a strong demand for interaction and cooperation. In this regard, there are also differences between Natural Science and Social Science. The former downloads data (DL) from interactive learning environment, while the latter is that learners tend to upload data (UL) for the platform, which is directly related to teaching requirements.

4 II: key features. As can be seen from Figure 2.7, the assessment methods of Natural Science learners are mainly MA and CA, and the computer-based approach has become an important part of the assessment. The Social Science learners adopt the teacher-based assessment (TA) that inherits the traditional methods. Therefore, the Natural Science is more conducive to automatic evaluation strategy.

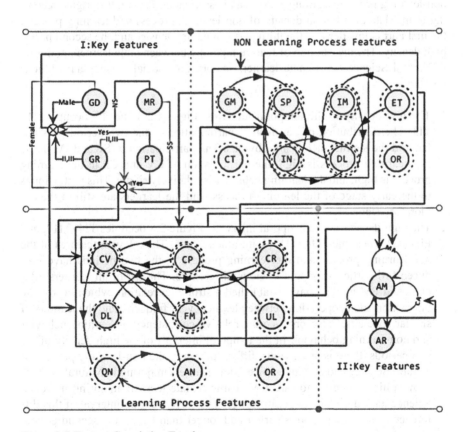

Figure 2.7 Feature Correlation Topology

Data analysis shows that the unification of learning process and non-learning process has strong correlation, and a fused topology is formed between the features.

According to the comprehensive analysis of the complete data in the first step, we locate the key features, deploy them in the whole learning process and train and analyze the feature correlation of each temporal interval. In the experiment, the male learners of Natural Science and female learners of Social Science in grades II and III in Figure 2.4 are taken as the experimental objects, and the feature correlation of multidimensional temporal intervals is calculated. The full data training shows that learners' interest trends in learning process and non-learning process are similar, and the strong correlation between different features occurs in the same or adjacent temporal intervals; the group of multidimensional temporal intervals in different periods remains relatively consistent, which is of great significance. Further, the results are visualized, and the topological fusion of multi-category features is obtained, as shown in Figures 2.8 and 2.9.

The features of Figures 2.7–2.9 are divided into three layers from top to bottom: non-learning process, learning process and assessment. From left to right, according to the data distribution density of non-learning process and learning process, the first part is low density, the third part is medium density and the second part is high density. The distribution of feature topology between male learners majoring in Natural Science and female learners majoring in Social Science has obvious regularity.

1 The low density in the temporal intervals: Figures 2.8 and 2.9 occupy TI1–TI3. The distribution of key feature participation in the two periods is similar, and the significance is not obvious. The participation of SP and IM in the non-learning process is high, the participation of CV and CP in the learning process is high, and the learning behavior is relatively single. This part belongs to the early stage of the learning process, and the learners are still in the exploratory stage.

2 The high density in the temporal intervals: Figure 2.8 occupies TI4–TI17, and Figure 2.9 occupies TI4–TI15, with a large span. The relevant features of the non-learning process and the learning process in the two periods have produced full participation and obvious differences. The IM of all learners after class and FM in class have established a strong correlation, which makes the interaction and cooperation between learners very frequent, and the learners of similar specialties also produce the relative consistency of learning behavior and non-learning behavior. In the temporal intervals of the high density of the two periods, there is an obvious differentiation in the non-learning process of Natural Science and Social Science. Male learners majoring in Natural Science show a high tendency toward GM, while female learners majoring in Social Science have a high enthusiasm for ET. The early warning interval of this difference in the first period is earlier and longer than that in the second period.

In the first period, the peak data is generated in the process of TI7–TI12, and in the second period, the peak data appears in TI8–TI11, learners' interaction, attention and participation last longer, and the impact weight is greater. At the same time, in the later stage, the learners majoring in Natural Science pay strong attention to the computer-based assessment and promote the learners' participation.

3 The medium density in the temporal intervals: Figure 2.8 occupies TI18–T20, and Figure 2.9 occupies TI16–T20. CA still gets the attention of Natural Science learners. In the process of participation, it drives learners to interact and cooperate with FM and IM. MA has also attracted Natural Science learners in this part. For Social Science learners, there is a strong correlation between CR and DL, but TA does not achieve advanced training and preparation.

The decision of the temporal intervals of two periods obtains the lower bound of the early warning, which is marked by the vertical bracket line of each temporal interval in Figures 2.8 and 2.9. For the first period, the lower bounds of early warning are TI4, TI7 and TI16, respectively; for the second period, the lower bounds of early warning are TI4, TI8, TI13 and TI17, respectively. CA enables the change of learning behavior.

In order to more clearly reflect the relevant features with different assessment results in the whole period, the learner's grade is taken as the observable variable to realize the feature mapping of learning process and non-learning process. Because there are few learners in "withdraw", there is no statistical significance. In a certain achievement level, the proportion of learners with high participation of a certain feature in all learners is a statistical index. For a feature, if a learner's participation is higher than the median of all learners' participation, then the learner's participation is higher. Through empirical experimental analysis and data statistics, the final results are obtained. Figure 2.10 shows the calculation from two different majors in two periods.

As can be seen from the four subgraphs in Figure 2.10, in different periods, learners of Natural Science and Social Science have similar distribution of broken lines in the proportion of key feature participation, but the feature participation of learners who pass the assessment (distinction, good, qualified) in the second period is closer, and the broken lines are more consistent. The learners who pass the assessment have controllable participation in games and entertainment and have higher enthusiasm in interaction and cooperation among learners. The learners who do not pass the assessment have high participation in GM and ET. Learners who fail the assessment in Social Science in the first period are more than that in the second semester. The data significance of non-learning process is more prominent, and their participation in interaction and cooperation, learning materials and tasks is relatively negative and universal. It shows that learners in the second period have stronger adaptability to the online interactive learning environment and have some teaching supervision, tracking, intervention and feedback to optimize the learning effect.

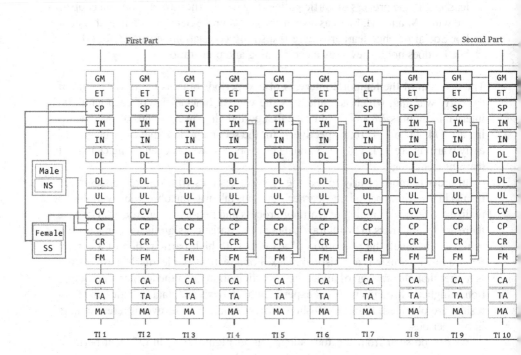

Figure 2.8 First Period: Topological Fusion of Features in Multidimensional Temporal Intervals

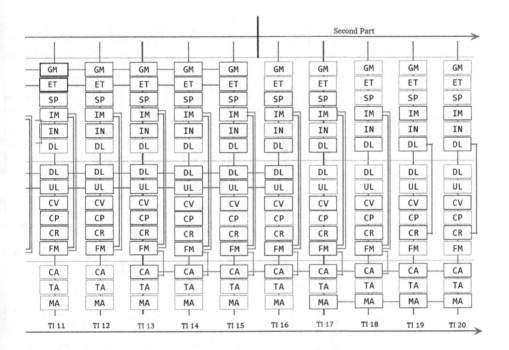

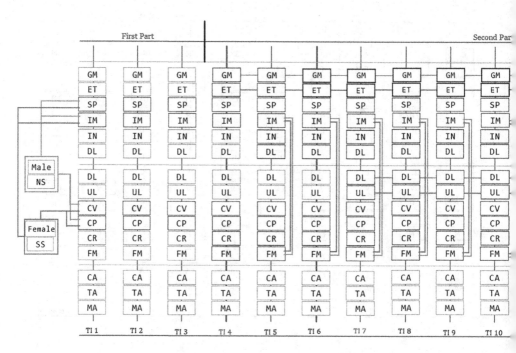

Figure 2.9 Second Period: Topological Fusion of Features in Multidimensional Temporal Intervals

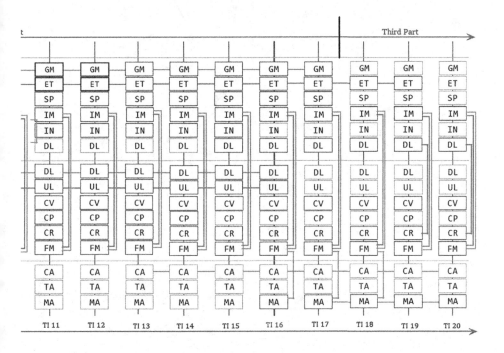

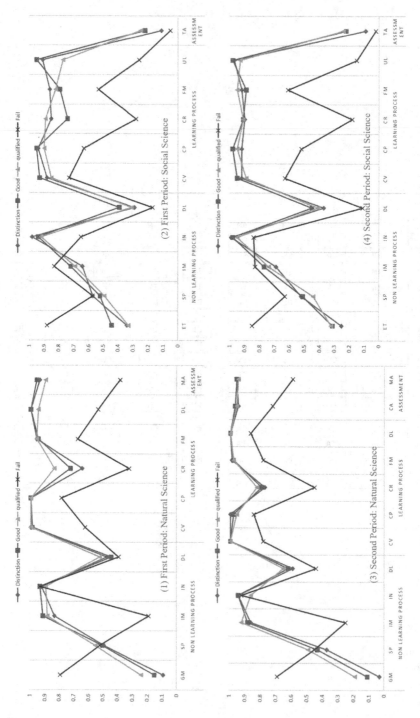

Figure 2.10 Proportion of Feature Participation Corresponding to Different Assessment Results

7 Discussion

Based on the massive data of the whole period, the multidimensional temporal topology fusion of interactive learning process is realized, and the experimental results are visualized and analyzed. Further, the learner behavior and participation process of interactive learning environment are summarized, mainly focusing on the multi-category features and risk prediction strategy.

7.1 Characteristics of Multidimensional Temporal Topology

Combined with the data analysis of learners in interactive learning environment and smart campus, it can be seen that the multi-category features have the following characteristics:

1 For non-learning process and learning process, learners of non-similar major have differences in interest preferences.

In this study, the majors of interactive learning environment are divided into two categories, i.e. Natural Science and Social Science. Through the fusion analysis of non-learning process and learning process, it can be seen that there are differences in learners' interest preference. For non-learning process, Natural Science learners pay more attention to games, while Social Science learners prefer various forms of entertainment. For the learning process, Natural Science learners cooperate and interact more frequently and submit a large amount of data to the platform; Social Science learners tend to obtain relevant resources.

2 For non-learning process and learning process, learners of similar majors have strong similarities in interest preferences.

It can be seen from Figure 2.7 that learners belonging to Natural Science or Social Science have similarity of the online participation process. There is a large overlap in interaction and cooperation, learning resources, assessment methods, etc. It shows that the learning process is affected by teaching methods, learning methods and learning contents. Learners form a more concentrated group after participating in each category features.

3 For non-learning process and learning process, learners of non-similar majors have some similarities in interest preferences.

About the multi-category features of non-learning process and learning process, learners of non-similar major also have certain similarities. The need for skill improvement, knowledge mastery and learning for application has made learners to have a strong cognition and formed a subtle influence and action. The similar features are mainly reflected in interaction, cooperation, leisure, training, auxiliary materials, relevant information and so on, which bring learners a strong participation.

4 For non-learning process and learning process, there are differences in learners' participation in the whole continuous temporal intervals.

As can be seen from Figures 2.8 and 2.9, learners' participation is different in the continuous temporal intervals composed of 20 weeks. According to the participation density, Figure 2.8 is divided into three parts and Figure 2.9 is divided into four parts, the participation density of the second part is the largest, the first part is the smallest and the third or fourth part is mainly driven by the assessment method. The participation of Natural Science learners has a moderate density. Therefore, the relatively early warning can be mined in the continuous temporal intervals, so as to enable learners' benign learning behavior and improve learning efficiency with the relatively optimal temporal node.

5   Assessment methods affect learners' participation in the learning process.

In Figure 2.8, the Natural Science majors introduce MA based on computer and teachers, which makes the later stage with continuous temporal intervals have a large amount of participation. In Figure 2.9, some Natural Science majors implement CA, which makes learners participate in assessment training earlier, resulting in a large degree of participation. The participation of online assessment also encourages the interaction and cooperation among learners and improves the participation of relevant features. Social Science learners mainly use the assessment method organized by teachers. Learners' participation is low, and there is no obvious participation significance around the assessment method.

6   The interaction and cooperation in non-learning process and learning process affect learners' participation.

Instant messaging in non-learning process and forum communication in learning process provide convenience for learners' cooperation and communication, and realize strong relevance. The active participation of such features also enables learners to participate in other features. The experiment shows that the full use of such features makes learners realize effective correlation across feature categories in non-learning process, learning process and assessment, and strengthens learners' interaction and cooperation.

7   There are some similarities in learners' interest preferences of the same kind of assessment results.

According to the four subgraphs in Figure 2.10, whether Natural Science or Social Science, the learners who pass the assessment and those who fail the assessment are similar in terms of key feature indexes, and the distribution of broken lines is consistent. In the second period, after taking certain intervention, this similarity is more significant. In addition, the non-effective learning features of learners who fail the assessment have high participation.

1   There is a strong correlation between the features of non-learning process and learning process.

The data analysis shows that the non-learning process can affect the learning process, and the learning process can also affect the non-learning process. In the second, third and fourth parts of Figures 2.8 and 2.9, IM of the non-learning process has a strong correlation with FM of the learning process, and FM has a strong correlation with the assessment method. This is a key conclusion to realize the early warning nodes and intervention strategy.

7.2 Risk Prediction Strategy

Based on the analysis of multidimensional temporal topology and combined with the behavior features of learners, the corresponding risk prediction strategy is proposed for the interactive learning process.

1 Build a timely early warning nodes for the interactive learning process.

A large number of data analysis shows that the temporary intervals is generally no more than the quarter of the learning period, which is of great significance for non-learning process and learning process. The middle of the learning period is generally located in the temporal intervals between the quarter and median, the median and the third quarter of the learning period; in these intervals, learners' participation in non-learning process and learning process is the largest. Learners' interaction and cooperation are generally carried out, the real-time tracking, mining and intervention of conditions and problems are very important. In the later stage, generally no later than the three-quarters of the temporal intervals, learners enter the preparation stage of learning assessment, track and adjust learning behavior and non-learning behavior, which helps to deepen the learning content. Therefore, in the whole interactive learning process, it is an effective measure for risk prediction to construct temporal early warning nodes with the boundaries of quarter, median and third quarter.

2 Build an interactive and cooperative teaching model.

Building effective interaction and cooperation among learners is very important to improve the efficiency of learning process and benign participation in non-learning process, and also the quality of learning (Steger & Kizilhan, 2021). Data analysis shows that in the learning process, matching the application of projects, whether Natural Science or Social Science, learners' interaction and cooperation are significant, and large-scale participation data will also be generated. While participating in the projects, it also drives the participation of other features. However, QA is not ideal; there are many questions and less answers, and the problem-solving is delayed; QA does not keep pace, which is unfavorable for interactive cooperation. Interactive learning environment should improve timely responsiveness in QA.

3 Build an applicable online assessment method.

The data analysis of this study shows that TA has not attracted the learners. Social Science generally adopts this traditional assessment method without computer. This is also an assessment method widely known to learners, but it is unfavorable to the collection of complete data. Therefore, setting applicable online assessment methods for different learning contents is a key business of interactive learning environment and will also provide more comprehensive and complete data for multi-category feature analysis.

4 Build the data fusion mechanism of non-learning process, learning process and other key features.

The current interactive learning environment is needed to achieve a complete learning process. The non-learning process is completed through many other platforms. Different platforms have different data structures and relationships, and the form of data is discrete (Chi, 2021). However, the data of non-learning process and learning process are all about the description of learners' behavior, and learners' behavior will be affected by some other static data (such as key features) to a certain extent. It is not feasible to generate and manage all learners' data through one platform, but it can take learners as the object and build the fusion mechanism of key data on different platforms to realize data tracking, mining, desensitization and calculation. This requires permissions, protocols and standard support for multi-platforms (Xia, 2020b).

5   Build a data-driven decision rule base.

Based on the data fusion mechanism of (4), it is needed to timely predict, warn and intervene the problems. Therefore, for some common problems and risks, the interactive learning environment should have certain applicable decision rules to realize independent and intelligent guidance, recommendation and prevention. The interactive learning environment generates data, which in turn will tune the potential behavior. In this process, it is necessary to build an intelligent decision rule base (Papa Dimitropoulos et al., 2021), realize knowledge mining and decision learning according to the problems and provide effective measures.

8   Conclusion

The main purpose of interactive learning process is to realize the construction of benign learning behavior, enable learners' enthusiasm and interest (S. J. Yu et al., 2021) and assess learning effect through applicable assessment methods. In this process, learning behavior is not the only behavior of learners (Jovanovi et al., 2021). Interactive learning process is constrained not only by the methods and resources but also by other static and dynamic features of non-learning process.

In this study, the behavior of learners in non-learning process and learning process is introduced, and the multidimensional temporal topology fusion of multi-category features is proposed. Therefore, we mine the massive data of interactive learning environment and smart campus, and design feasible methods. About the diversity of features and the complexity of relationships, an improved multidimensional temporal topology fusion neural network model is modeled and designed. After sufficient model training, experimental verification and parameter analysis, it is proved that the method is effective and reliable, and is suitable for multidimensional feature analysis and process tracking in multidimensional temporal intervals. Further, we visualize the experimental analysis results, demonstrate the significance and relevance of multi-category features, optimize learning process and formulate learners' risk prediction and early warning strategy.

The whole work of this study can provide a basis for intelligent early warning and decision of interactive learning environment (Blau & Shamir-Inbal, 2021). Relevant models and methods can be applied to empirical analysis and comparative test of approximate problems.

In the follow-up research, we will deepen the multidimensional temporal topology fusion scheme of interactive learning process, improve the strength and accuracy of early warning and intervention, and design the learning enthusiasm enabled dynamic early warning sequence model, in order to deepen the multidimensional temporal fusion and risk prediction in the interactive learning process.

References

Blau, I., & Shamir-Inbal, T. (2021). Writing private and shared annotations and lurking in Annoto hyper-video in academia: insights from learning analytics, content analysis, and interviews with lecturers and students. *Educational Technology Research and Development*. 69(2), 763–786. https://doi.org/10.1007/s11423-021-09984-5

Chaka, C., & Nkhobo, T. I. (2021). The use of a virtual personal assistant (FENNChat) as a platform for providing automated responses to ODL students' queries at UNISA. *Interactive Mobile Communication, Technologies and Learning. IMCL 2019*. Advances in Intelligent Systems and Computing, 1192. Springer, Cham. https://doi.org/10.1007/978-3-030-49932-7_28

Chi, M. (2021). Translating a theory of active learning: an attempt to close the research-practice gap in education. *Topics in Cognitive Science*. 13(3), 441–463. https://doi.org/10.1111/tops.12539

Cichiwskyj, C., Schmeier, S., Qian, C., Einhaus, L., Ringhofer, C., & Schiele, G. (2021). Elastic AI: system support for adaptive machine learning in pervasive computing systems. *Transactions on Pervasive Computing and Interaction*. 1–29. https://doi.org/10.1007/s42486-021-00070-6

Guo, W., Lei, Q., Song, Y., & Lyu, X. (2021). A learning interactive genetic algorithm based on edge selection encoding for assembly job shop scheduling problem. *Computers & Industrial Engineering*. 159(11–12), 107455. https://doi.org/10.1016/j.cie.2021.107455

Habib, M. N., Jamal, W., Khalil, U., & Khan, Z. (2021). Transforming universities in interactive digital platform: case of city university of science and information technology. *Education and Information Technologies*. 26(1), 517–541. https://doi.org/10.1007/s10639-020-10237-w

Hafez, R. M., Zaky, M. A., & Hendy, A. (2021). A novel spectral Galerkin/Petrov-Galerkin algorithm for the multi-dimensional space-time fractional advection-diffusion–reaction equations with nonsmooth solutions. *Mathematics and Computers in Simulation*. 190, 678–690. https://doi.org/10.1016/j.matcom.2021.06.004

Hameed, J. S., & Stünda, B. B. (2021). Hybrid intelligent technology for plant health using the fusion of evolutionary optimization and deep neural networks. *Expert Systems*. (2). https://doi.org/10.1111/exsy.12756

Hwang, G. J., Wang, S. Y., & Lai, C. L. (2021). Effects of a social regulation-based online learning framework on students' learning achievements and behaviors in mathematics. *Computers & Education*. 160(6), 104031. https://doi.org/10.1016/j.compedu.2020.104031

Jovanovi, J., Saqr, M., Joksimovi, S., & Gaevi, D. (2021). Students matter the most in learning analytics: the effects of internal and instructional conditions in predicting academic success. *Computers & Education*. 172(1), 104251. https://doi.org/10.1016/j.compedu.2021.104251.

Kabudi, T., Pappas, I., & Olsen, D. H. (2021). AI-enabled adaptive learning systems: a systematic mapping of the literature. *Computers and Education: Artificial Intelligence*. 2, 100017. https://doi.org/10.1016/j.caeai.2021.100017

Kaplar, M., Radovi, S., Veljkovi, K., Simi-Muller, K., & Mari, M. (2021). The influence of interactive learning materials on solving tasks that require different types of mathematical reasoning. *International Journal of Science and Mathematics Education*. https://doi.org/10.1007/s10763-021-10151-8

Kew, S. N., & Tasir, Z. (2021). Learning analytics in online learning environment: a systematic review on the focuses and the types of student-related analytics data. *Technology, Knowledge and Learning*. (3), 1–23. https://doi.org/10.1007/s10758-021-09541-2

Linh, V. T., & Vu, N. N. (2021). The impact of mobile learning on EFL students' learning behaviors and perceptions: from content delivery to blended interaction. *International Research in Higher Education*. 5(4), 25. https://doi.org/10.5430/irhe.v5n4p25

López-Zambrano, J., Lara, J. A., & Romero, C. (2021). Improving the portability of predicting students' performance models by using ontologies. *Journal of Computing in Higher Education*. https://doi.org/10.1007/s12528-021-09273-3

Moodi, M., Ghazvini, M., & Moodi, H. (2021). A hybrid intelligent approach to detect android botnet using smart self-adaptive learning-based PSO-SVM. *Knowledge-Based Systems*. 222(11). https://doi.org/10.1016/j.knosys.2021.106988

Musallam, Y. K., Al Fa Ssam, N. I., Muhammad, G., Amin, S. U., & Algabri, M. (2021). Electroencephalography-based motor imagery classification using temporal convolutional network fusion. *Biomedical Signal Processing and Control*. 69(December 1), 102826. https://doi.org/10.1016/j.bspc.2021.102826

Papa Dimitropoulos, N., Dalacosta, K., & Pavlatou, E. A. (2021). Teaching chemistry with Arduino experiments in a mixed virtual-physical learning environment. *Journal of Science Education and Technology*. 1–17. https://doi.org/10.1007/s10956-020-09899-5

Saeed, F., Khan, M. A., Sharif, M., Mittal, M., Goyal, L. M., & Roy, S. (2021). Deep neural network features fusion and selection based on PLS regression with an application for crops diseases classification. *Applied Soft Computing*. https://doi.org/10.1016/j.asoc.2021.107164

Steger, F., & Kizilhan, J. I. (2021). Usable and useful help in literature database search? A pedagogical implementation and the evaluation of an interactive screencast for Iraqi university students. *Technology, Knowledge and Learning*. https://doi.org/10.1007/s10758-021-09523-4

Tuma, F., Malgor, R. D., & Nassar, A. K. (2021). Actions to enhance interactive learning in surgery. *Annals of Medicine and Surgery*. 64, 102256. https://doi.org/10.1016/j.amsu.2021.102256

Xia, X. (2020a). Random field design and collaborative inference strategy for learning interaction activities. *Interactive Learning Environments*. Advance online publication 30 Dec 2020. 1–25. https://doi.org/10.1080/10494820.2020.1863236

Xia, X. (2020b). Learning behavior mining and decision recommendation based on association rules in interactive learning environment. *Interactive Learning Environments*. Advance online publication 4 Aug 2020. 1–16. https://doi.org/10. 1080/10494820.2020.1799028

Xia, X. (2021a). Decision application mechanism of regression analysis of multi-category learning behaviors in interactive learning environment. *Interactive Learning Environments*. Advance online publication 23 Apr 2021. 1–14. https://doi.org/10.1080/10494820.2021.1916767

Xia, X. (2021b). Interaction recognition and intervention based on context feature fusion of learning behaviors in interactive learning environments. *Interactive Learning Environments*. Advance online publication 17 Jan 2021. 1–19. https://doi.org/10.1080/10494820.2021.1871632

Yu, R., Ye, D., Wang, Z., Zhang, B., & Kurdahi, F. (2021). CFFNN: cross feature fusion neural network for collaborative filtering. *IEEE Transactions on Knowledge and Data Engineering.* 14(8), 1–13. https://doi.org/10.1109/TKDE.2020.3048788

Yu, S. J., Hsueh, Y.-L., Sun, J. C.-Y., & Liu, H. Z. (2021). Developing an intelligent virtual reality interactive system based on the ADDIE model for learning pour-over coffee brewing. *Computers and Education: Artificial Intelligence.* 2, 100030. https://doi.org/10.1016/j.caeai.2021.100030

3 Learning Enthusiasm Enabled Dynamic Early Warning Sequence Model

Abstract

Based on the conclusions of multidimensional temporal fusion and risk prediction in interactive learning process, the following work is to realize the tracking, prediction and decision of data-driven dynamic learning process, and improve learning enthusiasm and learning effectiveness; it is a key problem for the application of learning analytics in interactive learning environment. This chapter integrates the learning enthusiasm in the dynamic early warning process of interactive learning. Before constructing relevant methods, we design and integrate the multi-layer Bayesian model and hidden Markov chain model. Through the training and testing of massive learning data, it is proved that the method has good robustness and reliability. With the help of the learning enthusiasm enabled dynamic early warning sequence model, on the one hand, it associates, predicts and analyzes the massive data, mines the potential learning enthusiasm and laws, realizes the mapping between learning enthusiasm and the optimal early warning intervention sequence and deduces the corresponding early warning intervention strategies. The dynamic early warning sequence model plays a good role in optimizing the learning process. It is a key business capability to achieve the early warning value propagation for continuous learning behaviors, as well as the foundation for Chapter 4.

Keywords

Learning Enthusiasm; Dynamic Early Warning Sequence; Hidden Markov Chain; Bayesian Model; Learning Analytics; Interactive Learning Environment

1 Introduction

Online technology, database technology, sharing technology and computing technology have fully been implemented, which has greatly improved the business function and performance of the interactive learning environment, improved the learning process and behavior mode, generated new requirements and produced a large data set of learning behavior (R. S. Baker et al., 2021; Yang & Valcke,

DOI: 10.4324/9781003484905-3

2021). This learning mode breaks the shackles of time and space, realizes the full application of technology and media and brings great advantages in the personalization, autonomy and portability of learning behavior (Xia, 2021a). However, the application of technology also brings some problems. After all, the learning process is a complex topology (Lu et al., 2021) such as the interference of invalid or useless learning behavior data, the asymmetry and heterogeneity of data and the lack or inefficiency of data-driven precision teaching mechanism (Lazarides et al., 2021; Xia, 2020a). These problems make it difficult to highlight the key data value. Many micro-relationships and implicit data have not been effectively mined, accurately predicted and analyzed.

During COVID-19, the online interactive learning environment has become an important platform for the global teaching and learning process. Learners at different stages participate in the learning process through online technology, and complete the interaction and cooperation among learners, learning content and instructors. The whole learning process involves a complete learning period. From the beginning to the end of the period, learners' online behavior (including learning behavior) is in continuous change, reflecting certain negativity, enthusiasm, initiative and passivity, which has become a data-driven learner behavior trend. How to capture this change in time and make timely emergency response and decision feedback to track and the learning situation (Kaeophanuek & Chookerd, 2021). Therefore, it is needed to design the dynamic early warning and decision prediction; it is one key problem to realize the robustness and effectiveness of interactive learning process (Turcotte et al., 2021).

Based on the massive data generated by the interactive learning environment, this study designs the dynamic early warning sequence model (DEWSM) enabled by learning enthusiasm, and analyzes the feasibility and reliability of dynamic early warning. First, the feature topics and the explicit or implicit feature relationships are fully analyzed, the description features and interest trend are demonstrated, and the correlation of the dynamic early warning sequence is designed. Second, according to the decision and prediction requirements of the learning process, a multi-layer Bayesian decision mechanism is designed to optimize the hidden Markov chain, then realize effective fusion, used to support the learning enthusiasm classification and early warning sequence tracing. On the basis of testing the classification effect and early warning indicators, the optimal analysis results of the interactive learning process are derived. Third, according to the classification of different learning enthusiasm, the dynamic early warning points and intervention strategies are mapped. This research is a hot issue in the interactive learning environment from the perspective of educational big data. It aims to achieve data-driven decision and feedback. It is the innovation and application of learning analytics and is used to improve the accuracy, reliability and completeness of experimental schemes and conclusions.

2   Related Work

The dynamic early warning enabled by learning enthusiasm is a data-driven learning analytics. Relevant research results have been produced in theory, technology, practice and application (Henriksen et al., 2021; Licciardello et al., 2021). From the perspective of big data, the high integration requirements for interactivity, collaboration, sharing, real-time, adaptability and decision determine the complexity and heterogeneity, which poses a great obstacle to the application of few decision models and intelligent algorithms, resulting in inefficient or even useless data analysis (Fan et al., 2021). Based on some relevant references (Aguilar et al., 2021; Akçapınar et al., 2019; Krner et al., 2021), the application of learning analytics to dynamic early warning of interactive learning environment mainly has the following problems:

1　Related learning analytics is relatively simple, which is not conducive to the training and testing of massive data;
2　There are few complete and practical empirical research methods with great limitations;
3　The decision prediction model is mainly applicable to the analysis of static variables, and the systematic study of behavior sequences and temporal relationships is still in the exploratory stage.
4　There are few achievements on implicit variables, relationships and related influencing factors in the learning process, and the potential knowledge has not been fully studied, such as learning enthusiasm, emotions, interests and preferences, which will also implicitly affect learning behavior and learning effect, in the same time, bring potential risks.

About the problems existing in learning analytics about dynamic early warning, this study puts forward the learning behavior mining based on learning enthusiasm classification, introduces multi-layer Bayesian decision mechanism and improves the trend prediction effect of hidden Markov chain model, so as to realize dynamic early warning of learning process. For the decision learning, two problems need to be solved: one is that the model needs to have strong robustness, can realize relatively complete reasoning and adaptively select and calculate the prior knowledge and current observations between different sequences; second, we need to be able to sensitively perceive and feed back the changes, and accurately obtain the data change characteristics. Bayesian decision mechanism and hidden Markov chain model have been partially applied in decision (Bertolini et al., 2021; Tsiakmaki et al., 2021) and proved to be feasible. It is worth in-depth analysis and redesign.

1　Related work on Bayesian model
　　Bayesian model is based on probability theory and graph theory. It is an effective model to realize the uncertain cognition and reasoning of knowledge system. It can better support the fusion of prior knowledge and current observations, realize the association analysis of knowledge and complete the mining and retrieval of relevant rules. However, the data analysis process of the model is a NP problem. There are many restrictions and constraints in related applications, and it is very difficult to apply it in specific fields. According to the practical problems, the Bayesian model is improved and redesigned to improve

the applicability and reliability, and expand the breadth and depth of model application. However, the learning enthusiasm based on Bayesian model has not been actively and effectively analyzed and demonstrated.

2 Related work on Hidden Markov chain model

Hidden Markov chain model can better mine and show the change law of unstable temporal sequences. When the implicit temporal sequences are in the same state, an independent and verifiable sequence with the same distribution characteristics, namely stationary sequences, can be generated. When the implied temporal sequences change, the testable sequences will also transfer from one stable model to another. In this way, during model training, the testable unstable sequence is in the process of adaptive transformation of multiple heterogeneous stationary models, and this transformation satisfies Markov property. In order to record the transformation between various stationary models, this transformation process is usually described as an implicit stationary model. Hidden Markov chain model is a framework for describing unstable sequences by stationary sequences. Sequence classification is realized through the conversion between models. The basic mechanism is Bayesian decision, so as to construct the relationships between observation variables and category variables and judge the category of observation variables based on maximizing a posteriori probability. Due to the dynamics and complexity of the multidimensional observation variables and their relationships, although the hidden Markov chain model has a certain theoretical and technical basis, the analysis of the learning process has strict requirements, which cannot ensure that the key observation variables can be fully correlated and predicted.

Based on the massive data generated in the interactive learning environment, this study aims to realize the DEWSM, realize the elastic classification of learning enthusiasm, drive the improvement and integration of Bayesian model and hidden Markov chain model, timely mine the risk learners and risk learning behavior and implement active intervention and decision strategies, in order to reduce the bad learning effect, improve learners' satisfaction and interest, and realize the full utilization of relevant resources and businesses.

3   Data Processing and Problem Description

The data set comes from the online interactive learning environment of an adult education. The learning resources are mainly video, and the instructors participate in the guidance adaptively. Relevant learners have a certain academic level, and the learning goal is to pass the assessment in order to obtain high-level academic certification. On this basis, learners can achieve a certain degree or skill level of further study and specialization. The interactive learning environment records the data of multiple years, involving learners' basic data (such as demographic information), learning process (such as interactive activity records), learning assessment methods and assessment results. The data of seven majors in four semesters are extracted. The data scale is massive, reaching 1.7PB, 32,593 learners. The analysis of the whole data takes learner as the clue to realize the splicing and correlation, classify and analyze learning enthusiasm from five topics, i.e. basic educational level, interactive activities, learning duration, assessment method and assessment grade, and explore the laws and key features of dynamic early warning sequence in the complete learning process.

The distribution of basic educational level is shown in Figure 3.1, which is mainly divided into five categories: (1) "No Formal quals" means that learners have not obtained any education certification; (2) "Lower Than A Level" means that the educational level of learners is low, which usually means that they have not obtained a bachelor's degree; (3) "A Level or Equivalent" means that the learner has obtained the academic certification equivalent to undergraduate; (4) "HE Qualification" means ordinary bachelor degree; and (5) "Post Graduate Qualification" means graduate qualification. About the seven majors, the academic qualifications of learners are mainly distributed in two categories (2) and (3). For the five majors M2, M3, M4, M5 and M6, many learners' academic qualifications are in category (4). For categories (1) and (5), the minimum educational level and the highest education level, learners account for a very small number.

The learning process has different constituent features in different majors, and there are great differences. These features are the media of the interaction process between learners and the platform, which we define as interactive activities. It is directly related to the learning content and skill needs, and the semesters arranged by different majors are also different, but the features of the same major in different semesters are basically the same. The online learning behavior features and participation scale of the seven majors are shown in Figure 3.2. There are significant differences in interactive activities between the two semesters of M1; the "content" of M2 in the fourth semester is great compared with the other three semesters, but

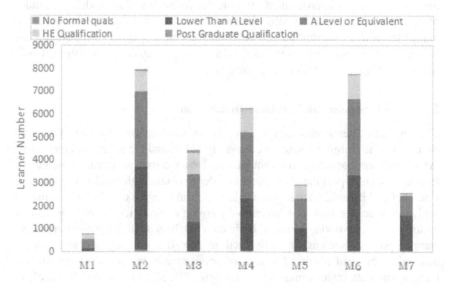

Figure 3.1 Basic Educational Level

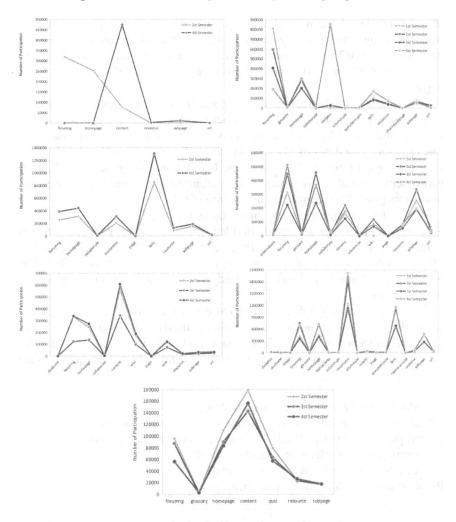

Figure 3.2 Constituent Features and Distribution of Online Learning Behavior

the "forumng" is the lowest. According to the statistical analysis, the tendency of interactive activities of the same major is basically the same.

Learning duration data comes from the log management of learning interactive environment, which mainly records the log data of three dimensions: major, interactive activities and learners. After data cleaning and classified statistics, the duration of interactive activities is M7>M5>M6>M2>M7>M1. There are differences in online participation among different majors, and M7's interactive learning process obtains the strongest adaptability and participation; about the participation duration of interactive activities, the distribution proportion of interactive duration of different majors is similar to that in Figure 3.1; there is an approximate trend between participation and learning duration. The duration of each learner's participation in each interactive activity is recorded, but mining each learner's whole online learning time length has no statistical significance. It is necessary to combine the behavior changes and assessment grades to realize the correlation test. In general, most learners of M7, M5, M6 and M2 have relatively high participation, while the enthusiasm of M7 and M1 is general; also the learners of M1 show a relatively negative attitude.

Assessment methods are mainly divided into three types: Computer Assessment (CA), Teacher Assessment (TA) or computer & teacher assessment (CTA). The assessment methods for different semesters of each major are shown in Table 3.1. The assessment methods of M1, M2, M3 and M7 are relatively fixed. M2 adopts CTA assessment mode in four semesters; M4, M5 and M6 practice CTA in the earlier semester and CA is generally adopted in the later semester. Learners and instructors generally enhanced the acceptance of CA.

As for the assessment grades, taking 60 as the qualification line, the assessment results of learners are mainly divided into four grades: withdraw (not participating in the assessment), Fail ($0<$, <60), Pass ($70<$, <85) and Distinction ($85\leqslant$, <100). At the end of one learning period, after assessment, each learner will have the assessment level. This study takes the assessment results as the target variable.

First, according to the data and distribution of these five topics, the dynamic early warning sequence enabled by learning enthusiasm is divided into six key questions, as shown in Figure 3.3; second, classify learning enthusiasm and construct the topology of dynamic early warning sequence. The six key questions are as follows:

R1: educational level affects learning duration;
R2: educational level affects the participation of interactive activities;
R3: the participation of interactive activities affects learning duration;
R4: learning process affects assessment method;
R5: learning process affects assessment grade;
R6: assessment method affects assessment grade.

Table 3.1 Assessment Method

Major	Semester	Assessment	Major	Semester	Assessment
M1	2nd	TA	M4	4th	CA
	4th	TA	M5	2nd	CTA
M2	1st	CTA		3rd	CA
	2nd	CTA		4th	CA
	3rd	CTA	M6	1st	CTA
	4th	CTA		2nd	CA
M3	3rd	TA		3rd	CA
	4th	TA		4th	CA
M4	1st	CTA	M7	2nd	TA
	2nd	CTA		3rd	TA
	3rd	CA		4th	TA

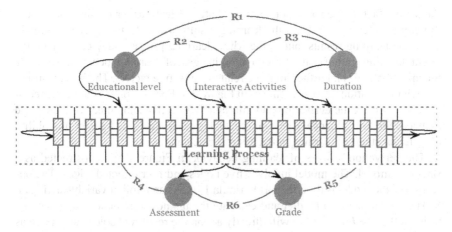

Figure 3.3 Association of Five Topics in the Learning Process

4   Method

The mining of learning enthusiasm and the realization of dynamic early warning need to carry out in-depth data analysis and decision prediction (R. Baker et al., 2021). Therefore, the Bayesian model is extended to become an iterative reasoning structure of multi-level correlation topology, realize feature learning and reasoning at different levels, and fit the likelihood function at different layers of the model. On this basis, the Logistic Growth process of hidden Markov chain is improved. Since the observation variables are presented as a discrete dynamic sequence, which will affect the prediction quality of the whole model, the optimization methods of parameter estimation and model evaluation are designed to predict the regression hidden variables, deal with the autonomous and changeable behavior changes, and realize the DEWSM.

4.1   Multi-layer Bayesian Network Model

The basic data structure of Bayesian network model includes Structure Diagram and Conditional Probability Table. The Structure Diagram is a directed acyclic graph. Nodes represent observation variables, directed arcs represent the relationship between nodes and acyclic indicates that there is no case in the graph where a node can point to itself through other nodes. The directed edge represents the relationship strength between two associated nodes that are expressed by conditional probability. For nodes without parent nodes in the graph, a priori probability is used to describe their distribution. Such nodes can be continuous variables or boolean variables.

For the analysis of learning enthusiasm, we need to consider the general features of learners' participation in the learning process. Learners' behavior is influenced by both objective factors and subjective factors. Objective factors are variables directly observed and can be used for reasoning and calculation such as not actively participating in interaction and cooperation and not fully consulting resources.

Subjective factors are some potential attributes or features, or conditions that are difficult to infer directly from the learning results. These factors may not directly affect the learning results, but in the whole learning process, they can reflect different learning enthusiasm through the changes of learning behavior (Blau & Shamir-Inbal, 2021). Further infer the related subjective factors. The basic learning behavior derivation process is shown in Figure 3.4. For the continuous sequence of learning process, the derivation and mining of subjective and objective factors are realized, and the influence of relevant factors is calculated. The transfer probability of different states of learning enthusiasm is calculated.

The derivation process of learning behavior in Figure 3.4 is constructed as a Bayesian model. The model involves five nodes and four directed edges. The operation of the model is described as Formula 1; ILS is an implicit variable acting on S. The model needs to predict and evaluate the unknown influence variables; the fitting influence I of S and O will directly act on the result variable C and serve as the potential influence variables of subjective factor S.

$$P(ILS,\ C \mid S,O,I) = \frac{P(ILS,C,S,O,I)}{P(S,O,I)}$$

$$= \frac{P(ILS)P(S \mid ILS)P(O)P(I \mid S,O)P(C \mid I)}{\int P(ILS)P(S \mid ILS)P(O)P(I \mid S,O)P(C \mid I)\,dILSdc}$$

$$= \frac{P(ILS)P(S \mid ILS)P(I \mid S,O)P(C \mid I)}{P(S)P(I \mid S,O)} = P(ILS \mid S)P(C \mid I) \quad \text{(Formula 1)}$$

$$argmax\ P(ILS,C \mid S,O) = argmax\ P(ILS \mid S)P(C \mid S,O) \quad \text{(Formula 2)}$$

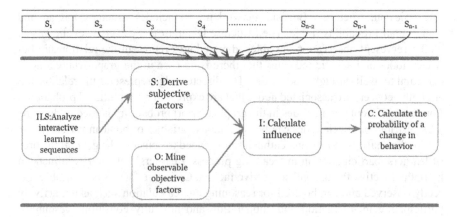

Figure 3.4 Derivation Process of Learning Behavior

In the analysis process of interactive learning process, if S and O can be observed, the observation result is the direct influence variable of C, then the derived model can obtain the composite likelihood function, expressed as Formula 2. The conditional distribution of ILS and C can be obtained by fitting two simple conditional distributions. The first conditional distribution is described as the state sequence of hidden Markov chain, and the second is designed as a regression function. Through the calculation of these two conditions, the fusion of estimation process and regression analysis is realized, and the influence of regression hidden variables is optimized.

4.2 Improved Hidden Markov Chain Model

The hidden Markov model (HMM) is used to count the change law of signal. The model includes two random processes: one process can be observed, namely the Markov process, and the relevant state sequence is a measurable. The state of the measurable sequence at each temporal point is a random variable. Another process cannot be observed. The state sequence corresponding to this process is a hidden sequence that comes from learners' subjective factors.

Assuming $ILS = \left(ILS_1, ILS_2, \cdots, ILS_k\right)^T$ is the sequence of learning process features, $C\left(ILS_i\right)$ represents the response variables on ILS_i; the Logistic Growth model is described as Formula 3:

$$\frac{\log P(Z=1|O,S)}{P(Z=0|O,S)} = O^T\beta + ST(S) \qquad \text{(Formula 3)}.$$

$S = \left(ST\left(ILS_1\right), ST\left(ILS_2\right), \cdots, ST\left(ILS_k\right)\right)'$ represents the sequence effect, $ST(S)$ is the unknown sequence state of S, which needs to be estimated with the help of the observation sequence. $S \sim HMM(\lambda)$ is the Logistic Growth model of HMM, $\lambda = (A, B, \pi)$, A is the state transfer matrix, B is the observation transfer matrix, π is the state initial probability, $C \in \{0,1\}$ is the response variable, $O = \left(O_1, O_2, \cdots O_d\right)^T \in R^d$ represents the d-dimensional covariate, $\beta = \left(\beta_1, \beta_2, \cdots, \beta_d\right)^T$ represents the d-dimensional regression vector.

The HMM is introduced into the Bayesian network model, and Formula 2 is expanded to obtain Formula 4,

$$P\left(C_t|O,S_t\right) = \frac{\exp\left(O^T\beta + ST(S_t)\right)}{1 + \exp\left(O^T\beta + ST(S_t)\right)} \qquad \text{(Formula 4)}$$

The process regression model of HMM is described as Formula 5,

$$\text{argmax} P\big(ILS, C \mid O, S\big) = \text{argmax} \; \frac{\exp\big(O^T \beta + ST(S_t)\big)}{1 + \exp\big(O^T \beta + ST(S_t)\big)} \qquad \text{(Formula 5)}$$

$$\prod P\big(ILS_t \mid ILS_{t-1}\big) P\big(S_t \mid \lambda\big)$$

The log likelihood function of Formula 5 is expressed as Formula 6, $L(\beta, \lambda) = \log\big(P(\beta)\big) + \log(\lambda)$ (Formula 6), $\beta = \big(\beta_0, \beta_1, \beta_2, \cdots, \beta_p\big)^T$ is a covariate estimation parameter.

4.3   Algorithm Design

Formula 6 includes two related but not independent iterative processes, and the simple least square method cannot be adopted. Here, a two-step method is adopted for decision estimation, which is described as Algorithm 1.

Algorithm 1

PROCESS

Step 1: Estimate λ according to HMM, output $\prod P\big(ILS_t \mid ILS_{t-1}\big)$ and $ST(S_t)$;

Step 2: Bring the calculation result of $ST(S_t)$ into Formula 4;
Step 3: Estimate β by the maximum likelihood method;
Step 4: if (Formula 6 does not get the maximum value)
　　　　Then Iteration Step 1 and Step 2
　　　　Else Break

Refinement Algorithm 1 applies the models of 3.1 and 3.2 to the analysis and prediction of learning process sequences, which is described as Algorithm 2.

Algorithm 2

Input: Interactive learning measurable sequence $S = \big(S_1, S_2, \cdots, S_T\big)$;

Output: $\lambda = \big(A, B, \pi, \beta\big)$, that might maximize $P\big(ILS, C \mid O, S\big)$;

PROCESS

Step 1:　During the iteration of Step 1 and Step 2 of Algorithm 1, the current parameter estimation obtained in step μ is $\lambda^\mu = \big(A^\mu, B^\mu, \pi^\mu, \beta^\mu\big)$;
Step 2:　Calculate the likelihood expectation of the whole hidden Markov process. The calculation formula is described as $L\big(\beta^\mu, \lambda^\mu\big) = \log\big(P\big(\beta^\mu \mid ST(S)\big)\big) + \log\big(ST(S) \mid \lambda^\mu\big) // \lambda^\mu$ is the parameter to be evaluated;

Step 3: The Logistic Growth regression parameters are calculated by maximum likelihood estimation, and the calculation formula is described as

$$Q_l = \prod_{i=1}^{n} \left\{ Pr\left(C_i = 1 \mid O_i^T \beta^\mu + ST^\mu \left(S_i \right) \right) \right\}^{C_i}$$

$$\left\{ 1 - Pr\left(C_i = 1 \mid O_i^T \beta^\mu + ST^\mu \left(S_i \right) \right) \right\}^{1-C_i};$$

Step 4: Fitting with HMM to obtain log likelihood, it is expressed as $Q = \log\left(P\left(S_i, ILS_i^\mu \right) \right) + \log\left(Q_l \right)$;

Step 5: Take Q_l into Q, and derivative $P\left(ILB_0 \mid \lambda^\mu \right) Q$ to get $P\left(ILS_0 \mid \lambda^\mu \right) = P\left(ILS_0 \mid \lambda^\mu, S \right)$;

Step 6: Realize the estimation that makes Q reach the maximum, $P\left(ILS_t \mid \lambda^\mu \right) = P\left(ILS_t \mid \lambda^\mu, S \right)$;

Step 7: Calculate $A\left(ILS_{t-1}^\mu = ST_k, ILS_t^\mu = ST_l \mid \lambda^\mu \right)$ and $B_{ILS_T}\left(Y_t \mid \lambda^\mu \right)$, respectively, the new parameter estimation that ensures that Q reaches maximum. The relevant calculation process is: $P\left(ILS_0 \mid \lambda^\mu \right) = P\left(ILS_0 = ST_k \mid S, \lambda^\mu \right)$;

$$A\left(ILS_{t-1}^\mu = ST_k, ILS_t^\mu = ST_l \mid \lambda^\mu \right) = \frac{\sum_{t=0}^{T-1} P\left(ILS_{T-1}^\mu = ST_k, ILS_t^\mu = ST_l \mid S, \lambda^\mu \right)}{\sum_{t=0}^{T-1} P\left(ILS_t^\mu = ST_l \mid S, \lambda^\mu \right)}, 1 \le k, l \le k$$

$$B_{ILS_T}\left(Y_t \mid \lambda^\mu \right) = \frac{\sum_{t=0}^{T} I\left(S_t \right) P\left(ILS_t^\mu = ST_l \mid S, \lambda^\mu \right)}{\sum_{t=0}^{T} P\left(ILS_t^\mu = ST_l \mid S, \lambda^\mu \right)};$$

Step 8: Derivative β and obtain $\beta^\mu = \beta^{\mu-1} +$

$$\alpha \sum_{i=1}^{n} O_i \left(C_i - P\left(C_i = 1 \mid O, \beta^{\mu-1}, ST\left(S_i \right) \right) \right);$$

Step 9: The K-fold cross validation method is used to select the number of states of the process sequence, $D = -2 \sum_{i=1}^{n} \sum_{t=1}^{T} \log\left(P\left(C_{it} = c_{it} \right) \right) / / c_{it}$ is the current state;

Step 10: The whole evaluation and prediction process obtains an estimated value of K test errors, $D_1, D_2, \cdots, D_K$, average these values, $\frac{1}{K} \sum_{i=1}^{K} D_i$, the results of K-fold cross validation are obtained.

The temporal sequence analysis of the DEWSM is the decision and prediction process realized by Algorithms 1 and 2.

5   Experiment

In this part, we fully analyze the data set of interactive learning environment, demonstrate the supporting basis of six key problems and draw the conclusion.

The DEWSM is used to deeply explore the data containing five topics. In order to fully test the effectiveness and reliability of the model, this study improves the RFM (Recency-Frequency-Monetary) model to better describe learning enthusiasm. The traditional RFM model includes three elements: recency, frequency and monetary. Based on the five topics of the learning process, the three themes in Figure 3.3, "Educational Level", "Interactive activities" and "Learning Duration" are taken as the three elements of RFM, respectively; then an RFM is applied to the analysis of the learning process, namely LP-RFM. The experiment is divided into two dimensions and implements three kinds of clustering strategies. Horizontally: (1) taking the median, upper quartile and lower quartile as the boundary, we implemented LP-RFM oriented hierarchical clustering; (2) LP-RFM oriented K-means clustering, K is set 6; (3) Penalty clustering. In the maximum likelihood solution of the clustering process, the penalty function $h_\lambda(\Theta)$ is subtracted, Θ is the penalty parameter that screens the variables of the clustering process again and directly eliminates the redundant variables that do not produce significance. Vertically, three aspects of the learning process are tested: (1) disordered sequence prediction of the learning process; (2) ordered sequence prediction based on traditional Markov chain; and (3) ordered sequence prediction based on DEWSM. The accuracy is used as the evaluation standard. After sufficient experiments, the prediction accuracy results of two dimensions and nine combination conditions are obtained, as shown in Table 3.2.

It can be seen from Table 3.2, horizontally, that the results of LP-RFM oriented hierarchical clustering and LP-RFM oriented K-means clustering are similar, and there is no significant difference. The penalty clustering can improve the prediction accuracy, which shows that the abnormal data generated in the learning process will have a significant impact on the clustering effect. The use of penalty term can reduce the interference of abnormal data and balance the clustering process, which

Table 3.2 Prediction Accuracy of Two Dimensions (Accuracy ± Standard Deviation)

Method Sequence	Disordered Sequence	Ordered Sequence Based on Traditional Markov Chain	Ordered Sequence Based on DEWSM
LP-RFM oriented hierarchical clustering	53.65%±0.015	62.44%±0.041	**69.72%±0.037**
LP-RFM oriented K-means clustering	55.09%±0.058	61.05%±0.049	**71.29%±0.025**
Penalty clustering	**68.80%±0.033**	**75.48%±0.060**	**89.42%±0.022**

Note: The standard deviation is 80% of 100 repeated samples and calculated by bootstrap iteration. The bold values represent the optimal results.

Table 3.3 Test Results of Six Key Problems

Key Problems	P Value	Condition
R1	0.0021**	<lower quartile: Temporal Sequences
R2	0.0047**	<upper quartile: Temporal Sequences
R3	0.0463*	lower quartile<, <upper quartile: Temporal Sequences
R4	0.0490*	<median: Temporal Sequences
R5	0.0004***	lower quartile<, <upper quartile: Temporal Sequences
R6	0.0069**	M1,M2,M3,M4: Major; 1st, 3rd: Semester

Note: $*P<0.05$; $**P<0.01$; $***P<0.001$.

is significant in tracking the related features of five topics. Vertically, compared with disordered sequence clustering and ordered sequence clustering based on traditional Markov chain, the prediction accuracy of ordered sequence clustering based on DEWSM has been significantly improved, the fitting of temporal sequences has been realized, different states of learning process are classified, the prediction results might be optimized and smoothed, and the online interaction trend and preference of learners is tracked on time; this is helpful for the accurate prediction of learning effect.

According to the analysis results of the temporal sequences of DEWSM, the correlation is calculated for the relevant features of the five topics. After sufficient experiments, the significance of the six key problems is shown in Table 3.3.

R1: in the temporal sequences less than the lower quartile, educational level will significantly affect learning duration;

R2: in the temporal sequences less than the upper quartile, educational level will significantly affect the participation of interactive activities;

R3: in the temporal sequences between the lower quartile and the upper quartile, the participation of interactive activities will significantly affect learning duration;

R4: in the temporal sequences less than the median, learning process will significantly affect assessment method.

R5: in the temporal sequences between the lower quartile and the upper quartile, learning process will significantly affect assessment grade;

R6: the impact of assessment method on assessment grade is mainly affected by major and semester, but not by other topic features.

It can be seen from Table 3.3 that these six key problems can show different significance under specific constraints, $P<0.05$, $P<0.01$ and $P<0.001$, respectively. With the change of temporal sequences, the correlation between relevant features fluctuates. The test results of the whole period prove that there is no significance, but under constraints, such as few temporal sequences or majors, there can be significance between topics. The learning needs of different sequences will also enable different learning enthusiasm. The test results of the six key problems can not only provide a basis for the change law of learning enthusiasm but also provide a feasible dynamic early warning sequence for the classification of learning enthusiasm.

6   Result

DEWSM makes the correlation and participation of the constituent features form different learning enthusiasm. The learning process sequence realizes the transfer of learning enthusiasm states by hidden Markov chain, including the learning behavior features corresponding to each sequence. Throughout the entire learning process, learning behavior has a certain degree of group nature; we used computer programs to track and analyze learners' participation, forming corresponding routing curves. The distribution of the curves showed different approximate changes, and combined with some theories of learning motivation, by predicting and analyzing the learning process sequences, we divided learning enthusiasm into six types. Following the whole learning process, the different trends of the six types of learning enthusiasm are visualized, as shown in Figure 3.5.

LE1: "Growth" learning enthusiasm. With the advancement of the learning process, learners' enthusiasm generally shows an upward trend;

LE2: "Attenuation" learning enthusiasm. With the advancement of the learning process, learners' enthusiasm generally decreases;

LE3: "Convex" learning enthusiasm. Learning enthusiasm presents two opposite situations in the whole learning process, falling in the middle and early stages and rising in the middle and late stages.

LE4: "Fluctuation" learning enthusiasm. Learning enthusiasm shows an alternating trend of rising and falling from time to time in the whole learning process;

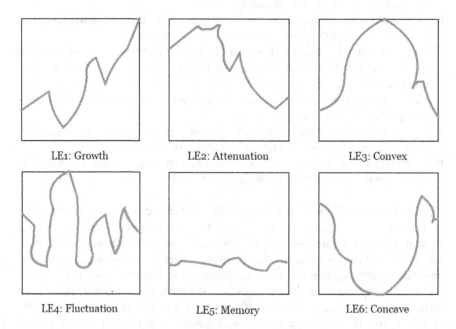

| LE1: Growth | LE2: Attenuation | LE3: Convex |
| LE4: Fluctuation | LE5: Memory | LE6: Concave |

Figure 3.5 Six Types of Learning Enthusiasm

LE5: "Memory" learning enthusiasm, which is relatively stable in the whole learning process; it is a relatively stable participation;

LE6: "Concave" learning enthusiasm. Learning enthusiasm shows a downward trend in the middle and early stages, and an upward trend in the middle and late stages.

There are differences in the distribution of these six types of learning enthusiasm of seven majors. Considering the distribution of different majors and the processing of penalty mechanism, learners' enthusiasm is described as three frequencies: Positive, General and Negative. The average observation value Q is used as the monitor, which is used as the median to form a continuous interval. When the participation of learners is higher than the upper quartile of the interval, it is a Positive state, when the participation of learners is lower than the lower quartile of the interval, it is a Negative state and when the participation of learners is between the lower quartile and the upper quartile, it is a General state.

The transfer between the three frequencies is shown in Figure 3.6. With the help of certain incentive measures, intervention mechanism or subjective initiative, the transfer or maintenance between different frequencies is realized. These three frequencies are also the state of learning enthusiasm at a certain time. Combined with the three frequencies, each type of learning enthusiasm has three states. In the training of DEWSM, clusters with the three states are generated. Each sequence of the learning process is composed of the hidden Markov chains of these three states, tracks the whole data and constructs the hidden Markov chain transfer matrix of six learning enthusiasm and three states, as shown in Table 3.4.

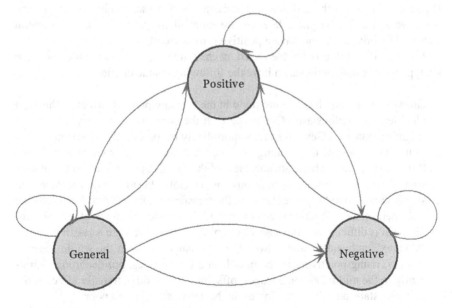

Figure 3.6 Three Frequencies of Learning Enthusiasm

Table 3.4 Hidden Markov Chain Transfer Matrix of Learning Enthusiasm

	LE1(Number: 5024)			LE2(Number: 6052)		
	<LQ	[LQ, UQ]	>UQ	<LQ	[LQ, UQ]	>UQ
1	12.4%	52.7%	35.9%	93.4%	5.2%	1.4%
2	27.3%	40.3%	32.4%	26.2%	71.8%	2.0%
3	9.9%	29.8%	60.3%	5.5%	13.1%	81.4%
	LE3(Number: 6733)			LE4(Number: 1386)		
	<LQ	[LQ, UQ]	>UQ	<LQ	[LQ, UQ]	>UQ
1	75.9%	24.0%	1.1%	60.9%	30.1%	9.0%
2	19.8%	77.5%	2.7%	25.5%	50.2%	24.3%
3	13.2%	36.4%	50.4%	33.0%	28.7%	38.3%
	LE5(Number: 5469)			LE6(Number: 7929)		
	<LQ	[LQ, UQ]	>UQ	<LQ	[LQ, UQ]	>UQ
1	63.6%	35.2%	1.2%	74.6%	17.4%	8.0%
2	3.3%	62.2%	34.5%	6.6%	59.1%	34.3%
3	0.9%	39.7%	59.4%	11.1%	23.7%	65.2%

Note: LQ, Lower Quartile; UQ, Upper Quartile.

Table 3.4 lists the possibility of mutual transfer among the three states of learning enthusiasm. Whether it is Negative or Positive, there is a relatively high transfer probability for General state, and the transfer possibility from Positive state to Negative state is generally small. It is more likely to maintain the original state. However, the "Growth" learning enthusiasm has a certain ability to absorb the Negative state. The Negative learners are more likely to transfer to the General state and Positive state and have a positive growth trend.

From the distribution of hidden Markov chain transfer matrix in Table 3.4, these six types of learning enthusiasm have the following characteristics:

1 Growth enthusiasm has a rising trend in the learning process, which is the most ideal learning enthusiasm. Compared with the other five types, whether it is a Negative state or a General state, it more likely becomes a Positive state.
2 In the early stage of the learning process, "Attenuation" enthusiasm is in a high Positive state, but with the advancement of the learning process, it shows a downward trend. The frequency of enthusiasm is General or Positive. Many learners will slowly change into Negative state, and the transfer probability from Negative state or General state to Positive state is very low. The positive transfer of learners' enthusiasm is difficult, and the absorptive ability of Negative state is relatively poor.
3 "Convex" enthusiasm shows two obvious change trends in the whole learning process, rising positively in the middle and early stages, but declining significantly in the middle and late stages, offsetting the positive transfer effect of the previous state, and the attraction of the Negative state is also poor.
4 "Fluctuation" enthusiasm fluctuates repeatedly in the learning process. The learning process or learners' subjective consciousness fluctuates obviously, and

the instability is very strong. Learners may have strong emotion, or the teaching methods are changeable frequently. There are fewer learners of this type.

5 "Memory" enthusiasm maintains strong stability and certainty in the learning process. Whether it is Negative, General or Positive, it is more likely to iterate in the same state, and the absorption ability of Negative state is also poor. Learners' learning consciousness is difficult to form a sustainable group effect.

6 "Concave" enthusiasm is a type with obvious ups and downs in the early, middle and late stages of the learning process. In the early stage, the Positive and General states are obvious. However, in the middle stage, the Positive and General states are obviously transferred into a strong Negative state. In the later stage, due to the traction of learning assessment, learners' enthusiasm is transferred positively.

Learners' participation in the learning process is influenced by different temporal sequences that have strong dynamics. Learners' subjective needs and objective traction of academic goals will affect their learning enthusiasm, resulting in different participation and collaborative interaction. Tracking the whole learning process, learning enthusiasm forms obvious differences, forms different frequencies and transfer parameter values, and constructs different Markov chain state transfer model. Different temporal sequences correspond to different learning enthusiasm frequencies; they need different state transfer conditions and have strong temporal dynamics. Through the clustering scale of six learning enthusiasm, it can be seen that in addition to "Fluctuation" enthusiasm, the other five types have produced a considerable number of learners, accounting for 95.75% of all learners. Learning enthusiasm has an obvious change law in the whole learning process. Learners' subjective consciousness will also be affected by many factors, and appropriate and timely early warning intervention is needed.

7   Discussion

Based on the analysis of learning enthusiasm and the prediction results of Markov chain transfer matrix, we further analyze the learning enthusiasm trend of seven majors and locate the corresponding dynamic early warning sequence from the whole learning process. In the full training and testing of data, a complete semester is divided into 20 equidistant temporal sequences. Based on the prediction and optimization of Markov chain transfer model, the mapping between learning enthusiasm and early warning intervention sequence is obtained.

It can be seen from Figure 3.7 that the seven majors have different learning enthusiasm: (1) the enthusiasm of M1 is concentrated in three types: "Attenuation", "Concave" and "Memory"; (2) the enthusiasm of M2 is concentrated in four types: "Growth", "Convex", "Attenuation" and "Memory"; (3) the enthusiasm of M3 is mainly concentrated in three types: "Concave", "Convex" and "Memory"; (4) the enthusiasm of M4 is concentrated in four types: "Growth", "Convex", "Concave" and "Fluctuation"; (5) the enthusiasm of M5 is concentrated in four types: "Growth", "Convex", "Memory" and "Fluctuation"; (6) the enthusiasm of M6 is concentrated in three types: "Growth", "Convex" and "Memory"; (7) the enthusiasm of M7 is mainly concentrated in three types: "Attenuation", "Concave" and "Memory".

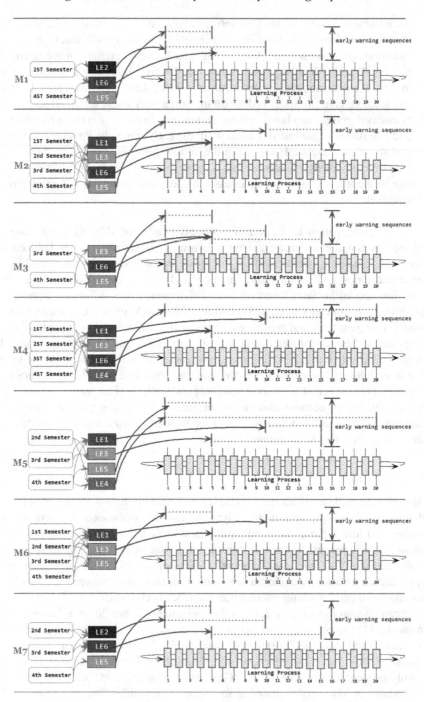

Figure 3.7 Mapping between Learning Enthusiasm and Early Warning Intervention Sequence

For example, M2 and M7 exhibit "Attenuation" enthusiasm, which is mainly determined by the analysis of learning behavior instances formed by learners in learning platform. The distribution of their participation is similar to the variation law of "Attenuation" enthusiasm. Due to the desensitization and standardization of some data descriptions on the learning platform, we are not very clear about the specific data descriptions. However, it can be determined that the learning content of M2 and M7 prefers theoretical abstract and technical practical types, respectively. The content of theoretical abstract type is usually obscure and difficult to understand, while the content of technical practical type requires strong mathematical theory and technical abilities, both learners need to have a relatively complete and solid background in precursor knowledge in order to facilitate the learning process of M2 and M7. However, as learning time goes by, the relevant knowledge points will become increasingly difficult, and the relevant principles and theories will also become more complex. Learners are prone to feeling frustrated and prone to "Attenuation" enthusiasm. Through training and evaluating a large number of learning behavior instances also predicts the occurrence of negative tendencies in this learning behaviors, which in turn proves that the difficulty is relatively high, and the learning behavior is far from enough simply by watching videos of the learning content. Therefore, we extracted interaction data from learners, and the frequency of M2 and M7 participating in Forum and Interaction was significantly higher. Learners received help from peers or answers from instructors and gradually feedback on changes in learning behavior routing and participation. Using the same method, the types of learning enthusiasm for M1, M3, M4, M5 and M6 can be analyzed.

The learning enthusiasm of these seven majors reflects certain laws as follows.

1 "Concave" enthusiasm is widely distributed. For the interactive learning environment that provides support for adult education, a considerable number of learners focus on the beginning and end of the learning process. In a long learning sequence, learners' participation in interaction and cooperation is relatively negative, but learners' enthusiasm will be driven by learning assessment. Therefore, in the later stage of the semester, their participation will be greatly improved. This is directly related to learners' positive subjective goals (i.e. passing the assessment).

2 "Convex" enthusiasm is also distributed. Learners show strong participation in the middle and early stages of the whole learning process, but their enthusiasm declines in the second half of the semester. Even at the end of the semester, this enthusiasm does not rebound effectively. Learners' attention to learning assessment does not produce a positive response. This is directly related to the learners' subjective consciousness of negative assessment.

3 "Memory" enthusiasm is more common. In the complete learning process, learners basically stay in a certain enthusiasm state. The data analysis shows that they mainly stay in the General state or the Negative state. Some learners directly give up the assessment (Withdrawn), and some do not pass the assessment. The demand for the subjective learning goal is not strong or clear, which is very easy to produce the feeling of slackness.

4 "Attenuation" enthusiasm mainly occurs in M1 and M7. The scale of learners in these two majors is relatively small, the learners' participation is relatively discrete and single, and the learning attitude is relatively negative. This is directly related to the learning content deployment and learning methods.

5 "Growth" enthusiasm mainly occurs in M4, M5 and M6. The learning organization methods of the three majors are similar, the project training is deployed in the learning process, which realizes a more sufficient flipped classroom mode, the learners' enthusiasm has a strong sense of consciousness and participation, and the participation and interaction are positive. This is directly related to the learning contents and learning methods.

6 "Fluctuation" enthusiasm mainly occurs in M4 and M5. It mainly appears in the first semester of the two majors, involving a small number of learners. Learners do not form independent learning interest. Due to the intervention of some external forces, their learning enthusiasm fluctuates constantly, and their self-consciousness is relatively passive. This is directly related to the learners themselves and the effectiveness of intervention.

According to the distribution of learning enthusiasm, the prediction analysis is carried out between different semesters of each major. The experiment shows that the learning enthusiasm still has obvious distribution changes in the subsequent semesters of the major. The learning enthusiasm trend of each semester is marked in Figure 3.7. It can be seen that in the later semesters, the enthusiasm has been significantly improved and the negative attitude has slowed down. The intervention measures have played an incentive role, but the effect of some improvement strategies is not obvious. Therefore, the data-driven learning enthusiasm is an important prerequisite for accurate early warning intervention. Based on the data analysis, the relevant early warning intervention strategies are mainly reflected as follows:

1 Different learning enthusiasm needs corresponding early warning intervention sequence. For the model design and decision mining driven by massive learning data, assuming that the length of the complete learning sequence in a semester is LP, the best early warning intervals of learning enthusiasm can be set: "Growth" enthusiasm→[0.5LP, LP], in the middle and late stages of the learning process; "Attenuation" enthusiasm→[1, 0.5LP], in the middle and early stages of the learning process; "Convex" enthusiasm, "Concave" enthusiasm, "Memory" enthusiasm→[0.25LP, 0.75/LP], in the sequences between the lower quartile and the upper quartile of the learning process, the early warning and intervention periods of "Convex", "Concave" and "Memory" are the same; "Fluctuation" enthusiasm→[1, LP], it occupies the whole learning process. According to the classification of learning enthusiasm, the tracking, intervention and optimization of learning process occur in the appropriate sequence intervals.

2 The three states of learning enthusiasm need to be benign transferred or maintained. It can be seen from Table 3.4 that the state transfer possibilities are different. To improve the transfer probability from Negative state to Positive state

in the Markov chain transfer matrix, we need to strengthen the intervention measures on the key early warning sequence and implement real-time data analysis and decision feedback.

3 The learning process might be needed to build an irregular assessment mechanism. Data analysis shows that learning assessment can improve learners' enthusiasm. In the whole learning process, we should strengthen the timely application of quiz, Q&A, etc. On the one hand, we can timely understand the learning effect; on the other hand, we can also play a certain role of supervision. Most learners still take passing the learning assessment as a strong subjective learning goal.

4 Learners' awareness of active interactive learning might be improved. In Figure 3.7, the learning process of M4, M5 and M6 has produced "Growth" learners of a certain scale, and the learners are highly motivated. Especially for M6, the learners have a strong awareness of actively participating in the learning process, which is directly related to the long-term project practice of the three majors. With the continuous updating of technology and tools, different majors should keep pace with the times. In combination with the current learning styles, organization methods and interest habits of learners, the combination of theory and practice should arouse learners' enthusiasm and participation, improve the probability of "Negative→General→Positive" and reduce the transfer time.

The above-mentioned methods are all discovered through a thorough analysis of learning behavior and related factors, which is also the true value of online learning data. However, they require the help of effective and appropriate analytical models to discover the potential risks. It is difficult to discover different learning passions solely from the explicit description. Therefore, learning platforms should also provide more measures to help learners improve their learning behavior and obtain more learning assistance, achieving effective intervention and positive guidance of learning enthusiasm.

Combined with the law of learning enthusiasm, the corresponding early warning intervention measures are formed for the research of dynamic early warning sequence enabled by learning enthusiasm (Er et al., 2021). Of course, these laws will reflect different data distribution characteristics with the corresponding early warning intervention, which will put forward new requirements and rules for data analysis methods and technologies, and also drive the improvement and adjustment of early warning intervention measures, so as to realize the benign incentive effect between learning enthusiasm and early warning intervention and truly realize the goal of data-driven learning process (Mangaroska et al., 2021; Xia, 2021b).

8   Conclusion

Lifelong learning has become the purpose of today's education and learning. The development of educational information science and technology has provided more convenient tools and platforms, used to support for the deepening and popularization of lifelong learning (Silvola et al., 2021; Xia, 2020b), online learning and interactive learning that have been more comprehensively and timely integrated and applied; the implementation of intelligent, personalized and autonomous interactive learning environment has produced great needs and requirements (Whitelock-Wainwright et al., 2021). At the same time, the interactive learning environment also produces massive data, which provides sufficient training and testing data for learning analytics, and provides a basis for realizing data-driven dynamic learning process tracking, prediction and decision.

Based on the integration of improved multi-layer Bayesian model and hidden Markov chain model, this research analyzes sufficient data and demonstrates relationships in terms of learning enthusiasm, needed to optimize the autonomous learning process, and realize the DEWSM; the data analysis and prediction of the model are fully compared. Based on the correlation and standardization of the features of the five themes in the learning process, two parts of work are completed by using the DEWSM: first, through the correlation prediction analysis, six types of learning enthusiasm and the transfer possibility between different states are mined, and the potential laws are summarized; second, it realizes the mapping between learning enthusiasm and early warning intervention sequences and deduces the early warning intervention strategies. The whole work realizes the dynamic early warning sequences and adaptively solves the problems of complexity, variability, discreteness, multiple interference and multiple factors of the learning process sequence (Ameloot et al., 2021). The data analysis and prediction process have good robustness and reliability.

There is still possibility for improvement and deepening of the DEWSM enabled by learning enthusiasm, which is mainly reflected in the generalization ability and adaptability, the attribution interpretation and decision feedback of early warning, and effectively extended to the classification and prediction of relevant data in interactive learning environment. The following work is to achieve the dynamic early warning value propagation driven by DEWSM, in order to enable efficient learning enthusiasm and improve the effectiveness and reliability of early warning and intervention.

References

Aguilar, S. J., Karabenick, S. A., Teasley, S. D., & Baek, C. (2021). Associations between learning analytics dashboard exposure and motivation and self-regulated learning. *Computers & Education*. 162, 104085. https://doi.org/10.1016/j.compedu.2020.104085

Akçapınar, G., Altun, A., & Aşkar, P. (2019). Using learning analytics to develop early-warning system for at-risk students. *International Journal of Educational Technology in Higher Education*. 16(1), 1–20. https://doi.org/10.1186/s41239-019-0172-z

Ameloot, E., Rotsaert, T., & Schellens, T. (2021). The supporting role of learning analytics for a blended learning environment: exploring students' perceptions and the impact on relatedness. *Journal of Computer Assisted Learning*. 38, 1–325. https://doi.org/10.1111/jcal.12593

Baker, R., Nasiar, N., Ocumpaugh, J., Hutt, S., & Biswas, G. (2021). Affect-targeted interviews for understanding student frustration. *International Conference on Artificial Intelligence and Education*. Utrecht, The Netherlands, June 14–18. 52–63. https://doi.org/10.1007/978-3-030-78292-4_5

Baker, R. S., Gaevi, D., & Karumbaiah, S. (2021). Four paradigms in learning analytics: why paradigm convergence matters. *Computers and Education: Artificial Intelligence*. 2. https://doi.org/10.1016/j.caeai.2021.100021

Bertolini, R., Finch, S. J., & Nehm, R. H. (2021). Testing the impact of novel assessment sources and machine learning methods on predictive outcome modeling in undergraduate biology. *Journal of Science Education and Technology*. 30(2), 1–17. https://doi.org/10.1007/s10956-020-09888-8

Blau, I., & Shamir-Inbal, T. (2021). Writing private and shared annotations and lurking in Annoto hyper-video in academia: insights from learning analytics, content analysis, and interviews with lecturers and students. *Educational Technology Research and Development*. 69(2), 763–786. https://doi.org/10.1007/s11423-021-09984-5

Er, E., Dimitriadis, Y., & Gašević, D. (2021). Collaborative peer feedback and learning analytics: theory-oriented design for supporting class-wide interventions. *Assessment & Evaluation in Higher Education*. 46. https://doi.org/10.1080/02602938.2020.1764490

Fan, Y., Matcha, W., Uzir, N. A., Wang, Q., & Gaevi, D. (2021). Learning analytics to reveal links between learning design and self-regulated learning. *International Journal of Artificial Intelligence in Education*. 1–42. https://doi.org/10.1007/s40593-021-00249-z

Henriksen, D., Creely, E., Henderson, M., & Mishra, P. (2021). Creativity and technology in teaching and learning: a literature review of the uneasy space of implementation. *Educational Technology Research and Development*. 69, 2091–2108. https://doi.org/10.1007/s11423-020-09912-z

Kaeophanuek, S., & Chookerd, N. (2021). A development of the flipped learning model using the critical inquiry process to enhance research skills. *International Journal of Interactive Mobile Technologies (iJIM)*. 15(3), 70. https://doi.org/10.3991/ijim.v15i03.17905

Krner, T., Warwas, J., & Schumann, S. (2021). A learning analytics approach to address heterogeneity in the classroom: the teachers' diagnostic support system. *Technology, Knowledge and Learning*. 26(1), 31–52. https://doi.org/10.1007/s10758-020-09448-4

Lazarides, R., Fauth, B., Gaspard, H., & Gllner, R. (2021). Teacher self-efficacy and enthusiasm: relations to changes in student-perceived teaching quality at the beginning of secondary education. *Learning and Instruction*. 73. https://doi.org/10.1016/j.learninstruc.2020.101435

Licciardello, F., Consoli, S., Cirelli, G., Castillo, C., & Taguas, E. V. (2021). Technology-enhanced learning for promoting technical and social competences in hydrological science. *Technology, Knowledge and Learning*. 26, 985–997. https://doi.org/10.1007/s10758-021-09510-9

Lu, O., Huang, A., & Yang, S. (2021). Impact of teachers' grading policy on the identification of at-risk students in learning analytics. *Computers & Education*. 163(1), 104109. https://doi.org/10.1016/j.compedu.2020.104109

Mangaroska, K., Martinez, R., Aldonado, C. M., Vesin, B., & Gaevi, D. (2021). Challenges and opportunities of multimodal data in human learning: the computer science students' perspective. *Journal of Computer Assisted Learning*. 37(3). https://doi.org/10.1111/jcal.12542

Silvola, A., Nykki, P., Kaveri, A., & Muukkonen, H. (2021). Expectations for supporting student engagement with learning analytics: an academic path perspective. *Computers & Education*. 168(12). https://doi.org/10.1016/j.compedu.2021.104192

Tsiakmaki, M., Kostopoulos, G., Kotsiantis, S., & Ragos, O. (2021). Fuzzy-based active learning for predicting student academic performance using autoML: a step-wise approach. *Journal of Computing in Higher Education*. 33, 635–667. https://doi.org/10.1007/s12528-021-09279-x

Turcotte, N., Hollett, T., Dan, M., Wager, S., & Handley, E. (2021). The co-construction of data in-time: collaborative pedagogical encounters of golf instructors and students with data. *Learning Media and Technology*. 47(2), 216–234 https://doi.org/10.1080/17439884. 2021.1960560

Whitelock-Wainwright, A., Tsai, Y. S., Drachsler, H., Scheffel, M., & Gaevi, D. (2021). An exploratory latent class analysis of student expectations towards learning analytics services. *The Internet and Higher Education*. 51. https://doi.org/10.1016/j.iheduc.2021.100818

Xia, X. (2020a). Random field design and collaborative inference strategy for learning interaction activities. *Interactive Learning Environments*. Advance online publication 30 Dec 2020. 1–25. https://doi.org/10.1080/10494820.2020.1863236

Xia, X. (2020b). Learning behavior mining and decision recommendation based on association rules in interactive learning environment. *Interactive Learning Environments*. Advance online publication 4 Aug 2020. 1–16. https://doi.org/10.1080/10494820.2020.1799028

Xia, X. (2021a). Decision application mechanism of regression analysis of multi-category learning behaviors in interactive learning environment. *Interactive Learning Environments*. Advance online publication 23 Apr 2021. 1–14. https://doi.org/10.1080/10494820.2021.1916767

Xia, X. (2021b). Interaction recognition and intervention based on context feature fusion of learning behaviors in interactive learning environments. *Interactive Learning Environments*. Advance online publication 17 Jan 2021. 1–19. https://doi.org/10.1080/10494820.2021.1871632

Yang, J., & Valcke, M. (2021). Online classroom environments and students' learning enthusiasm in China college English under the influence of corona. *15th International Technology, Education and Development Conference. Online Conference*, 8–9 March, 2021. https://doi.org/10.21125/inted.2021.0847

4 Early Warning Value Propagation Network for Continuous Learning Behaviors

Abstract

Based on the conclusions of learning enthusiasm enabled dynamic early warning sequence model, the following work is to achieve the dynamic early warning value propagation. After all, the dynamic early warning propagation of interactive learning process is an important part of improving learning behavior, and also the key issue to realize the relative optimal learning paths. This chapter proposes and designs a diversion inference model of learning effectiveness supported by differential evolution strategy. First, we analyze and design the definition and principle of differential evolution strategy; second, convolution neural network is improved and optimized based on differential evolution strategy, the multi-level inference process of convolution neural network is transformed into the task topology of learning behavior and the diversion inference model of learning effectiveness is realized; third, the algorithm corresponding to the model is applied to the full training and testing of big data sets. The experimental results show that the model is reliable and feasible; finally, based on the visualization of the experimental results, we analyze the problems and rules found in the diversion inference results, and put forward the intervention measures suitable for the interactive learning environment. The whole research process of this chapter not only provides a set of feasible solutions for the dynamic early warning propagation but also demonstrates some key conclusions, which provides theoretical support and practical for early warning pivot space, as well as the foundation of the work in Chapter 5.

Keywords

Interactive Learning Process; Early Warning; Value Propagation Network; SIR Model; Learning Behavior; Learning Analytics

1 Introduction

Educational big data comes from the education and teaching process and feeds back in order to improve the learning quality (He et al., 2021; Yilmaz, 2020). According to the distribution law and statistical results of existing data, we mine

DOI: 10.4324/9781003484905-4

the learning behavior trend of learners, demonstrate the implementation effect of teaching methods and achieve early warning (Dietrich et al., 2021). This is the key issue in the research and application of learning analytics, and it is also a powerful guarantee for the data-driven education and teaching process (Er et al., 2021; Xia, 2020a). With the wide application and continuous optimization of online learning platform, the completeness, accuracy and continuity of educational big data have been well improved, which provides important and complete data. However, the adaptability and effectiveness of analysis methods determine the breadth and depth of data value. How might we mine more useful information from data and realize the systematization and continuity of education and teaching process? That has a great challenge for the technical means and research problems (Aguilar et al., 2021).

The early warning of interactive learning process is an important aspect of data-driven education and teaching process. How to design and use early warning is related to the application effect of educational big data (Xia, 2020b). With the emergence of interactive learning environment, especially the online learning platform that has gradually become the main mode, realizing the effective accumulation and full collection of learning data, there are a large number of logs, forming a dynamic continuous description of learning process; it provides more bases for the early warning (Israel-Fishelson, 2021). At the same time, learning behavior is associated with a large number of description items, attributes and characteristics, resulting in massive data with different structures, conditions and correlations. It has formed many application cases, which is also an important component of early warning. The most applicable early warning is designed through sufficient training of data, which is the expanded application of learning analytics (Song et al., 2021). Therefore, the early warning is to transform the interactive learning process into a propagation process that continuously mines data value and adapts to feedback. Through the selection of key nodes and the construction of effective relationships, we might realize an open and shared elastic network of the interactive learning process. Then, the early warning is guided by the value propagation of the interactive learning process; it is no longer a linear topology, but a multidimensional network topology.

The data value of interactive learning process includes two aspects: one is to train learners' behavior model and predict the learning effect; the second is to analyze the learning behavior in a period, judge the state change of learners and generate the behavior profile. The value validity and reliability of these two aspects involve the accurate and complete analysis of key nodes and effective relationships. Based on the massive data set generated in the interactive learning process, this study constructs an applicable early warning value propagation network, takes data as the driving force, fully trains network nodes and relationships, explores the relatively optimal parameters of key nodes, positive paths and negative paths, and further uses data to test network performance, analyze the effective tracking topology of interactive learning process and evaluate the multidimensional early warning value propagation strategy.

2   Related Work

The early warning of interactive learning process continuously tracks the real-time change that takes the dynamic temporal sequences as the clue; it is directly related to the description elements of learning process (Clark et al., 2020). At the same time, learners' participation in the interactive learning process is also affected by other stable elements such as learners' own learning background, teaching methods and assessment methods. These elements are usually relatively stable; the data value will not or is not easy to change in a period. Realize multi-level correlation calculation and analysis for the key elements and send timely early warning information to learners, according to the data analysis results; instructors and platform supervisors track the learning process in an effective temporal interval (Main et al., 2021). The design and application of early warning might better understand the data-driven learning behavior (Xia, 2021a), find the problems and potential risks in advance, make effective decisions, guide learners to create more appropriate learning behavior or provide more effective learning suggestions to give full play to data value. The elements for early warning is directly related to the description methods of process, data and features, it is also necessary to locate the appropriate element range based on the research objectives.

As for the theoretical research on early warning, some researchers have made more achievements. Some educational institutions have developed locally early warning prototypes and have obtained better suggestions in the actual learning process. It can play a positive role in reducing learners' early leave (Granberg et al., 2021; Havu-Nuutinen et al., 2021). Early warning needs to take learning analytics as the premise. Learning analytics focuses on the evaluation of learning process, evaluates learning ability and participation status. Early warning is a continuous and dynamic interactive participation. It continuously predicts to find learners with high-risk in time. Early warning is an iterative data analysis and decision feedback of different temporal sequences. Both data features and relationships are multidimensional complex structures that have high requirements.

As for the application research on early warning, the first application mainly serves the R&D of learning system and is also the auxiliary optimization mechanism of learning system, in order to identify high-risk learners by analyzing some logs generated by the learning system or predict expected learning results through the evaluation of learning behavior. Previous studies mainly focus on the construction and optimization of performance evaluation model, but do not really effectively bind the early warning and tracking strategy that is not useful for the accurate prediction, mining and intervention of high-risk learners (Li et al., 2021; Xia, 2021b). The second application is the Learning Dashboard that has been applied in the course teaching process. The Learning Dashboard analyzes the current learning status by building a learning behavior model, presents it in a visual way, or analyzes targeted data according to the application requirements. Combined with data value, it adopts different models and technologies to provide analysis results. However, the data scale of the learning dashboard is limited, and it is not suitable for the learning behavior of multi-course and multi-interactive process.

The early warning of interactive learning process is essentially a comprehensive research topic in theory and application. The interactive learning process is no longer limited to a single platform, realizes data sharing and integration of multiple mixed interactive learning environments, tracks the temporal sequences of the learning process, and constructs a data value propagation system, so as to timely discover and identify potential risks, and issue early warning to predict possible adverse consequences (Fischer et al., 2020; Luo, 2021; Zainuddin et al., 2020). The interactive learning process involves multi-features, categories, structures and processes; it is not the linear structure. Therefore, this study proposes an early warning value propagation network, demonstrates the early warning based on multidimensional relationships and nodes, and mines and analyzes massive data more comprehensively and accurately. It will also bring great difficulty to the research of technology and methods.

3   Data Processing and Problem Description

The data in this study comes from an online learning interactive environment, which is the logs and records of college teaching activities during COVID-19. According to the learning periods, three complete learning processes and six learning contents with certain relevance are selected. This relevance is reflected in the large-scale overlapping learners; these five learning contents belong to compulsory learning contents. For learners, they have strong learning tendency and participation. After data statistical analysis, these learners mainly involve six majors, and the data covers the whole process from registration to assessment. A learning period consists of 20 weeks. The data scale of these three learning processes has reached tens of millions and includes a large number of incomplete data, even empty data. For example, the learning process logs are vacant or lost, which has caused great obstacles to data analysis. Therefore, it is inefficient or ineffective to use all records for the analysis and prediction; it is necessary to define the key elements, so as to formulate data cleaning and standardization rules and design effective data mining algorithms.

After sufficient data analysis, purification and merging, the experimental data is obtained, which is about 1.67PB, involving 23,470 learners. The distribution of key elements of three learning processes, five learning contents and six majors is shown in Table 4.1.

As can be seen from Table 4.1, each learning period involves two different learning contents, and the main five majors are classified. These learning contents overlap among majors, especially the learning contents with strong basic principles, which are common compulsory items. For some learning contents with more obvious major direction, the learners are more concentrated. In the selection of some learning contents, there are a small number of learners who are exempted or abandoned. The main reason is directly related to the academic background of learners.

Table 4.1 Element Distribution

Learning Process	Learning Content	Content Category	Major	Learner Scale
I	C1	Statistics (SS)	M1	4,950
			M2	3,111
			M3	3,902
			M4	5,319
			M5	5,933
	C2	Mathematics (MS)	M1	4,791
			M2	3,084
			M3	3,944
			M5	5,970
II	C3	Economics (ES)	M2	3,130
			M4	5,310
	C4	Computer Science (CS)	M1	4,915
			M3	3,922
			M5	5,977
III	C5	Software Engineering(SE)	M2	3,030
			M4	5,469
	C6	Management (MT)	M3	3,808
			M4	5,460
			M5	5,935

Learners of different majors have different learning objectives about the same learning content, some prefer application, some prefer principle, the focus of learning content is different, and the learning problems and assessment needs will also be different. Learners' academic background and learning needs will also affect learning cognition and trend, resulting in different learning behaviors. Therefore, learning behaviors based on "Learning period-Learning content-Major-Learner" have certain personalization. For learning behaviors with similar conditions, there will also be some overlap and similarity.

Based on the elements in Figure 4.1, the key elements and possible relationships of the interactive learning process are defined. In addition to the conditions in Table 4.1, the interactive learning process depends on the functions of the learning platform. After data analysis, the interactive learning process is mainly divided into ten types of interactive activities, as shown in Table 4.2. Assessment is also an interactive activity. At the same time, assessment produces learning evaluation results. As can be seen from Table 4.2, learners' interactive activities have strong groupness, resulting in high participation in "Watch video", "Click content page", "Search resources", "Forum" and "Interactive and Cooperation". The participation of the other five types of interactive activities is general, but they are an important part, and have correlation or significance with other interactive activities. As the nodes of interactive learning process, these interactive activities have different influence weights. The correlation and significance between interactive activities constitute the relationships.

Table 4.2 Interactive Activities

NO.	Interactive Activity	Description	Frequency of Participation
1	WV	Watch video	4,026,019
2	CP	Click content page	4,280,003
3	SR	Search resources	2,120,700
4	QA	Question&answer	916,544
5	IC	Interactive and cooperation	1,725,555
6	FD	Forum discussion	2,210,936
7	DM	Download materials	595,223
8	UA	Upload assignments	448,729
9	QZ	Quiz	299,050
10	PR	Presentation	54,653
11	OA	Other activities	22,910

For the paths of interactive learning process, we need to consider several factors: the weight of nodes, the correlation or significance of relationships, assessment methods and results. This study takes the assessment method as the end node, the assessment results as the observation variables; combined with the learning period, learning content and major, we design the learning process topology driven by interactive activities and deduce the positive path and negative path. Positive path refers to the interactive activity route that can bring good assessment results, which has a positive guiding force for learners. Negative path refers to the interactive activity route that produces significant negative assessment results, which has a negative force on learners. The distribution and relationships between key elements and interactive activities are shown in Figure 4.1.

Based on the temporal sequences in Figure 4.1, as well as the relevant elements, interactive activities and possible relationships, the key problems in data analysis are determined as follows:

R1: Correlation between majors and learning contents in different learning periods;

R2: Correlation between interactive activities in the same learning period, involving cross test between five majors;

R2': Correlation between interactive activities in different learning periods, involving cross test between five majors;

R3: Significance of assessment methods on assessment results;

cR1,2,3: Based on the test results of R1, R2 and R3, the significance of positive path on the assessment results;

cR1,2',3: Based on the test results of R1, R2' and R3, the significance of positive path on the assessment results;

Rr1,2,3: Based on the test results of R1, R2 and R3, the significance of negative path on the assessment results;

Rr1,2',3: Based on the test results of R1, R2' and R3, the significance of negative path on the assessment results.

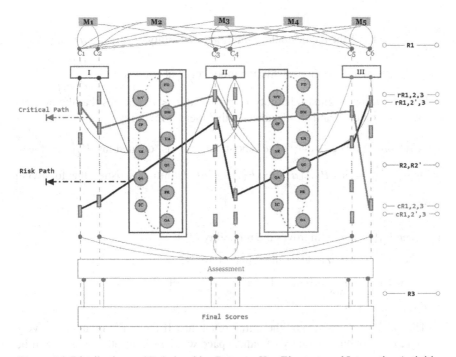

Figure 4.1 Distribution and Relationships Between Key Elements and Interactive Activities

The demonstration process of these key problems takes learners' good assessment results as the clue of value propagation and realizes the test of correlation and significance. Therefore, the value propagation of interactive learning process has become the key technical demand.

4   Method

The early warning value is essentially an aspect of data value, which is reflected in changing or forming the reliability of relevant objects. The Large Number Theorem shows that, under the same experimental conditions and repeated experiments for many times, the frequency of random events tends to be consistent with its probability. Based on a large number of repeated conditions, random events are easy to show the hidden characteristics or laws behind them. For the multidimensional data distribution in Figure 4.1, within a certain temporal sequences, the intention and motivation of data generation might have strong randomness and autonomy. Learners generate their own interactive learning process. The early warning value propagation needs to prove the importance of data value. The relevant definitions are as follows:

Definition 1: Supposing Y is an event with multiple possible cases $Y = (A_1, A_2, \cdots, A_n)$, and each case corresponds to a priori reliability $P(A_i)$,

$\sum\limits_{i=1}^{n} P(A_i) = 1$, a is the data, and the conditional reliability of A_i about a is expressed

as $P(A_i \mid a)$, then the utility calculation model of A_i about a is $U = \dfrac{P(A_i \mid a)}{P(A_i)}, U > 1$

indicates that the original reliability is improved, $U < 1$ indicates that the original reliability is reduced and $U = 1$ indicates that there is no utility.

Definition 2: The value of a about case A is defined as $V_A(a) = \log U$

$= \log \dfrac{P(A \mid a)}{P(A)} = \log P(A \mid a) - \log P(A)$. This definition satisfies the following rules:

1   When $V_A(a) > 0$, a improves the reliability of A;
2   When $V_A(a) < 0$, a reduces the reliability of A;
3   If $\left(\log P(A \mid a)\right)_{\max} = 0$, then $V_A(a)_{\max} = -\log P(A)$;
4   $V_A(a)_{\min} = -\infty$;
5   The value of a depends on the initial reliability. If the initial reliability is very high, the growth possibility of value space will be small; otherwise, it will be large.

Let $D = (d_1, d_2, \cdots, d_s)$ be a data sequence; then, the value of D is defined as

$V_A(D) = \dfrac{1}{s} \log \dfrac{P(A \mid D)}{P(A)}$, $P(A \mid D)$ is the conditional probability of case A about D

and the value of D reflects the average of the reliability change for case A.

Based on the basic description models of Definition 1, Definition 2 and Definition 3, it is proved that the data value propagation will meet three theorems, namely:

Theorem 1: Suppose a data sequence $D = (a_1, a_2, \cdots, a_n)$ in the interactive learning

process is independently distributed; then $V_A(a_1, a_2, \cdots, a_n) = \dfrac{1}{n} \sum\limits_{i=1}^{n} V_A(a_i)$. The

data value is cumulative, which is useful to the value calculation, but the premise needs to meet the data independence.

Theorem 2: Let $\xi_1, \xi_2, \cdots, \xi_r$ be a group of random variables, and for every d_i satisfy $P(d_i) > 0$. If the random variable produces two data sequences, $D_n = (d_1, d_2, \cdots, d_n)$ and $D_{n+s} = (d_1, d_2, \cdots, d_{n+s})$, respectively, then $\lim\limits_{n \to \infty} P(|V_A(D_{n+s}) - V_A(D_n)| \leq \varepsilon) = 1$. This reflects the decrement of data value. When the data increases, the value decreases.

Theorem 3: If data sequence $D = (a_1, a_2, \cdots, a_n)$ satisfies Theorem 1 and Theorem 2, then $P(|V_A(a_1, a_2, \cdots, a_{n+s}) - V_A(a_1, a_2, \cdots, a_n)| < \varepsilon) > \left(1 - 2^{\left(-\frac{n\varepsilon^2}{(c-b)^2}\right)}\right)^2$.

If n represents the number of samples, ε and $\left(1 - 2^{\frac{n\varepsilon^2}{2(c-b)^2}}\right)^2$ represent the value difference and confidence, respectively, according to Theorem 2, when the amount of data reaches n, it is the confidence of $\left(1 - 2^{\frac{n\varepsilon^2}{2(c-b)^2}}\right)^2$, the value provided by the subsequent increased data will not exceed ε.

Based on the above definitions and theorems, an early warning value propagation model suitable for interactive learning process is constructed. Traditional information propagation mainly includes three basic states: Susceptible(S), Infected(I) and Removed(R). A network composed of interactive activities and multiple elements is defined as $G = (V, E)$, V is the node set and E is the relationship set. It is assumed that in the initial temporal sequence, all nodes may process S state, and then set some nodes to the I state. The correlation between nodes makes the S nodes vulnerable to the influence of the I nodes, and gradually turn into I nodes. I nodes will also return to R or S nodes with a certain probability. According to the transfer characteristics of S, I and R states, different value propagation models are formed. The correlation between interactive activities is reflected in a network topology, which is described as the state transition sequence of S-I-R; it is called SIR value propagation model; each node will reflect different propagation directions and strategies under the SIR model.

The value propagation model of interactive learning process is described as follows:

$$
\begin{cases}
\dfrac{dS}{dt} = -\alpha SI + \beta R \\[2mm]
\dfrac{dI}{dt} = \alpha SI - \gamma I \\[2mm]
\dfrac{dR}{dt} = \gamma I - \beta R
\end{cases}
$$

α is the probability that S node turns into I node, β is the probability that the immune node turns into S node and γ is the probability that I node turns into the immune node.

The process of *SIR* value propagation model is described as Algorithm SIR.

Algorithm SIR

Input: Adjacency matrix LS; //LS represents interactive activities, elements and relationships;

Sequence diagram structure TS; //TS represents the temporal sequences, the corresponding interactive activities and elements;

Output: Value propagation abilities

PROCESS

Step 1: The elements in LS are defined as nodes, and the graph structure of LS and TS is constructed according to the relationships;

Step 2: According to the temporal sequence distribution of TS, the node set corresponding to the initial sequence is retrieved;

Step 3: Iteratively calculate the correlation between nodes in LS, analyze learners' participation in each node and set the thresholds of correlation and participation, respectively. When the average correlation between nodes and other nodes is not less than the threshold, and the participation is not less than the threshold, the node is defined as the initial node;

Step 4: Initializing one part of the nodes of the initial sequence as S nodes, the other part as I nodes;

Step 5: I nodes activate adjacent nodes with a certain probability p;

Step 6: **if** a S node has k adjacency nodes and $k_1 \left(k_k \le k \right)$ I nodes

Then in the next temporal sequence, the probability of the node turning into an I node is $1 - \left(1 - p \right)^{k_1}$;

Step 7: The probability that S node turns into the immune node in each temporal sequence is q;

Step 8: Set $\beta = 0$ to make immune nodes maintain stable participation and correlation;

Step 9: **if** the number of I nodes and the immune nodes is not stable, p and q do not converge to stable values

Then goto Step 3;

Else the sum of the number of I nodes and immune nodes is expressed as the propagation ability, and output.

End Process

5   Experiment

In order to test the effectiveness of SIR model and algorithms, an experimental process is constructed. In order to effectively track the performance of the algorithms for the value propagation process, three indexes are selected: AUC (Area Under

Curve), Precision and Correlation. The measurement process of these three indexes follows the following rules:

1 AUC, in the measurement of this index, each "node pair" in the interactive learning process corresponds to a similarity value. Randomly select n "node pairs" with real relationships and "node pairs" without relationships, and compare the similarity between them. The case number with high similarity is n_1. The case number with equal similarity is n_2. Then, the calculation model of AUC is $AUC = \left(n_1 + 0.5n_2\right)/n$.
2 Precision, it is used to evaluate the overlap between the reconstructed network topology and the real network topology. It is a supplement to AUC.
3 Correlation, it is mainly described by Pearson correlation coefficient. It is used to measure the reconstructed and the original topology nodes, which is reflected in the Pearson correlation coefficient between nodes.

The value propagation process involves two parameters: infection probability μ and propagation probability f. It is proved by adjacency matrix that the network parameter space $\left(\mu, f\right)$ will affect the indexes. AUC, Precision and Correlation correspond to different $\left(\mu, f\right)$, which will affect the performances after network reconstruction. Therefore, it is necessary to fully train the data set to find the best value of each performance. After sufficient data analysis, when $\mu \approx 0.16$, AUC and Precision are relatively optimal at that time; when $\mu \approx 0.23$, the Correlation is relatively optimal at that time.

This study uses the node similarity to reconstruct the network in line with the SIR model. The basic principle is that the nodes receiving a large amount of common information are similar, the activities with common correlated activities are similar, and these nodes have a strong relationship in the network. For the dependence of similar "node pairs" in the interactive learning process, it is necessary to consider the temporal sequences of SIR model. Therefore, four feasible and efficient comparison methods are selected and improved: SIR+CN(common neighbor, CN), SIR+Jaccard(Jac), SIR+RA(Resource Allocation, RA) and SIR+LHN(Leicht-Holme-Newman, LHN). The whole experimental process is mainly divided into three steps: the first step analyzes the interactive learning process in the same period, and calculate the average of the performance indexes in the three periods; the second step is to combine the interactive process of three learning periods of each major, and analyze the interactive activity crossing between different majors; the third step analyzes the interactive learning processes to realize the temporal sequence crossing in different learning periods. Relevant program codes are implemented in Python 3.9.

In the first step, we test the dependence of AUC, Precision and Correlation on μ. The experimental results are shown in Figures 4.2–4.4, respectively. This method can achieve high performance indexes, AUC and Precision are limited by μ, while the correlation test, SIR+CN and SIR+Jac get the best results. The data analysis of the whole experiment shows that when $f = 0.45$, there is a strong data tendency. The experimental result is the average of 500 independent training results; it

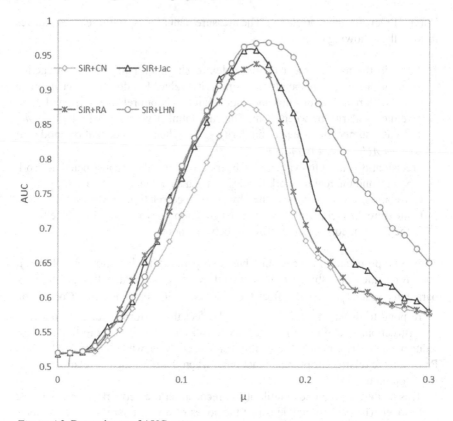

Figure 4.2 Dependence of AUC on μ

satisfies $N = 1,000$, $p = 0.15$, $k = 15$. In addition, the experimental results show that no matter which similarity calculation method, when the infection rate of the interactive learning process exceeds the optimal critical value, AUC, Precision and Correlation are in a declining state, which cannot improve the effectiveness and credibility of value propagation. According to Figures 4.2–4.4, the Correlation values of CN and Jac are better, while that of SIR+CN and SIR+Jac are more robust. Therefore, in the data analysis of the next two steps, these two methods are used for comparative experiments.

In the second step, based on the optimal μ obtained in the first step, the interactive activity crossing between different majors is analyzed, in order to test the node similarity and relationship similarity of the SIR model, applied to the interactive learning process of different majors. We need to consider the feasible combination between majors. The relevant combination test follows one principle: there may be similarity in the interactive learning process between majors with common learning content. Since the similarity probability of interactive activities of two majors is greatest, this study combines with the corresponding relationships between the majors and the learning contents; it is found that there are nine major combinations with two or more common learning contents. The performance indexes are

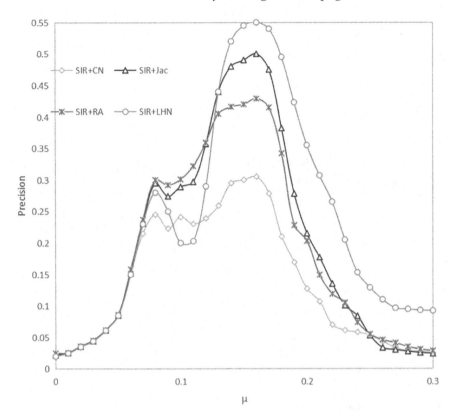

Figure 4.3 Dependence of Precision on μ

obtained, as shown in Table 4.3. The test results show that SIR+Jac can get better performance indexes.

In the third step, based on the optimal μ obtained in the first step, the temporal sequences of five majors spanning three periods are analyzed, in order to test the node similarity and relationship similarity, when SIR model is applied to the temporal sequence crossing. While satisfying good AUC, Precision and Correlation, we can get more stable node similarity. Therefore, in the value propagation of temporal sequences, we track and calculate the indexes of value propagation to each node. The experimental results are shown in Table 4.4. For the temporal sequences crossing of different majors, the advantages of the two methods are different. From Table 4.4, it can be seen that the advantages of SIR+Jac are more obvious.

Through the complex experiments of the above three steps, it is proved that the combination of SIR+Jac similarity method is helpful to the temporal sequence crossing, as well as the activities crossing of multi-majors, and can well support the tracking of the value propagation. The test results of performance indexes show that the application of this method can ensure the reliability and credibility of data analysis. Therefore, based on SIR+Jac, this study will construct the early warning value propagation network and make the best path of early warning.

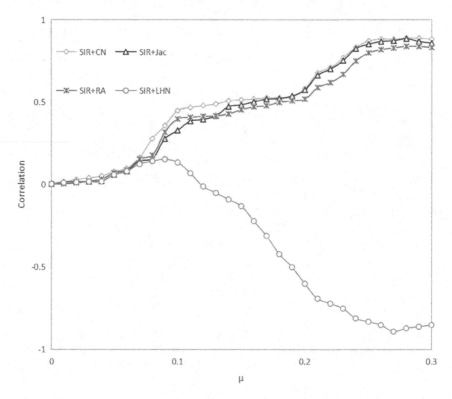

Figure 4.4 Correlation

Table 4.3 Performance Indexes of Interactive Activity Crossing Between Majors

Composition	Topology Properties		AUC		Precision		Correlation	
	Node	Edge	SIR+CN	SIR+Jac	SIR+CN	SIR+Jac	SIR+CN	SIR+Jac
M3↔M5	2,781	19,809	0.915	**0.950**	0.323	**0.337**	0.771	**0.784**
M2↔M4	1,270	7,011	0.870	**0.919**	0.374	**0.426**	0.720	**0.767**
M1↔M3	1,584	6,129	0.878	**0.900**	0.255	**0.268**	0.823	**0.841**
M1↔M5	598	1,028	0.926	**0.988**	0.420	**0.687**	0.571	**0.763**
M1↔M2	496	2,215	0.922	**0.935**	0.515	**0.522**	0.839	**0.844**
M2↔M3	402	1,106	0.905	**0.934**	0.427	**0.448**	0.816	**0.827**
M2↔M5	337	895	0.822	**0.830**	0.461	**0.482**	0.835	**0.840**
M3↔M4	369	952	0.865	**0.873**	0.422	**0.606**	0.789	**0.813**
M4↔M5	294	937	0.843	**0.926**	0.529	**0.633**	0.721	**0.783**

Note: The bold values represent the optimal results.

Table 4.4 Performance Indexes of Temporal Sequence Crossing

Major	Topology Properties		AUC		Precision		Correlation	
	Node	Edge	SIR+CN	SIR+Jac	SIR+CN	SIR+Jac	SIR+CN	SIR+Jac
M1	2,865	6,009	0.754	**0.832**	0.342	**0.459**	0.637	**0.709**
M2	1,482	8,441	0.675	**0.679**	0.273	**0.295**	0.350	**0.627**
M3	5,090	17,909	0.755	**0.782**	0.199	**0.223**	0.336	**0.632**
M4	8,087	49,168	0.691	**0.719**	0.114	**0.185**	0.593	**0.668**
M5	13,638	90,155	0.852	**0.864**	0.202	**0.216**	0.804	**0.815**

Note: The bold values represent the optimal results.

6 Result

The early warning value propagation is to realize the effective optimization and guidance of learning behavior, promote the recommendation and selection of effective interactive activities, determine the appropriate early warning sequences, timely mine risks, construct appropriate learning and teaching methods, help learners to determine the adaptive ways to participate in the learning process as soon as possible and improve learning efficiency and effect. This is not only the value of interactive learning process research but also the decision of learning behavior given by data analysis. The early warning value propagation requires continuous tracking and timely feedback of complete temporal sequences, in order to achieve the analysis of appropriate data and the prediction of reasonable decision.

There are three-step value propagation analysis results in the experiment that will serve the multidimensional temporal sequence tracking and dynamic early warning. Through the tracking of the data change, the appropriate early warning sequences of the temporal sequences will be located to form the positive path and negative path. Through experiments, the empirical test results of the key problems are obtained, as shown in Tables 4.5 and 4.6, respectively.

Table 4.5 shows the correlation of R1, R2 and R2'; we fully analyze the relevant elements, calculate the combinations between different elements and list the value ranges with strong correlation. For R1, different majors have specific or common learning contents with strong correlation, indicating the key role of these learning contents, which is compulsory contents for professional ability, and C1 is the basis of the five majors. For R2, important rules are found in the data distribution of different interactive learning processes, and the combinations with strong correlation are mined from 11 interactive activities, the participation of one activity will have a significance on other activities, which is universal, and there is also a certain correlation between these combinations. For R2', including the cross test of three interactive learning processes, five groups of combinations with strong correlation are obtained. From the analysis results, it can be seen that similar interactive activities or combinations can realize the potential trends of learners' participation

Table 4.5 Correlation

Category	Hypothesis Test	Correlation Interval	Corresponding Items
Correlation	R1	[0.808, 0.873]	M1→(C1,C2) M2→(C1,C2) M3→(C1,C4) M4→(C1,C3,C5) M5→(C1,C2,C4)
	R2	[0.712, 0.799]	CP↔WV IC↔FD SR↔DM QZ↔PR
	R2'	[0.650, 0.743]	I:UA↔II:UA↔III:UA I:(CP↔WV)↔II:(CP↔WV) II:(CP↔WV)↔III:(CP↔WV) II:(IC↔FD)↔III:(IC↔FD) II:(SR↔DM)↔III:(SR↔DM) I:(QZ↔PR)↔II:I:(QZ↔PR)↔ III:(QZ↔PR)

Table 4.6 Significance

Category	Hypothesis Test	P	Corresponding Items
Significance	R3	>0.05	No significance
	cR1,2,3	<0.01	Significance
	cR1,2',3	−0.05<, <0	Significance
	rR1,2,3	<0.01	Significance
	rR1,2',3	−0.05<, <0	Significance

and learners can build a stable interactive learning mode earlier; this will affect the participation in the follow-up learning process.

Table 4.6 shows the significance of R3, cR1,2,3, cR1,2',3, rR1,2,3 and rR1,2',3. The data analysis results show that the assessment method does not have a significance on the assessment results. However, the positive paths of the same and different interactive learning processes have a positive significance on the assessment results, and the negative paths of the same and different interactive learning processes have a negative significance on the assessment results. The effective interactive learning process can promote the learning effect, while the negative interactive learning process will also have an adverse impact on the learning effect.

Based on the eight key problems and taking the final assessment results as observation variables, the data analysis results are statistically calculated and visualized, integrated into the key elements required for the early warning, and demonstrated the feasibility of value propagation in multiple dimensions. After full training and testing of complex relationships, the early warning value propagation topology in Figure 4.5 is obtained. The three interactive learning processes are composed of 20 temporal sequences (each temporal sequence is a week). Each interactive learning process distributes the interactive activities corresponding to the relevant learning content.

The early warning value propagation process in Figure 4.5 involves three-level routes and corresponding temporal sequences. Three-level routes have certain commonalities and differences. Learning contents, learning periods, majors and interactive activities affect the construction of routes, and also have special needs and objectives for the selection of early warning sequences. Relevant features are summarized as follows:

1 Route of different majors (positive path+negative path)

The routes between different majors are directly related to the learning content. The routes of different majors in different learning periods jointly form the positive and negative paths. To a certain extent, the learning content and organization mode will affect the learners' participation, and more stable groupness will be formed over time. Through the analysis, it is found that M1, M3 and M5 have high coincidence in the positive path, and M2 and M4 also have some similarities. The activities based on interaction and cooperation have played a positive role. QA and OA do not have a positive impact in interactive learning. Excessive participation in this aspect affects the construction and implementation of learners' key routes, resulting in adverse assessment results.

2 Route of interactive activities in the same learning period (positive path+ negative path)

In the same learning period, analyzing the learners' participation in interactive activities, it is found that the 11 interactive activities in Table 4.2 produce obvious local clusters. From the construction of learning behavior, there is a certain strong correlation between these interactive activities. The test results in Table 4.6 are obtained, namely WV and CP, IC and FD, SR and DM, QZ and PR; there is a potential correlation between two activities. In Figure 4.5, these four clusters are formed in the three learning periods, but these four clusters do not necessarily become the positive path of a certain learning content. For example, IC and FD are not included in the positive path of SS, MS and ES, but IC and FD play a key role in the positive path of CS and SE. The negative path of each learning period mainly includes QA and OA. They have no direct correlation, but have an adverse impact on the assessment results.

3 Route of interactive activities in different learning periods (positive path+negative path)

For the same major, there is the propagation of interactive activities in different learning periods, the learning behavior in the previous learning period will have significance on the subsequent learning behavior, forming the routes between interactive activities in different learning periods. For the positive path, UA is a key node of the three learning period route. WV and CP in the first learning period strongly affects WV and CP in the second and third learning period. IC and FD, SR and DM in the second learning period affect the corresponding clusters of the third learning period. QZ and PZ have a joint impact on the participation in the three learning periods, These interactive activities or clusters become the key nodes of the positive path. For the negative path, OA is the only node, but its participation has a related impact, which has become the key to adverse assessment results. The data analysis results show that learners' participation in QA will also have a malignant impact in different learning periods.

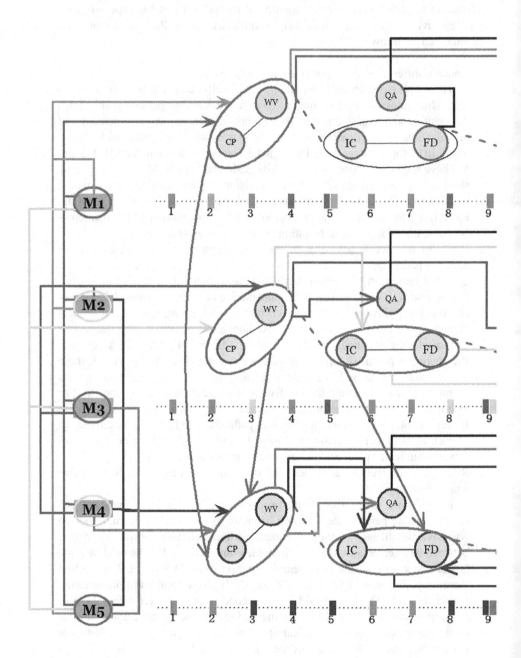

Figure 4.5 Early Warning Value Propagation Topology of Interactive Learning Process

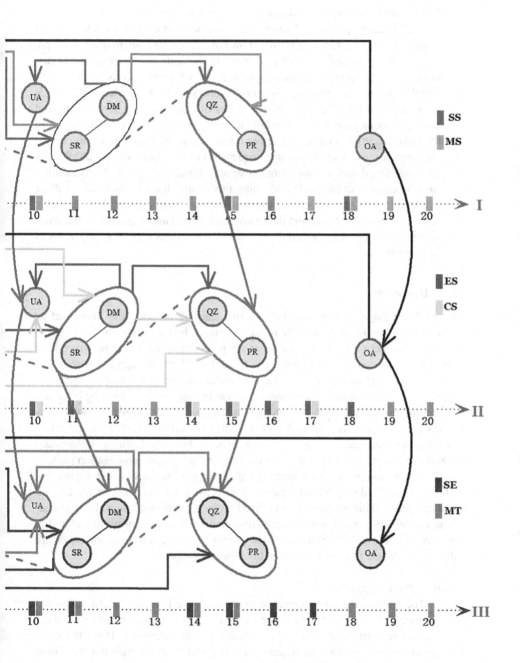

4   Early warning sequences of different learning contents

Each learning period is divided into 20 weeks, and each week is a temporal sequence. The experimental results show that a learning content needs multiple early warning sequences. Different learning contents may correspond to different or overlapping early warning sequences, which is directly related to the correlation between learning contents, Different marks are made in Figure 4.5; it can be seen that the temporal sequences of early warning form a compact and continuous process. If the whole learning process is divided according to the lower quartile, median and upper quartile, four parts can be obtained, and each part has a key early warning sequence. For example, MS has an obvious early warning demand in the second temporal sequence; CS and SE have similar early warning sequences. The teaching modes and learning methods of these two learning contents have great commonality, which brings very homogeneous risks. In other aspects, around the lower, median and upper quartile of the interactive learning process, a certain interval of continuous early warning needs to be constructed.

7   Discussion

By studying the early warning of interactive learning process, it is found that its value propagation path is directly related to major, learning content, learning period and interactive activities, and there are potential relationships between these elements. However, it is not feasible to mine the unified law applicable to all interactive learning processes, because the generation and presentation of data are affected by the autonomy, discreteness and goal inconsistency of learning behavior. Therefore, the early warning of interactive learning process needs to comprehensively analyze the data, and make an accurate evaluation according to the actual process and historical data, as well as the associated majors, learning contents and learning periods, so as to build a feasible early warning value propagation path.

The relationships of key elements in value propagation are shown in Figure 4.6. Through the scheduling and integration of early warning, the elements are learned and analyzed. Although there is no unified law for the early warning value propagation, a relatively general method can be designed. In order to improve the reliability and availability of early warning value propagation, the improved measures are discussed that are mainly reflected in the following aspects:

1   Relevance of majors

The major crossing is becoming more and more frequent, which makes the interaction and cooperation between different majors closer and closer, and the interactive learning processes have similarity and relevance. Then, the cross research topics involve the requirements and factors of multiple majors. These topics are also fed back to knowledge cognition and skill training. The research on the early warning value needs a comprehensive analysis and decision on the multiple similar or related majors, as well as multidimensional influence conditions and expected objectives.

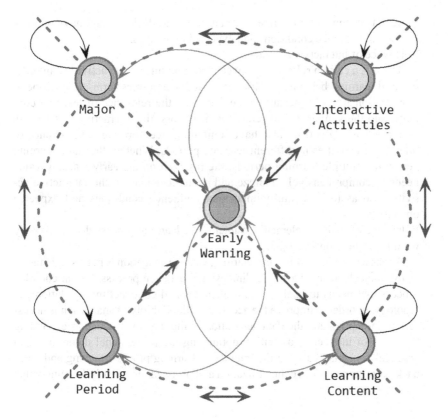

Figure 4.6 Relationships Between Relevant Elements of Interactive Learning Process in Value Propagation

2 Relevance of learning contents

There is knowledge relevance between different learning contents, which needs to follow a certain topological order. For example, before learning CS and SE, it is needed to learn SS and MS first. Or some learning contents need compulsory courses of a major, and their interactive learning process should serve the learning, practical and cognitive objectives. Relevant research on the early warning value requires comprehensive analysis and decision on the learning contents that are relevant or similar majors, as well as multidimensional influence conditions and expected objectives.

3 Relevance of learning periods

Learning behavior is constantly changing in a learning period with different trends. The same learning period is divided into different temporal sequences. Different temporal sequences correspond to related learning behavior. Along the learning period, multiple early warning sequences are generated. Different learning contents will be learned in different learning periods. The relevance of learning contents determines the relevance of learning periods. The research on the early warning value needs to serialize multiple learning periods for the same major, conduct comprehensive analysis and decision, and have multidimensional influence conditions and expected objectives.

4   Relevance of interactive activities

There is a certain relevance between learning interactive activities, in order to build learning behavior, multiple interactive activities form close cooperative relationships. At the same time, based on the relevance of learning contents, and the similarity and relevance of majors, the interactive activities in multiple learning periods also have some influence, forming the relevance of interactive activities in different learning periods. Whether the same learning period or multiple learning periods, the research on the early warning value needs to comprehensively analyze and make decisions on the interactive activities, so as to have multidimensional influence conditions and expected objectives.

5   Relevance of multiple elements in interactive learning process driven by early warning value propagation

As shown in Figure 4.6, early warning value propagation is not a single factor analysis mechanism or a single-dimensional decision process, but an complex process that needs to analyze multi-elements and construct multi-relationship topology. In order to improve the accuracy and reliability of analysis, it is necessary to in-depth study the data generation of these elements such as expanding the types of interactive activities, optimizing the professional theoretical and practical contents, realizing the interactive learning process tracking and feedback, in order to improve the utilization and propagation of early warning value propagation.

8   Conclusion

The full practice of interactive learning environments supported by various software and hardware provides a large amount of data, used to support early warning research and learning analytics, but it still faces various challenges (Xia, 2021c). Few researchers have done some work at the theories of early warning, but there are few relevant achievements on how to improve the data-driven early warning, and there is also a lack of analysis and test of the actual application scenarios. For the continuous learning behavior tracking, there is still more problems to analyze the change of learning behavior and adaptive early warning. In particular, there are many difficulties in the exploration of practical application algorithms and methods (Donker et al., 2021).

Based on the previous research results of early warning, this study puts forward early warning based on the multidimensional temporal sequences that fuses multidimensional elements, breaks through the linear early warning of single temporal sequences and demonstrates the early warning value propagation of interactive learning process. First, taking an actual interactive learning environment as the data collection platform, the key elements are mined from massive data, and the correlation and significance test problems are constructed; secondly, the elements are defined as nodes, the correlation or significance between elements is defined as relationships, the assessment results are observation variables and the early warning requirements are defined as the node value. A value propagation model is designed, and the relevant algorithms are realized. Through a large number of data training and testing, the optimal method applied to value propagation is derived to support the multiple temporal sequences. The experiments show that it can well support the value propagation of nodes and relationships; thirdly, according to the results of data analysis, the visualization of early warning value propagation is realized. Driven by data, the positive and negative paths of nodes and relationships are retrieved, and the relevant characteristics and existing problems are summarized. Finally, we evaluate the early warning value propagation process. The whole research provides a feasible learning analytics for the dynamic early warning. The conclusions might provide theoretical support and practical basis for the similar issues.

In the follow-up research, it will further deepen the exploration and application of learning analytics in the dynamic early warning, expand the analysis categories and calculation attributes, construct the practical for early warning pivot space, improve the accuracy and reliability of early warning and better serve the tracking, adjustment and optimization of interactive learning process.

References

Aguilar, S. J., Karabenick, S. A., Teasley, S. D., & Baek, C. (2021). Associations between learning analytics dashboard exposure and motivation and self-regulated learning. *Computers & Education*. 162, 104085. https://doi.org/10.1016/j.compedu.2020.104085

Clark, J. A., Liu, Y., & Isaias, P. (2020). Critical success factors for implementing learning analytics in higher education: a mixed-method inquiry. *Australasian Journal of Educational Technology*. 36(6), 89–106. https://doi.org/10.14742/ajet.6164

Dietrich, J., Greiner, F., Weber-Liel, D., Berweger, B., Kmpfe, N., & Kracke, B. (2021). Does an individualized learning design improve university student online learning? A randomized field experiment. *Computers in Human Behavior*. 106819. https://doi.org/10.1016/j.chb.2021.106819

Donker, M. H., Lian, V. V., Hessen, D. J., Gog, T. V., & Mainhard, T. (2021). Observational, student, and teacher perspectives on interpersonal teacher behavior: shared and unique associations with teacher and student emotions. *Learning and Instruction*. 73(4), 101414. https://doi.org/10.1016/j.learninstruc.2020.101414

Er, E., Dimitriadis, Y., & Gašević, D. (2021). Collaborative peer feedback and learning analytics: theory-oriented design for supporting class-wide interventions. *Assessment & Evaluation in Higher Education*. 46(2), 169–190. http://doi.org/10.1080/02602938.2020.1764490

Fischer, C., Pardos, Z. A., Baker, R. S., Williams, J. J., & Warschauer, M. (2020). Mining big data in education: affordances and challenges. *Review of Research in Education*. 44(1). https://doi.org/10.3102/0091732X20903304

Granberg, C., Palm, T., & Palmberg, B. (2021). A case study of a formative assessment practice and the effects on students' self-regulated learning. *Studies in Educational Evaluation*. 68(3). https://doi.org/10.1016/j.stueduc.2020.100955

Havu-Nuutinen, S., Kewalramani, S., Veresov, N., Pntinen, S., & Kontkanen, S. (2021). Understanding early childhood science education: comparative analysis of Australian and Finnish curricula. *Research in Science Education.* 52(1). https://doi.org/10.1007/s11165-020-09980-4

He, Y., Harper, S., & Vigo, M. (2021). Modeling micro-interactions in self-regulated learning: a data-driven methodology. *International Journal of Human-Computer Studies.* 151(3), 102625. https://doi.org/10.1016/j.ijhcs.2021.102625

Israel-Fishelson, R. A. (2021). Micro-persistence and difficulty in a game-based learning environment for computational thinking acquisition. *Journal of Computer Assisted Learning.* 37(3), 839–850. http://doi.org/10.1111/jcal.12527

Li, H., Majumdar, R., Chen, M., & Ogata, H. (2021). Goal-oriented active learning (goal) system to promote reading engagement, self-directed learning behavior, and motivation in extensive reading. *Computers & Education.* 171(2), 104239. https://doi.org/10.1016/j.compedu.2021.104239

Luo, Z. (2021). Using eye-tracking technology to identify learning styles: behaviour patterns and identification accuracy. *Education and Information Technologies.* 26, 4457–4485. https://doi.org/10.1007/s10639-021-10468-5

Main, J. B., Wang, Y., & Tan, L. (2021). Preparing industry leaders: the role of doctoral education and early career management training in the leadership trajectories of women STEM PhDs. *Research in Higher Education*, 1–25. https://doi.org/10.1007/s11162-021-09655-7

Song, D., Hong, H., & Oh, E. Y. (2021). Applying computational analysis of novice learners' computer programming patterns to reveal self-regulated learning, computational thinking, and learning performance. *Computers in Human Behavior.* 120(6), 106746. https://doi.org/10.1016/j.chb.2021.106746

Xia, X. (2020a). Random field design and collaborative inference strategy for learning interaction activities. *Interactive Learning Environments.* Advance online publication 30 Dec 2020. 1–25. https://doi.org/10.1080/10494820.2020.1863236

Xia, X. (2020b). Learning behavior mining and decision recommendation based on association rules in interactive learning environment. *Interactive Learning Environments.* Advance online publication 4 Aug 2020. 1–16. https://doi.org/10.1080/10494820.2020.1799028

Xia, X. (2021a). Decision application mechanism of regression analysis of multi-category learning behaviors in interactive learning environment. *Interactive Learning Environments.* Advance online publication 23 Apr 2021. 1–14. https://doi.org/10.1080/10494820.2021.1916767

Xia, X. (2021b). Interaction recognition and intervention based on context feature fusion of learning behaviors in interactive learning environments. *Interactive Learning Environments.* Advance online publication 17 Jan 2021. 1–19. https://doi.org/10.1080/10494820.2021.1871632

Xia, X. (2021c). Sparse learning strategy and key feature selection in interactive learning environment. *Interactive Learning Environments.* Advance online publication Nov 2021. 1–25. https://doi.org/10.1080/10494820.2021.1998913

Yilmaz, O. (2020). The human muscular arm avatar as an interactive visualization tool in learning anatomy: medical students' perspectives. *IEEE Transactions on Learning Technologies.* 13(3), 593–603. http://doi.org/10.1109/TLT.2020.2995163

Zainuddin, Z., Shujahat, M., Haruna, H., & Chu, S. (2020). The role of gamified e-quizzes on student learning and engagement: an interactive gamification solution for a formative assessment system. *Computers & Education.* 145(Feb), 103729. https://doi.org/10.1016/j.compedu.2019.103729

5 Early Warning Pivot Space Model of Multi-Temporal Interactive Learning Process

Abstract

Based on the conclusions of Chapters 2–4, the following work is to deepen the early warning needs and decision applications brought about by imbalanced learning behavior instances. The online learning platform not only promotes the teaching objectives but also realizes the enthusiasm and autonomy of learners. However, it also breaks away from the direct supervision and tracking of instructors in the traditional classroom, so the learning behavior presents a strong discreteness, and the generated data has a strong imbalance. This chapter explores MT-BCSSCAN applied to the early warning of unbalanced learning behavior. It divides interactive learning behavior into three types: generative, browsing, as well as interactive and collaboration, and introduces other online behaviors into the feature calculation, realizing unbalanced multi-source data fusion. The experimental results show that MT-BCSSCAN can effectively support the prediction of interactive learning behavior based on high performance, and further draw the conclusion of relevant test problems. After fusing other online behaviors of learners, the three types of learning behavior form significant relationships, and the corresponding early warning model and decision application strategy are derived. The whole research adopts deep learning method, creatively constructs the prediction method of massive unbalanced interactive learning behavior, realizes the fusion calculation of multi-source data and improves the quality of early warning that might be the important basis for implementing the temporal tracking and decision intervention of unbalanced learning behaviors. It is of great significance for precipitation prediction in the early warning, as well as the foundation of the work in Chapter 7.

Keywords

Multi-temporal Sequence; Early Warning Pivot Space Model;   Learning Analytics; Space Division; Interactive Learning Process

DOI: 10.4324/9781003484905-5

1   Introduction

The online learning platform realizes the digitization and traceability of the learning process; these data might be used to describe historical learning behavior, provide a basis for studying potential learning behavior and reflect the particularity and complexity of educational data (Li et al., 2021; O'Neill et al., 2021; Song et al., 2021). Online technology, software technology and data technology are fully implemented, which strengthens the business robustness of the online learning platform, realizes the full description of the interactive learning process and produces massive dynamic data and multi-relationships: on the one hand, it has the characteristics of significant multidisciplinary, multi-temporal, multi-scene and multi-semantics (Xia, 2021a); on the other hand, it perfectly ensures the individualized learning behavior and interactive mode, rather than a learning environment under controlled rules and requirements (Lai et al., 2020). Moreover, the multi-elements and relationships are opportunities and challenges for studying and deepening learning analytics (Koeslag-Kreunen et al., 2020). Effective data mining and prediction is an important basis for improving, optimizing and intervening learning. In a series of related studies, the new demand for learning analytics brought by the early warning has always been a research difficulty (Alemany et al., 2020).

The rapidly accumulated massive learner behavior logs and items provide complete data for the research of early warning (Xia, 2020a). These data contain rich information, which is an important basis for describing the temporal sequences and correlations. The online learning platform drives the development and application of early warning, which is mainly reflected in two aspects: one is the practical research and development of relevant software and hardware systems (Ober et al., 2021); the second is to analyze learning behavior in different dimensions, judge the current state and possible trend of learning behavior, generate problem reports and make targeted decision (Cerezo et al., 2020). The early warning is to compare the current learning situation with a certain measurement standard, and find that there has been or will be some inconsistency or violation, and the learning behavior has potential risks. It is necessary to give warning and guiding in advance. In this process, early warning needs to form a closed-loop strategy "tracking-analysis-prediction-intervention". With the help of applicable big data technology, it might ensure benign learning behavior and learning effect as much as possible.

However, the existing theoretical and applied research on early warning mainly focuses on the tracking and feedback of a single learning period. The early warning between multiple learning periods has not been fully analyzed and demonstrated. Based on the massive data set of learning behavior with multiple complete learning periods, this study will build a topology supported by multi-elements to realize the early warning pivot space model. Each learning period is defined as a complete interactive learning process; we mine interrelated elements between different interactive learning processes, demonstrate the critical path of early warning pivot and the corresponding temporal sequence strategy, so as to realize the linkage early warning mechanism of multi-interactive learning process.

2 Related Work

Based on the relevant references on the early warning of interactive learning process (La Gatta et al., 2021; Ruiz et al., 2020). The core problems of early warning are mainly reflected in three aspects: (1) accurate and efficient positioning and identification of risk learners; (2) setting appropriate early warning domain for continuous learning behavior; and (3) providing accurate and effective learning intervention measures. Some references focus on the early warning research scheme, take the assessment needs as the precursor condition of the interactive learning process and consider the constituent characteristics of the interactive learning process in advance; however, this scheme ignores the learners' own conditions and learning background, and ignores the learners' individuality and autonomy; or take the assessment results as the subsequent force, demonstrate the risks and problems according to the various indicators of the assessment results and summarize the feasible early warning schemes and intervention measures. Is it applicable to the next interactive learning process? It is difficult to achieve accurate evaluation in advance, which is not dynamic and relevant (Rui et al., 2016).

The interactive learning process is continuous and progressive, not an endpoint or single line structure. Therefore, early warning needs to be transformed into a multi-element metric space model, which is more helpful to improving the traceability, dynamics and relevance of early warning.

The advantage of the metric space model is its high applicability. It has no restrictions on data, and only needs to meet the distance function (Gregory, 2021). In the data analysis, the trigonometric inequality of distance function might be mainly deduced. The data is abstracted into some points in the metric space, which improves the universality, but also loses the coordinate and semantic information. The only available information is distance. The lack of coordinates and semantics makes the metric space have many shortcomings, and it also causes many obstacles (Olmanson et al., 2021). Therefore, mapping data from metric space to pivot space is a focus of many big data analysis and applications. It is mainly reflected in the following two aspects.

1 The pivot-based metric space index structure is used to manage data with uniform distance distribution and relative concentration. However, in the process of data search, if the search space is too large, the search efficiency will be greatly reduced. Therefore, in the training process of some commercial or network data, some subspace partition techniques are usually used to divide the metric space, the adjacent nodes are selected in metric space and European space to build a two layer topology and then fast routing is realized through the cooperation of routing table and local index tree.

2 For non-centralized data, a similar data index structure based on dynamic clustering is constructed. The metric space object is used as the node, the relationship is organized according to the nature of the metric space and the subspace is divided by data insertion. For the asynchrony of node insertion and data insertion, heuristic search is used to improve the hit rate of key nodes. This method

realizes the independence of data and maintains a relatively stable hit rate. With the help of heuristic algorithm, the analysis complexity can be significantly reduced.

The research of these two aspects has been demonstrated in the interactive learning process. However, for the data distribution and relationship construction. It is not only a network structure but also there are complex elements and hierarchical structure, which needs to be deeply designed.

3   Data Processing and Problem Description

Interactive learning process is to strengthen the interaction and cooperation between learners and instructors, learners and learning content, and learners in the learning process (Xia, 2020b). When studying the interactive learning process, it is necessary to ensure the continuity, relative integrity and long periodicity of interaction and cooperation, so as to mine the laws and significant problems. Since 2020, this study has tracked 3,657 learners of a university for three semesters, and collected the online behavior traces through the campus network, involving ten majors, consisting of online and offline data. According to the privacy protection requirements, the unified desensitization and standardized processing are realized through program design, and the abnormal data and noise are cleaned and deleted. The final data scale is 1.36PB. The basic information of 15 majors is shown in Table 5.1.

It can be seen from Table 5.1, History major has the least number of learners, and Economics, Computer Science, Mathematics and Software Engineering have more. The data scale is the largest in Software Engineering and the smallest in History. In the learning process of these majors, there are differences in interactive modes which mainly produce seven interaction modes. Among them, System Development is mainly reflected in the R&D of software system. Learners are divided into R&D groups. This interactive mode is mainly applied to the two majors of Computer Science and Software Engineering; Survey is a comprehensive

Table 5.1 Data Description

Major	Learner Scale	Data Scale	Interaction Mode (IM)
Computer Science (CS)	466	0.172PB	System Development***
Software Engineering (SE)	430	0.181PB	System Development***
Mathematics (MS)	434	0.151PB	Homework*
Physics (PS)	380	0.159PB	Experiment*
Management (MT)	303	0.125PB	Practice**
Pedagogy (PY)	252	0.131PB	Practice**
History (HY)	207	0.096PB	Survey***
Economics (ES)	472	0.099PB	Investigation and Research***
Journalism (JM)	398	0.141PB	Investigation and Research***
Literature (LE)	315	0.105PB	Survey***

*offline, **online, ***offline&online.

investigation, classification and organization of the learned content. In this interactive process, learners can form a relatively complete topic research by querying online and offline materials, books and documents. Learners can complete it independently or form a small group, which is mainly used in History and Literature. Homework is a practice topic set for the learning content to improve learners' cognition, which is completed offline by learners. This interactive mode is mainly applied to Mathematics. Practice refers to the theory and rules of the learning content and the experience of learners. This interactive model is mainly applied to Management and Pedagogy; Investigation and Research is the combination of theory and practice. It mainly applies to Economics and Journalism by summarizing and tracing the current phenomena or existing problems, finding the corresponding principles and putting forward improvement measures and effective decisions. Experiment is a specific experiment based on specific equipment and reagents, which is mainly used in Physics.

These interactive modes cover the basic professional contents of ten majors and three learning periods, and these interactive modes produce a continuous and lasting interaction and cooperation. In this study, learners' interactive activities are mainly online, and some majors have completed some online assessments, as shown in Table 5.2; it mainly involves 14 kinds of activities. Different activities have different modes and objects; the participation and preference of these activities are different, which is directly related to the professional learning content and learning needs. These activities describe the frequency of learners' participation through the click rate. The assessment results are viewed as observation variables to demonstrate the significance of interactive activities, so as to judge the law and existing problems of interactive activities.

Table 5.2 Interactive Activities

Activity	Form	Interactive Objects
Video&audio (VD)	Click	learner↔video and audio
Interaction (IN)	Comment without time limit	learner↔platform/lecturer/learner
Forum (FM)	Instant comment	learner↔platform/lecturer/learners
Content (CT)	Click	learner↔contents
Resource (RE)	Click	learner↔contents
Illuminate (IL)	Search engine	learner↔platform
Glossary (GY)	Search engine	learner↔platform
Folder (FR)	Click	learner↔platform
DataSet (DS)	Upload/download	learner↔platform
Task Submit (TS)	Upload/download	learner↔platform
Wiki (WK)	Search engine	learner↔platform
Questionnaire (QN)	Question&answer(unfixed duration)	learner↔platform/lecturer
Quiz (QZ)	Question&answer(fixed duration)	learner↔platform/lecturer
Assessment	Question&answer(fixed duration)	learner↔platform/lecturer

Table 5.3 Assessment Method

Major	1st Semester	2nd Semester	3rd Semester
Computer Science (CS)	Online, offline	Online, online&offline	Online, online&offline
Software Engineering (SE)	Online, offline	Online, online&offline	Online, online&offline
Mathematics (MS)	Online	Online, offline	Offline, online&offline
Physics (PS)	Offline	Online, online&offline	Offline
Management (MT)	Offline	Offline, online&offline	Offline
Pedagogy (PY)	Offline	Online, offline	Offline
History (HY)	Offline	Offline, online&offline	Offline
Economics (ES)	Online&offline	Online, online&offline	Online, online&offline
Journalism (JM)	Online&offline	Online, online&offline	Online, online&offline
Literature (LE)	Offline	Offline, online&offline	Offline

The final assessment methods of all majors are online and offline, which is related to the learning content. The same major has different learning contents in different semesters, which corresponds to different assessment methods. Then, when collecting data, we need to comprehensively consider the assessment methods and the standardization of assessment results. The assessment methods of different majors in different semesters are shown in Table 5.3. It can be seen that in these three semesters, the online assessment has been explored in different majors. The combination of online and offline assessments is more widely used, but the offline method is still used in some learning contents. The assessment results are regarded as the learning effectiveness of learners. Different assessment methods also stimulate the participation and repetition of interactive activities, resulting in different learning behaviors and corresponding risks. During data analysis, the activities, assessment methods and comprehensive assessment results need to be included in the calculation and evaluation.

Each semester is a continuous temporal process, which is composed of interrelated sequences. In this study, a week is defined as a temporal sequence so that each semester can be divided into 20 temporal sequences. A multi-correlation calculation domain is formed between the activities, assessment methods and assessment results of the three semesters, as shown in Figure 5.1. The second semester is defined as the transition period of interactive activities between the first and third semesters, and the early warning pivot space of temporal sequence, majors and interactive activities of the three semesters is constructed. In data analysis and pivot mining, we take the final assessment results as observation variables to demonstrate the following six problems:

P1: key temporal sequence of each semester;
P2: relevant interactive activities of key temporal sequences;
P3: correlation between key temporal sequences of different majors in each semester;
P4: correlation between key temporal sequences of the same major in different semesters;

P5: critical path of interactive activities formed by the key temporal sequences of each semester of each major;

P6: critical path of interactive activities formed by the key temporal sequence of different semesters of each major;

Based on the test results of P1–P6, the key interactive activities, critical paths and key temporal sequences are defined as the pivots and relationships, and the pivot space of temporal early warning is constructed.

4 Method

According to the distribution and potential correlation of multi-temporal sequences, interactive activities, majors and assessments in Figure 5.1, the pivot space model of interactive process is constructed. However, in the pivot space model, the distance between data is different from that in the metric space, and there is distortion, which is not suitable for constructing the topology of interactive learning process. It is necessary to improve the basic rules of pivot space and optimize space relationship of interactive learning process that might solve the distortion.

First, relevant definitions are given.

4.1 Pivot Space

The metric space is represented as (M, d), M is a finite non-empty data set, d is a distance function about M and satisfies three properties:

1 Positive definiteness: if $x, y \in M$, $d(x,y) \geq 0$, then $d(x,y) = 0 \Leftrightarrow x = y$.
2 Symmetry: if $x, y \in M$, then $d(x,y) = d(y,x)$.
3 Triangular inequality: if $x, y, z \in M$, then $d(x,y) + d(y,z) \geq d(x,z)$, $d(x,z) + d(y,z) \geq d(x,y)$, $d(x,y) + d(x,z) \geq d(y,z)$.

Let S be a finite subset composed of elements in M; then $S = \{x_i \mid x_i \in M, i = 1, 2, \cdots, n\}$, P is the pivot set $P = \{p_1, p_2, \cdots, p_k\}$, its length is k, $P \subseteq S$. For any element x in S, the distance to all pivots is its coordinates; we define a mapping x^P from M to k; then, the pivot space is defined as:

$$F_{p,d}: M \to R^k : x^P \equiv F_{p,d}(x) = \left(f_1(x), \cdots, f_k(x)\right)$$
$$= \left(d(x, p_1), \cdots, d(x, p_k)\right) \in F_{P,d}(M)$$

The pivot space of S is a mapping in R^k, expressed as:

$$F_{p,d}(S) = \left\{x^P \mid x^P = F_{p,d}(x) = \left(d(x, p_1), \cdots, d(x, p_k)\right), x \in S\right\}$$

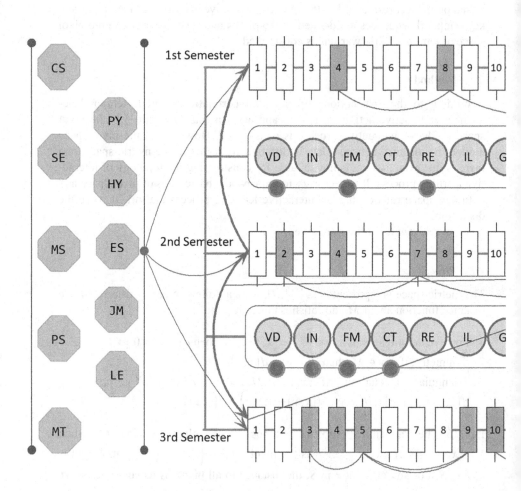

Figure 5.1 Correlation Topology of Multi-temporal Interactive Learning Process

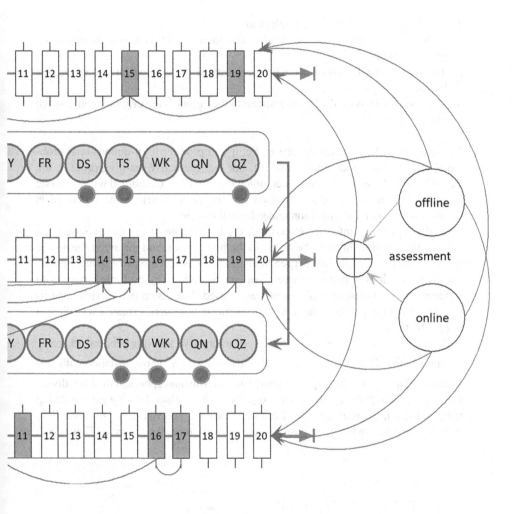

4.2   Complete Pivot Space

Complete pivot space (CPS) is obtained after all points in the data set are selected as pivots, expressed as $F_d^c(S)$. The distance between any two points in the CPS is equal to their distance in the original data space and meets the following properties:

1 The dimension of CPS is equivalent to S.
2 Only one value in the coordinates of each point of CPS is 0, and the others are positive numbers.
3 The points of CPS correspond to the points in the original metric space one by one.
4 The coordinate axes of CPS correspond to the points in the original metric space one by one.

CPS can avoid the distance distortion, but it will produce high-dimensional problems, so dimension reduction is needed. For the interactive learning process, the data division of the metric space is completed in the CPS. Combined with the basic topology of Figure 5.1, the data division method of the metric space is defined as the fusion of hyperplane division and spherical division.

In the process of interactive learning, the hyperplane of the metric space is a straight line passing through the origin in the pivot space, and the arc in the metric space becomes a straight line perpendicular to the x axis in the pivot space. Spherical division achieves that the same pivot can be divided by multiple circles with different radius so that multiple pivots can be used. The fusion of hyperplane partition and spherical partition can make the partition boundaries rotate each other in the pivot space.

Given the metric space data set (S,d) of interactive learning process, the early warning range $R(q,r)$ is to find out all elements x in S whose distance with q is within r, $d(q,x) \le r$. The original hyperplane division and spherical division divide the data into two parts. If one of the two parts can be excluded during early warning range retrieval, the retrieval speed can be improved; otherwise, the retrieval time will be increased, which is a case of poor performance. As shown in Figure 5.2,

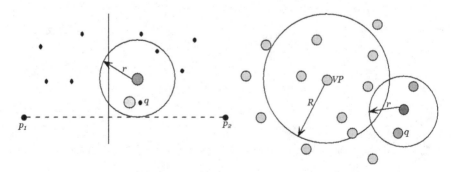

Figure 5.2 Poor Performance of Early Warning Range

when the arc of range retrieval intersects the division boundary, these two parts cannot be excluded.

Therefore, in the CPS of the interactive learning process, the effective early warning range of single semester is realized through hyperplane division. For the effective early warning range of multi-semesters, the boundary location is realized through spherical division, and the probability of the intersection of the retrieval arc and the division boundary is taken as an parameter to measure the retrieval performance. This probability is directly proportional to the number of elements near the division boundary. This study uses the r −neighborhood $|N_r(L)|$ as a measure of retrieval performance, the smaller the value, the better.

In the pivot space of interactive learning process, the boundaries of hyperplane partition and spherical partition become straight lines. The r −neighborhood is determined by the parallel lines on both sides of the dividing boundary, $|N_r(L)|$ is determined by the width of the r −neighborhood, as well as the linear density of data in the direction perpendicular to the boundary. In this way, in the metric space of multi-semesters, the early warning range with radius r is spherical. The shape of the sphere after mapping to the pivot space cannot be determined, but it will be completely contained in a cube with center q^p and side length $2r$, as shown in Figure 5.3.

Thus, it can be proved that the r − neighborhood satisfies the following theorem:

1 The r −neighborhood width of spherical partition in pivot space is $2r$;
2 The r −neighborhood width of hyperplane division in pivot space is $2\sqrt{2}r$;
3 The line with slope $a(1 < a < 1)$ in pivot space is used to divide the boundary, and its r −neighborhood width is $2\dfrac{1+a}{\sqrt{1+a^2}}r$.

According to the principles of hyperplane partition and spherical partition, the partition process of metric space in the whole interactive learning process is described as Algorithm 1.

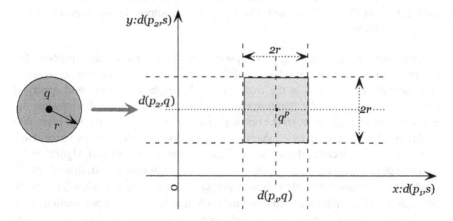

Figure 5.3 Transformation of Metric Space into Pivot Space Contained by Cube

Algorithm 1

Step 1: The temporal sequences of a single semester are defined as a process, which uses hyperplane division to retrieve the early warning range and the corresponding pivot set, and iteratively calls the optimal pivot selection algorithm (i.e. Algorithm 2);

Step 2: Construct the pivot space respectively, and calculate the corresponding warning range according to the r −neighborhood theorem; calculate $\left| N_r \left(L \right) \right|$ of the corresponding early warning range.

Step 3: If the hyperplane division is not completed in three semesters, go to Step 1, otherwise go to Step 4;

Step 4: Define the temporal sequences and relationships of three semesters as a multi-correlation system;

Step 5: Take early warning range of the single process as the boundary, analyze correlation on the temporal sequences, interactive activities, assessment methods and other elements of the three semesters, and construct related data subsets;

Step 6: Iteratively use spherical division to retrieve the early warning range of each data subset, determine the pivot set, respectively, and iteratively call the optimal pivot selection algorithm (i.e. Algorithm 2);

Step 7: The pivot space comprehensively adopts the suitability of hyperplane division and spherical division, and constructs the early warning range and pivots of different data subsets;

Step 8: Calculate the early warning range $\left| N_r \left(L \right) \right|$ of all data subsets according to the r −neighborhood theorem;

Step 9: Sort $\left| N_r \left(L \right) \right|$ in ascending order. According to the early warning requirements of the interactive learning process, select the applicable early warning range and set effective $\left| N_r \left(L \right) \right|$;

Step 10: According to the selected early warning range, determine the final early warning topology and the corresponding temporal sequences, key interactive activities, assessment methods and other elements.

Step 11: Build the early warning pivot space and output the corresponding key elements.

To construct the early warning pivot space in the interactive learning process, the key problem is to realize the selection of the optimal pivots. This is a multi-iterative operation of Algorithm 1 in the two steps of hyperplane division and spherical division. In this study, the iterative enumeration method is used that ensures the effectiveness and reliability of the optimal pivots and obtains the overall pivot distribution. Therefore, the whole experimental process is divided into two processes: one is the pivot selection, the second is the experimental analysis of Algorithm 1.

The optimal pivot selection process needs the common constraints of multi-conditions. Suppose we need to select m pivots; the data scale is $n \left(n \geq m \right)$, and there are r query radii. m data are used as pivots each time to form C_n^m combination; each combination is viewed as pivots; we calculate the average distance times for each query radius. In the calculation process, each data in the dataset is defined as the query object, but some data can be excluded by triangular inequality. If it cannot be excluded, the distance needs to be calculated and the calculation times are accumulated. After traversing the combination of all pivots, the combination corresponding to the minimum distance calculation times is selected as the optimal pivot combination. The calculation process is described as Algorithm 2.

Algorithm 2

Step 1: While every m data is combined as pivots
Step 2: While each query radius
Step 3: While each query object
Step 4: While every data in set
Step 5: Use triangular inequality to exclude or include data. For data that cannot be excluded, calculate the distance to judge whether it is within the query radius. The number of query results and the number of distance calculations are obtained.
Step 6: End while
Step 7: The average distance calculation times of the pivot combination in the current radius are obtained;
Step 8: Record results
Step 9: End while
Step 10: End while
Step 11: End while
Step 12: Output pivot combination with minimum distance calculation times

5 Experiment

According to the learning period, major, interactive activities, assessment methods and assessment results, the data of multi-temporal sequences of interactive learning process is divided into five dimensions, and then full experiments are carried out. The range of query radius is [0.05,0.5], and the interval is 0.05. One to five pivots are selected for each dimension to form 25 combinations. The amount of data corresponds to the number of pivots, so the number of pivots and the amount of data are the key factors limiting the experiment time. When the pivot number is gradually increased, the amount of data should be reduced. In addition to saving the calculation results, it is necessary to count the maximum distance calculation times (maxDCT), the minimum distance calculation times (minDCT), the distance calculation time sum (DCTsum) and the distance calculation time square sum (DCTss) on each radius.

In order to improve the operation efficiency of the experiment, parallel computing is realized, and multi-process parallelism is adopted among computing nodes. According to the sample size and the pivot number, the number of calculation nodes and running time are shown in Table 5.4. The running time means to complete the operation and selection of pivots, which is directly related to the pivot number, sample size and calculation nodes. When the pivot number increases and the sample size decreases, the workload of data analysis can be greatly reduced and the identification ability of key data can be improved.

Table 5.4 Corresponding Experimental Data

Pivot Number	Sample Size	Calculation Nodes	Running Time
1	5,000	3	120s
2	5,000	5	35m
3	5,000	70	25h
4	1,000	80	34h
5	500	80	5h

Ten-fold cross validation realizes random sampling of interactive learning process, program iteratively calculates, sort out all items obtained in each program iteration, and deduces the optimal pivot distribution. Experiments show that when the data dimension is 4 and the query radius is 0.05, the probability of optimal pivot distribution is the largest, and the data analysis on other dimensions and radii is basically similar. Figures 5.4–5.8 show the distributions of the optimal 1 pivot, 2 pivots, 3 pivots, 4 pivots and 5 pivots. For each distribution, it shows the optimal value. The relevant characteristics are as follows:

1 In Figure 5.4, the optimal pivots are mainly distributed at both ends of the diagonal of the two-dimensional plane; when one pivot is selected from the data set, the optimal pivot distribution is mainly concentrated at the two endpoints of the data set;
2 In Figure 5.5, a pair of pivots are distributed near the four corners of the square; when two pivots are selected from the data set, the two data points at the adjacent endpoints are easier to become better pivots;
3 In Figure 5.6, when three pivots are selected from the data set, the optimal pivots are basically distributed around the data set rather than at the endpoints, which is different from the case of one or two pivots. The space of each three pivots is approximately equivalent to the three vertices of isosceles triangle;
4 In Figure 5.7, when four pivots are selected from the data set, the optimal pivots are not only distributed around the data set but also the inner data is easy to be selected as the pivots. The quadrilateral composed of the sidelines of the four pivots is similar to a diamond;
5 In Figure 5.8, when five pivots are selected from the data set, the distribution interval of the optimal pivots is mainly concentrated in the interior of the data set rather than the periphery.

It can be seen from Figures 5.4–5.8 that the distribution of 1–5 optimal pivots is relatively scattered, so it is necessary to further analyze the internal topology of multi-elements. Taking the distribution of two optimal pivots as an example, 5,000 original data are mapped to the optimal CPS with Euclidean distance. The mapped data distribution is shown in Figure 5.9. The data distribution in the optimal pivot space is wide and uniform, the distortion degree of the original data mapped to the optimal pivot space is smaller, and it is easier to distinguish the data and obtain the best data performance.

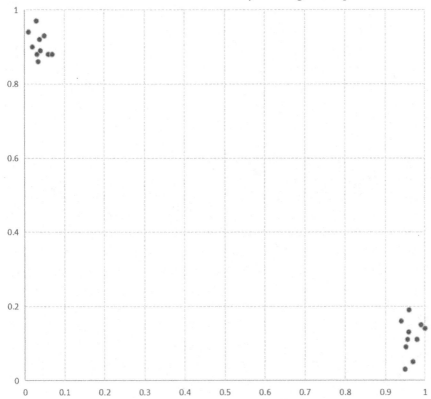

Figure 5.4 One Optimal Pivot

Furthermore, according to the change of division radius, the relevant indicators are calculated by statistical distance. The interval of division radius is 0.05. The calculation results of the four statistics are shown in Table 5.5. With the increase in division radius, maxDCT, minDCT, DCTsum and DCTss will increase, and some even increase exponentially.

As for the changes of the number of data combinations and the distance calculation times, data tracking is also done in the experiment. (1) and (2) of Figure 5.10 are the change trend of distance calculation times when the radius is 0.03 and 0.3, respectively, and the number of data combinations reaches 473,711. The calculation times are arranged in the descending order, and the maximum distance times and minimum distance times of radius are marked. In the (1) subgraph of Figure 5.10, the whole change trend is a relatively stable curve. However, the front section of the curve decreases significantly at 9,735 combinations, and the decline frequency of all sections in the rear section is gentle, indicating that the reliability and stability of most random combinations are good. The (2) subgraph of Figure 5.10 is the trend after the radius increases to 0.5. When the radius increases, the change trend is more gentle and the distribution of distance calculation is more extensive. From this aspect, the algorithms designed in this study can be applied to the data analysis of interactive learning process that can ensure good performance.

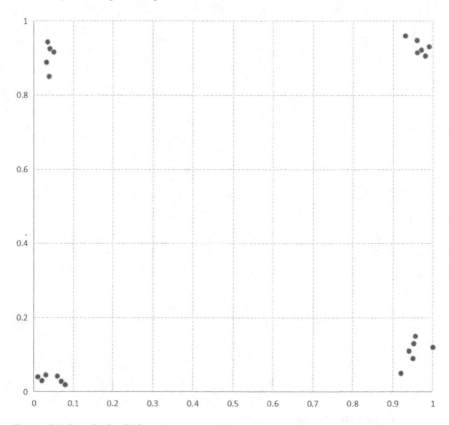

Figure 5.5 Two Optimal Pivots

6 Result

As some existing pivot selection methods are more mature, the possibility of optimizing the multi-interactive learning process might be difficult, which is not suitable to the multi-element analysis. The existing mature technology is not suitable for the effective learning analysis (Schüttpelz-Brauns et al., 2020). About the interactive data described by five elements, this study puts forward the mapping idea of the CPS model and adopts hyperplane division and spherical division. It can improve the efficiency of data analysis and explore the feasibility of the pivot space of interactive learning process. Through the full experiments, we find that the key measurement indicators are much good, and can ensure the robustness and reliability of the analysis results.

According to the data analysis results, taking assessment results as the observation variables, the assessment results score ≥85 are excellent, and score ≥60 are passed; otherwise, they will not pass. We demonstrate the test problems proposed in the third section, visualize the conclusions obtained from each problem and describe the relationship of early warning pivot space in the multi-temporal interactive learning process, as shown in Figure 5.11.

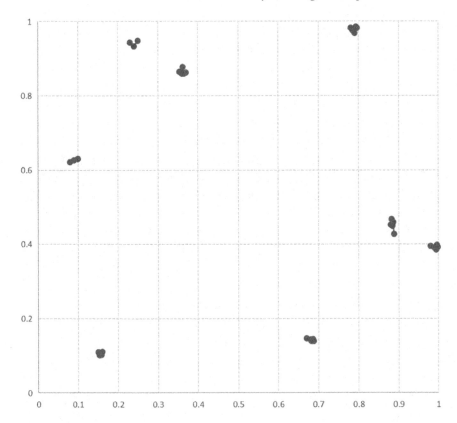

Figure 5.6 Three Optimal Pivots

Based on Figure 5.11, the test results of the six problems in the third section are obtained, which are respectively:

1 P1: key temporal sequence of each semester.

Through the full learning and division of early warning pivot space, the iterative calculation of learning behavior of ten majors is realized, and the key temporal sequence of each semester is divided into different stages. It can be seen from Figure 5.11 that each week does not necessarily become a significant key sequence; the continuous sequence of early warning might improve the intervention effect. In the first semester, there are three locally continuous early warning stages. The 4th and 5th weeks constitute the first stage, the 9th–11th weeks constitute the second stage, and the 14th–17th weeks constitute the third stage. In the second semester, the 3rd–6th weeks constitute the first stage, the 8th–12th weeks constitute the second stage and the 15th–19th weeks constitute the third stage. In the third semester, the 1st–4th weeks constitute the first stage, the 7th–15th weeks constitute the second stage, and the 18th–20th weeks constitute the third stage. In the three semesters, there are three stages of early

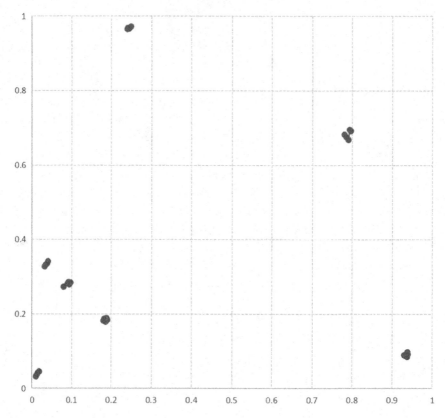

Figure 5.7 Four Optimal Pivots

warning period, but the corresponding temporal sequences are different. The early warning stages of the second semester and the third semester are much larger than that of the first semester. The three semesters also have the same temporal sequences in the same early warning stage.

2 P2: relevant interactive activities of key temporal sequences.

The key temporal sequences of the three semesters mainly produce two types of interactive activities and relationships. There are obvious differences between the first semester and the third semester. At the same time, the significant interactive activities of the ten majors in the second semester are between the first semester and the third semester, which is directly related to the major and the professional learning content. In general, all interactive activities have a strong correlation around VD. After statistical analysis, the correlation between interactive activities is shown in Table 5.6. VD, CT and RE related to learning content occupy an important position in the three semesters; they have been widely concerned by learners. Science and Engineering majors have a strong participation in interactive and collaborative activities such as FM and IN. No matter which semester, QZ has been fully applied in all majors. In the second

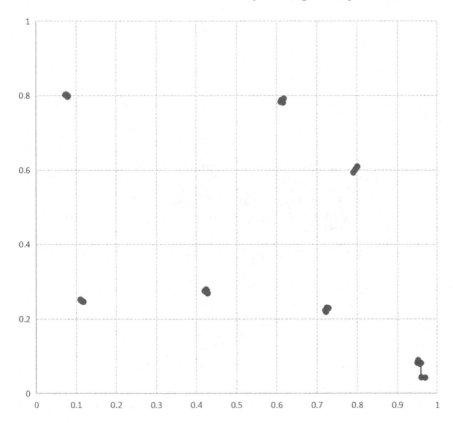

Figure 5.8 Five Optimal Pivots

and third semesters, learners of Science and Engineering majors have a strong demand for participation and application trend in DS and TS.

3 P3: correlation between key temporal sequences of different majors in each semester.

    In the three semesters, there are obvious commonness and differences in the key temporal sequences of different majors. The commonness of the first semester is the largest, and the difference of the second semester is the largest. According to the key temporal sequences of early warning, different major groups are formed in three semesters. In the first semester, the six majors of PS, MS, Se, CS, MT and ES are similar, and the three temporal stages form a strong progressive correlation. JM, PY, LE and HY have commonness, and all have strong correlation in the second and third temporal sequence stages. In the second semester, the major is divided into three groups. PS, MS, Se and CS correspond to the three temporal stages, resulting in progressive strong correlation. MT and ES have strong correlation in the second and third sequence stages, respectively. The early warning of JM, PY, LE and HY is only related to the third temporal stage. In the third semester, the majors form five groups, PS and MS form a

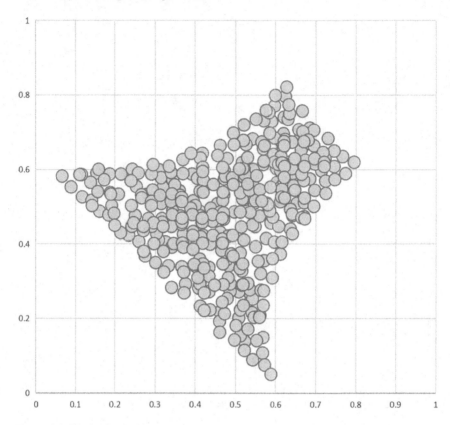

Figure 5.9 Six Optimal Pivots

Table 5.5 Calculation Results of Four Statistics

Radius	maxDCT	minDCT	DCTsum	DCTss
0.05	99.74	6.93	6.22e+06	1.01e+08
0.10	184.03	16.95	1.21e+07	8.39e+08
0.15	267.63	33.11	2.94e+07	2.44e+09
0.20	342.50	53.34	3.26e+07	6.35e+09
0.25	468.87	79.45	7.59e+07	1.03e+10
0.30	553.06	104.08	8.64e+07	2.67e+10
0.35	626.17	144.39	9.53e+07	3.63e+10
0.40	709.35	180.44	1.23e+08	4.88e+10
0.45	783.55	225.05	1.84e+08	7.07e+10
0.50	860.72	253.17	1.93e+09	8.81e+10

progressive strong correlation in the first and second temporal stages and SE and CS form a strong correlation in the three temporal stages. LE and HY form one group, and C and D also form a whole, they are all only related to the second temporal stage, because of the obvious difference of interactive activities, different groups are formed respectively. JM and PY form a strong progressive

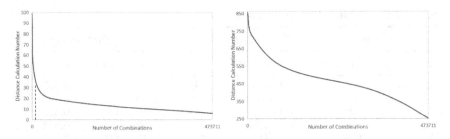

Figure 5.10 Distance Calculation Times with Different Radii. (1) radius = 0.03 (2) radius = 0.30

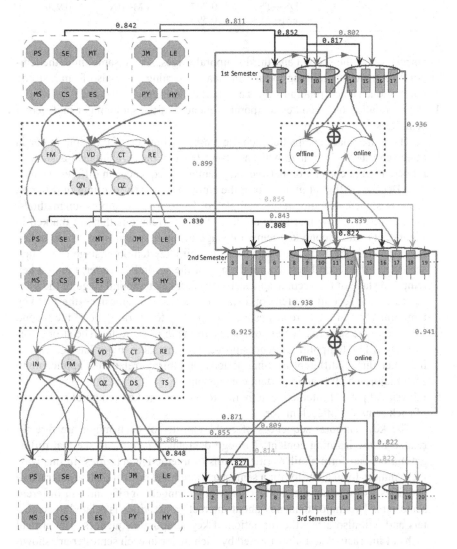

Figure 5.11 Early Warning Pivot Space Topology in Multi-temporal Interactive Learning Process

Table 5.6 Correlation of Interactive Activities

1st Semester		2nd Semester		3rd Semester	
Activities' Item	*Correlation*	*Activities' Item*	*Correlation*	*Activities' Item*	*Correlation*
VD→CT	0.842	VD→CT	0.793	VD→CT	0.877
VD→RE	0.831	VD→RE	0.761	VD→RE	0.892
VD↔FR	0.804	VD↔FR	0.735	VD↔FR	0.823
VD→QZ	0.866	VD↔IN	0.640	VD↔IN	0.802
VD→QN	0.569	VD→QZ	0.817	VD→QZ	0.844
		VD→DS	0.652	VD→DS	0.905
		VD→QN	0.509	DS↔TS	0.928
		DS↔TS	0.707	FM↔IN	0.936
		FM↔IN	0.594		

correlation in the second and third temporal stages. At the same time, the temporal sequences belonging to the same early warning stage also form a strong correlation. The correlation values are marked in Figure 5.11.

4 P4: correlation between key temporal sequences of the same major in different semesters.

There are relationships between the learning contents of the same major in three semesters. Combined with the above (1)–(3), these relationships are also reflected in the correlation between key temporal sequences in different semesters. Because different majors form the similarity of early warning in different semesters, the correlation test is completed. There are 27 combination methods; the test results show that there are five strong correlations that are marked in Figure 5.11: the second key temporal stage of the first semester→the first key temporal stage of the second semester; the third key temporal stage of the first semester→the second key temporal stage of the second semester; the first key temporal stage of the second semester→the first key temporal stage of the third semester; the second key temporal stage of the second semester→the first key temporal stage of the third semester; the third key temporal stage of the second semester→the second key temporal stage of the third semester. The strong correlation of key temporal sequences proves that the same major has correlation influence during different learning periods, and this correlation is applicable to each major, which is an important conclusion.

5 P5: critical path of interactive activities formed by the key temporal sequences of each semester of each major.

The key temporal sequences of each semester of each major are directly related to the learning content. Through data analysis, we can see that different majors can form similar critical paths of interactive activities. In this way, these majors form a cluster for a semester. Taking the critical path of interactive activities as the clue, the major cluster has changed significantly in different semesters. The major tendency about interactive activities is related to semesters and will also affect the formation of key temporal sequences. The critical paths of interactive activities formed by each major in each semester are shown in Table 5.7; "(·)" shows that the two interactive activities have a significant

Table 5.7 Critical Paths of Interactive Activities in Each Semester

Semester	Major	Interactive Critical Path
1st Semester	PS,MS,SE,CS,MT, ES	FM↔VD→((CT↔RE),QZ)
	JM, PY, LE, HY	VD→((CT↔RE),QN,QZ)
2nd Semester	PS, MS, SE, CS	(FM∥(FM↔IN))↔VD→((CT↔RE),QZ)
	MT, ES	VD→((CT↔RE),QZ)
	JM, PY, LE, HY	VD→((CT↔RE),QN)
3rd Semester	PS, MS	(FM↔IN)↔VD→((CT↔RE),QZ)
	SE, CS	(FM↔IN)↔VD→((CT↔RE),(DS↔TS))
	MT, ES	FM↔VD→((CT↔RE),QZ)
	JM, PY	IN↔VD→((CT↔RE),QZ)
	LE, HY	VD→((CT↔RE),QZ)

Table 5.8 Critical Paths in Different Semesters

Major	Interactive Critical Path Among Different Semesters
PS, MS	FM↔VD→((CT↔RE), QZ)
SE, CS	FM↔VD→((CT↔RE)
MT, ES	VD→((CT↔RE),QZ)
JM, PY	VD→(CT↔RE)
LE, HY	VD→(CT↔RE)

positive correlation, one activity will drive another activity, and the two activities have a positive impact on each other. As can be seen from Table 5.7, with the continuous change of major clusters, there are obvious differences in the critical paths, and the nodes and relationships of the critical paths have changed greatly in the third semester.

6 P6: critical path of interactive activities formed by the key temporal sequence of different semesters of each major.

Through the data analysis of (1)–(5), it can be seen that there are common nodes in the critical path of interactive activities of each major in different semesters, and the approximate correlation also occurs between the nodes. The majors in different semesters and different learning contents can form the same, stable and appropriately learning behavior. A potential critical path is formed between the key temporal sequences of different semesters, so as to drive the transfer of learning behavior in different semesters. Since majors have formed clusters in different semesters, and five major clusters have been formed in the third semester, the critical paths during different periods form five categories; the critical paths of interactive activities of different majors in Table 5.7 are selectively merged; in this way, the critical paths of interactive activities in different semesters are obtained, as shown in Table 5.8. Data analysis shows that JM, PY, LE and HY have the same critical path in different semesters, and their learning behaviors are quite similar.

In addition, based on the test and analysis of the above-mentioned six problems, the interactive activities, the critical path, the temporal sequence of early warning will be affected by assessment methods. After the second and third semesters, the online assessment method has been more comprehensively applied, which will also affect the pivot distribution as shown in Figure 5.11. Different behavior preferences and trends determine the composition of early warning temporal sequences and the choice of interactive activities, which will affect the learning and analysis results of early warning pivots, and different pivots will also correspond to different nodes and relationships. It also further shows that the learning behavior formed by any major in different semesters is not isolated (Greene et al., 2020; Xia, 2021b). The early warning is affected by various factors, which will affect the critical paths of early warning pivot space and the correlations between pivots.

7   Discussion

The multi-temporal interactive learning process involves multi-elements, including time, major, interactive activities and assessment methods. These elements are interrelated and limited to each other, forming the regularity, collectivity and complexity of the interactive learning process (Brandmiller et al., 2020). It also gradually constructs effective learning behavior, and the early warning pivot space model is designed to realize the correlation calculation of multi-elements, and the key multi-early warning strategies are deployed. Based on the early warning pivot model, the early warning strategy of multi-temporal interactive learning process is discussed, which is mainly reflected in the following aspects:

1 In the same learning period, the interactive learning process has strong correlation with the key temporal sequences of early warning.

   After massive data analysis, including the existing research results (Er et al., 2021), it is further verified that in a complete interactive learning process, an effective early warning sequence is not an event, but forms a continuous stage, and multiple stages may be required. It is usually distributed in three important stages of interactive learning process, i.e. early, middle and late. From the assessment results of learners, these stages have strong correlation and continuity; the effective early warning and intervention in these stages can effectively play a positive guiding role. At the same time, it is also found that learners of different majors may have similar temporal sequences of early warning, indicating that learning content, learning needs and objectives, teaching methods and assessment methods may have a group similar impact on learning behavior (Herodotou et al., 2021), which also produces early warning needs of the same period.

   Therefore, for majors with similar temporal sequences of early warning in the same period, we can explore the commonness and repeatability among many majors, which is of great significance for the research of cross topics. We can strengthen the interaction and cooperation among majors in the same learning period. It can not only improve learners' learning enthusiasm and interest but also provide reference suggestions for learners' choice of second major.

2 In different learning periods, the interactive learning process has strong correlation with the key temporal sequences of early warning.

The cultivation of professional skills generally involves multiple learning periods. In different learning periods, different learning contents need to be set. Between these contents, there is a limited relationship between the topological order of learning time and the knowledge itself. For example, before setting up a course, it is necessary to complete the related precursor courses; the learning quality of a course will have a significant impact on the construction of follow-up learning behavior, affect the learning needs and objectives of the course, and even react on the teaching methods and assessment methods, which makes the interactive learning processes of different learning periods of the same major have a correlation, which may be positive or negative. There must also be potential correlations between the key temporal sequences. The application of early warning temporal sequences is to build a vertical effective latency between different learning periods (Xia, 2021c). The data analysis shows that the early warning stage in the middle or late stage will form strong correlations with the early or middle stage of the subsequent interactive learning process.

Therefore, to give full play to the vertical influence of early warning sequence, it is necessary to build effective learning relationships of professional contents, learning objectives, assessment methods, interactive activities and teaching methods, strengthen the applications of pre and post learning contents, and through the correlations between early warning sequences, learners are driven to gradually form and strengthen the professional knowledge context, and realize the integration of different interactive learning processes.

3 In the same learning period, the learning process has strong correlation with the interactive critical path of early warning.

The key work of early warning is to optimize learning behavior and the dynamic elements directly related to learning behavior, which is mainly reflected in the interactive activities. In the same learning period, the construction of learning behavior has an obvious tendency; there is a need for resources related to learning content, which drives learners to participate in multiple corresponding interactive activities. Through data analysis, in the process of online interactive learning, "Video" has been actively participated by learners. For the learning content with strong interactivity and collaboration, learners form strong correlations between different interactive activities, which has become a critical path for early warning. These paths help to trace the interactive learning process in the same learning period.

Therefore, in the same learning period, clustering majors or learners according to the interactive critical path of early warning, it serves the recommendation of approximate learning behavior and the prediction of potential learning preferences, and mines the similarities and differences of different major clusters or learner clusters. Meanwhile, by analyzing the tendency and personalization, we might demonstrate the advantages and disadvantages of learning behavior, improve the timeliness of early warning and the reliability of intervention, and improve the relevance of interactive learning process (Israel-Fishelson, 2021).

4 In different learning periods, the learning process has strong correlations with the interactive critical path of early warning.

Learners learn different professional contents in different learning periods. According to the above aspects (1)–(3), these professional contents are related and progressive, so learners will form relatively stable learning behavior in different learning periods. Learning interests, habits, behavior patterns and preferences will be reflected in different interactive learning processes. For most learners, learning behavior will not be easy to change in a short time; the interactive critical paths are formed with large coincidence in different learning periods. The experimental results of this study show that there are great similarities in the interactive critical paths in the three learning periods, indicating that there are strong correlations between the critical paths. The difference is mainly due to the change of the individual interactive activities. In this regard, it shows that the change of other key elements in different interactive learning processes can bring significant guiding effect, for example, assessment methods and objectives, learning needs and objectives, teaching methods and evaluation indicators may affect the participation of interactive activities.

Therefore, based on the strong correlations of interactive critical paths in different learning periods, the potential learning behavior risks can be evaluated in advance in the temporal sequences, the possible problems in the interactive process can be predicted and the participation of key interactive activities can be guided and optimized (Tsiakmaki et al., 2021). In the construction of interactive learning process, it is necessary to analyze the changes of key elements and explore feasible and adaptive improvement strategies.

8   Conclusion

Interactive learning process produces massive dynamic data and multidimensional complex relationships, enriches the characteristics and attributes of learning behavior, and also provides a complete data for the improvement and innovation of learning analytics. The significance of data to the interactive learning process is to realize data-driven adaptive learning behavior, produce effective learning assessment results, timely find the risks and problems, and improve learners' participation and interest. To achieve this goal, the early warning model based on multi-elements is a key problem. The traceable early warning and intervention is also a difficult problem in the research of interactive learning process, because it needs to consider the dynamics, autonomy and continuity of learning behavior, involving multi-element correlation analysis and relationship prediction.

Based on the CPS theory, this study designs one early warning pivot space model of multi-temporal interactive learning process that integrates hyperplane partition and spherical partition, expands the research framework of linear early warning mechanism, mines the early warning pivot and relationships from multi-elements and designs the space topology. First, about the multi-elements of interactive learning process, the complete data of three semesters are mined, the data is standardized and the test problems for possible correlations and topological relationships are put forward; second, an early warning pivot space model is constructed, and the corresponding learning rules and analysis algorithms are designed. Sufficient parallel experiments show that the model is effective and reliable for the pivot learning and training; third, the analysis results are summarized, the test conclusions of related problems are derived and the early warning pivot space topology in multi-temporal interactive learning process is visualized. On this basis, the implementation law and improvement aspects are discussed. This study explores a novel early warning mechanism based on multi-temporal interactive learning process, which is helpful for correlation analysis and relationship calculation, enriches the dimension and depth of early warning of learning behavior, and can more comprehensively support the dynamic analysis and decision feedback.

However, there are still some limitations in this study. The data only involves three learning periods, and further experimental tests are needed for data tracking and analysis of more learning periods. For the analysis and calculation of more key elements, the model needs to be fully trained and optimized. For the interdisciplinary, the early warning strategies also need the support of more learning platforms and massive data. Early warning model of unbalanced interactive learning behaviors might be the next key issue that requires in-depth research.

References

Alemany, J., Del Val, E., & Garcia-Fornes, A. (2020). Assessing the effectiveness of a gamified social network for applying privacy concepts: an empirical study with teens. *IEEE Transactions on Learning Technologies*. 13(4), 777–789. https://doi.org/10.1109/TLT.2020.3026584

Brandmiller, C., Dumont, H., & Becker, M. (2020). Teacher perceptions of learning motivation and classroom behavior: the role of student characteristics. *Contemporary Educational Psychology*. 63(2020), 101893. https://doi.org/10.1016/j.cedpsych.2020.101893

Cerezo, R., Bogarín, A., Esteban, M., & Romero, C. (2020). Process mining for self-regulated learning assessment in e-learning. *Journal of Computing in Higher Education*. 32(1), 74–88. https://doi.org/10.1007/s12528-019-09225-y

Er, E., Dimitriadis, Y., & Gašević, D. (2021). Collaborative peer feedback and learning analytics: theory-oriented design for supporting class-wide interventions. *Assessment & Evaluation in Higher Education*. 46(2), 169–190. http://doi.org/10.1080/02602938.2020.1764490

Greene, J. A., Copeland, D. Z., & Deekens, V. M. (2020). A model of technology incidental learning effects. *Educational Psychology Review*. 33(2), 1–31. https://doi.org/10.1007/s10648-020-09575-5

Gregory, S. (2021). Requirements for the new normal: requirements engineering in a pandemic. *IEEE Software*. 38(2), 15–18. https://doi.org/10.1109/MS.2020.3044403

Herodotou, C., Maguire, C., Mcdowell, N. D., Hlosta, M., & Boroowa, A. (2021). The engagement of university teachers with predictive learning analytics. *Computers & Education*. 173(c), 104285. https://doi.org/10.1016/j.compedu.2021.104285

Israel-Fishelson, R. A. (2021). Micro-persistence and difficulty in a game-based learning environment for computational thinking acquisition. *Journal of Computer Assisted Learning*. 37(3), 839–850. http://doi.org/10.1111/jcal.12527

Koeslag-Kreunen, M., Bossche, P., Klink, V. D., & Gijselaers, W. H. (2020). Vertical or shared? When leadership supports team learning for educational change. *Higher Education*. 82(2), 1–19. https://doi.org/10.1007/s10734-020-00620-4

La Gatta, V., Moscato, V., Postiglione, M., & Sperlì, G. (2021). PASTLE: pivot-aided space transformation for local explanations. *Pattern Recognition Letters*. 149, 67–74. https://doi.org/10.1016/j.patrec.2021.05.018

Lai, S., Sun, B., Wu, F., & Xiao, R. (2020). Automatic personality identification using students' online learning behavior. *IEEE Transactions on Learning Technologies*. 13(1), 26–37. https://doi.org/10.1109/TLT.2019.2924223

Li, H., Majumdar, R., Chen, M., & Ogata, H. (2021). Goal-oriented active learning (goal) system to promote reading engagement, self-directed learning behavior, and motivation in extensive reading. *Computers & Education*. 171(2), 104239. https://doi.org/10.1016/j.compedu.2021.104239

Ober, T. M., Hong, M. R., Rebouas, D. A., Carter, M. F., & Cheng, Y. (2021). Linking self-report and process data to performance as measured by different assessment types. *Computers & Education*. 167(2), 104188. https://doi.org/10.1016/j.compedu.2021.104188

Olmanson, J., Liu, X., Heselton, C. C., Srivastava, A., & Wang, N. (2021). Chinese character recognition and literacy development via a techno-pedagogical pivot. *Educational Technology Research and Development*. 69(2), 1299–1324. https://doi.org/10.1007/s11423-021-09976-5

O'Neill, L., Rasyidi, R., Hastings, R., & Bayern, A. V. (2021). Innovative problem solving in macaws. *Learning & Behavior*. 49(1), 106–123. https://doi.org/10.3758/s13420-020-00449-y

Rui, M., Peihan, Z., Xingliang, L., & Liu, X. (2016). Pivot selection for metric-space indexing. *International Journal of Machine Learning & Cybernetics*. 7(2), 311–323. https://doi.org/10.1007/s13042-016-0504-4

Ruiz, G., Chavez, E., Ruiz, U., & Tellez, E. S. (2020). Extreme pivots: a pivot selection strategy for faster metric search. *Knowledge and Information Systems*. 62(6), 2349–2382. https://doi.org/10.1007/s10115-019-01423-5

Schüttpelz-Brauns, K., Hecht, M., Hardt, K., Karay, Y., & Kmmer, J. E. (2020). Institutional strategies related to test-taking behavior in low stakes assessment. *Advances in Health Sciences Education*. 25(3), 1–15. https://doi.org/10.1007/s10459-019-09928-y

Song, D., Hong, H., & Oh, E. Y. (2021). Applying computational analysis of novice learners' computer programming patterns to reveal self-regulated learning, computational thinking, and learning performance. *Computers in Human Behavior*. 120(6), 106746. https://doi.org/10.1016/j.chb.2021.106746

Tsiakmaki, M., Kostopoulos, G., Kotsiantis, S., & Ragos, O. (2021). Fuzzy-based active learning for predicting student academic performance using autoML: a step-wise approach. *Journal of Computing in Higher Education*. 33, 1–33. https://doi.org/10.1007/s12528-021-09279-x

Xia, X. (2020a). Random field design and collaborative inference strategy for learning interaction activities. *Interactive Learning Environments*. 2020(12), 1–25. https://doi.org/10.1080/10494820.2020.1863236

Xia, X. (2020b). Learning behavior mining and decision recommendation based on association rules in interactive learning environment. *Interactive Learning Environments*. 2020(8), 1–16. https://doi.org/10.1080/10494820.2020.1799028

Xia, X. (2021a). Sparse learning strategy and key feature selection in interactive learning environment. *Interactive Learning Environments*. 2021(11), 1–25. https://doi.org/10.1080/10494820.2021.1998913

Xia, X. (2021b). Interaction recognition and intervention based on context feature fusion of learning behaviors in interactive learning environments. *Interactive Learning Environments*. 2021(1), 1–19. https://doi.org/10.1080/10494820.2021.1871632

Xia, X. (2021c). Decision application mechanism of regression analysis of multi-category learning behaviors in interactive learning environment. *Interactive Learning Environments*. 2021(4): 1–14. https://doi.org/10.1080/10494820.2021.1916767

6 Early Warning Model Design and Decision Application of Unbalanced Interactive Learning Behaviors

Abstract

The online learning platform not only promotes the teaching objectives but also realizes the enthusiasm and autonomy of learners. However, it also breaks away from the direct supervision and tracking of instructors in the traditional classroom, so the learning behavior presents a strong discreteness, and the generated data has a strong imbalance. This study explores MT-BCSSCAN applied to the early warning of unbalanced learning behavior. It divides interactive learning behavior into three types: generative, browsing, as well as interactive and collaboration, and introduces other online behaviors into the feature calculation, realizing unbalanced multi-source data fusion. The experimental results show that MT-BCSSCAN can effectively support the prediction of interactive learning behavior based on high performance, and further draw the conclusion of relevant test problems. After fusing other online behaviors of learners, the three types of learning behavior form significant relationships, and the corresponding early warning model and decision application strategy are derived. The whole research process adopts the deep learning method, creatively constructs the prediction method of massive unbalanced interactive learning behavior, realizes the fusion calculation of multi-source data and improves the quality of early warning; implementing the temporal tracking and decision intervention of interactive learning behavior might be important.

Keywords

Unbalanced Interactive Learning Behavior; Early Warning Model; Online Learning Platform;

Multi-source Data Prediction Framework; Learning Analytics

1 Introduction

Online interactive learning has become a new form of education, breaking through the limitations of time and space, ensuring the convenience and timeliness of the interactive learning process (Roldán et al., 2021). It has also generated the interest of instructors and learners, generated new interaction and collaboration, and

DOI: 10.4324/9781003484905-6

become an important practice of big data-driven education. The data application of interactive learning behavior has become an important issue of learning analytics (Ugalde et al., 2021). Through data mining technology and analysis model, the massive data is transformed into valuable information, which in turn interferes with or improves the interactive learning behavior (Yoon, 2021), timely provides instructive and enlightening suggestions for instructors and learners, constructs a benign iterative interactive learning process and improves the learning effect and teaching quality (Xia, 2021a).

The online learning platform has made the online interactive learning fully applied in the teaching process (Mangaroska et al., 2021a). Based on data technology, the effective integration of traditional teaching and online courses has become a key attempt of educational reform and curriculum innovation (Eberle & Hobrecht, 2021). Practice has proved that the full application of online interactive learning environment can not only ensure the teaching quality but also improve the enthusiasm and participation of learners so that learners have more flexible time and interactive methods, can independently navigate the learning process, form their own learning behavior and better ensure and support the personalization. But it also brings new challenges (Xia, 2020a, 2020b). However, the interactive learning behavior needs to be timely tracked, which is different from the traditional offline classroom. The online interactive learning process is separated from the direct supervision of the instructors, and it is difficult to capture the knowledge comprehension (Sailer et al., 2021). Therefore, it is necessary to analyze and feedback massive learning data in real time with the help of technical means (Ouyang et al., 2021) so as to effectively evaluate the risk that may occur in the interactive learning process and make appropriate predictions; the interactive learning process needs to set up an effective tracking and early warning mechanism (Xia, 2022a).

The early warning of interactive learning process cannot be separated from the interaction and cooperation between learners and online learning platform. The accurate prediction of learning effect requires sufficient learning behavior data. At the same time, the construction of learning behavior is also affected by the orientation of teaching objectives, such as demographic information, forming a personalized and obvious learning behavior (Xia & Qi, 2022). The research in this area mainly turns the early warning into a binary problem such as the prediction of learners' dropout rate or the prediction that the learning effect conforms to the Gaussian distribution (Geyer, 2021). The premise of these research branches is based on relatively balanced samples (Xia, 2021b) that meet the analysis model. However, due to the autonomy and personalization of learning behavior, it is very easy to form unbalanced data samples, and unrealistic and unscientific to simply attribute the early warning to binary classification. Therefore, this study is to design a strategy from problem definition to method design, as well as decision application, design an applicable early warning model, and analyze the multi-source data including online interactive learning data and other online data. The early warning and intervention of risk learners can achieve accurate and reliable classification prediction.

2   Related Work

The data distribution of interactive learning process might be unbalanced (McKenna et al., 2021). When it is necessary to locate risk learners and take timely and effective early warning, it is very easy to produce data imbalance. At the same time, risk assessment and prediction require relatively comprehensive calculation in order to improve the reliability and integrity of data support (Razmerita et al., 2020). Therefore, the key problem of early warning is to improve the analysis quality of unbalanced interactive learning data and build a reliable early warning strategy and decision application mechanism (Xia, 2021c).

About the data imbalance of interactive learning behavior, it is necessary to collect multi-source data, including interactive learning behavior and other behaviors, and achieve classified prediction and intervention for risk learners who need early warning (Carter & Egliston, 2021). The relevant model design mainly focuses on the Sequence Classification with Adversarial Nets (SCAN). This model is to predict risk learners by analyzing the interactive learning behavior and improve the analysis accuracy of unbalanced data with the help of multi-source data. This research is mainly divided into the following three dimensions:

1 Analysis of multi-source data

   In order to realize the fusion of multi-source data, during data analysis, it is necessary to carry out continuous feature mining for the learning behavior and other online behaviors, and form the effective distribution of relevant features and temporal sequences (Ruipérez-Valiente et al., 2022). In this respect, it is necessary to use LSTM (Long Short-Term Memory) to map the features of multi-source data to the hidden space, analyze the correlation between different behaviors and obtain the complete continuous interactive learning behavior.

2 Early warning of interactive learning behavior

   In order to realize the early warning of interactive learning behavior, corresponding methods are generally designed to realize the multi-classification of learning behavior. This requires multi-source data samples to build a training set. Once the samples contain only a few risk learners, these data are easily classified as outliers, resulting in the imbalance of data distribution. This makes some classification methods not applicable to the early warning and prediction (Xia, 2022b). This research can be defined as the abnormal diagnostic prediction of interactive learning behavior. We can consider using the single classification method to design the strategy of retrograde backtracking derivation; we analyze the data of non-risk learners to deduce the relevant risk data samples and then build a data-driven technical framework.

3 Over fitting in data analysis

   Because the formation of learning behavior has strong uncertainty, it is easy to produce over fitting. In the case of massive data, this effect is more significant. According to the randomness and autonomy of interactive learning behavior and other online behaviors (Ameloot et al., 2021), it can be considered to adopt a recursive neural network to independently train multiple LSTMs with different network structures. Because each LSTM can analyze the feature dependence in different temporal intervals, it can provide multiple representation vectors of different features for each original input sample. This scheme can enhance the effect of data training and greatly reduce the possibility of over fitting.

Combined with the research aspects of these three dimensions, this study proposes a complete early warning model based on the fusion of adversarial network, and autonomous encoder might realize the risk analysis of multi-source learners' behavior. On the one hand, it is used to solve the data imbalance; on the other hand, it is used to realize the timely prediction and intervention. Moreover, while improving the accuracy and reliability of data prediction, we need to more accurately mine multiple risks and possible trends, and provide more accurate data basis for early warning.

3   Data Processing and Problem Description

We mine the interactive learning behavior data set and other online behavior data sets of 5,432 anonymous learners. The interactive learning behavior data set is mainly from an online learning platform. The data period is one semester in 2021, including 20 online learning weeks. The scale of interactive learning behavior data is 2.15PB in total. After preliminary data analysis, it is found that there is an obvious imbalance in these data, and the distribution of features shows a strong discreteness and autonomy, so it is difficult to realize the mining of continuous behavior. So we consider the data supplement of other online behaviors that mainly comes from the log records, and is composed of the data that the learner browses or participates in other online resources.

Online interactive learning behavior mainly includes the relevant interactive activities of learners. The click or link transfer behavior will be converted into the data records of interactive learning behavior. Table 6.1 lists the relevant descriptive features, mainly forms three types: browsing learning behavior, generative learning behavior as well as interactive and collaborative learning behavior. Each type captures several key features. From Table 6.1, we can see that each key feature involves a large number of pages. For a complete learning period, each learner generates frequent participation on each page.

In mining learning behavior data, we mainly focus on the learning behavior data of online course projects; the participation of such data is higher. The setting of course projects is carried out in groups. Different course projects have different group sizes. At the same time, quiz of learning content is arranged every two weeks in each learning period. At the end of the semester, learners report the projects in groups. The final score includes three parts: the average score of quiz, the project score and the comprehensive assessment score. The proportion of the scores is 3:3:4. If the scores of quiz each time are in the last quarter of the same level learners, or the learners who leave early do not participate or significantly lack project participation, they are defined as risk learners; there is a clear lack of theory or practice of learning behavior, which needs to carry out timely early warning.

Table 6.1 Descriptive Features and Statistical Results

Type	Corresponding Features and Description		Page Number
Browsing learning behavior	B_content	Browse the theoretical knowledge related to the learning course	14703
	B_project	Browse training projects related to the course	4911
	B_attachment	Browse and download files, data, materials, etc.	2437
	B_post	Browse the posts in the forum	3795
	B_review	Browse the reviews of relevant posts in the forum	7088
	Others	Browse other pages	844
Generative learning behavior	G_content	Generate the new theoretical knowledge related to the learning course	10915
	G_project	Create or modify requirements and content for the project	3317
	G_attachment	Upload relevant documents, data, materials, etc.	8922
	G_post	Post your own opinion in the forum	2778
	G_review	Review other users' opinions in the forum	5427
	G_others	Create or modify other page contents	320
Interactive and collaborative learning behavior	Chat	Immediate discussion among learners	23188
	Presentation	Immediate reporting of learning	2056
	Design	Learners' interactive design of learning content	10351
	Program	Learners' interactive implementation of learning content	9417
	Quiz	Online instant quiz	3551

Other online learning behaviors mainly come from the network logs of the campus network, and the statistical time of data is equal to the interactive learning behavior. It mainly records the categories of web pages visited by learners and the corresponding time stamps. The relevant web page features are mainly reflected in 12 categories such as news, games, music, film and television, search engines, small videos, uploading, downloading, shopping, e-mail, payment tools and instant messaging. The pages have a huge click rate and involve privacy needs, which is not suitable for specific data statistics. Therefore, we only analyze the categories of page features.

Based on the anonymous ID of the learners, the interactive learning behavior is integrated with other online behaviors, and merged into the online behavior sequence of the learners according to the temporal sequences. In order to ensure that the interactive learning behavior is consistent with other online behaviors, the learning behavior sequence is improved by zero filling for the time gaps so that the behavior sequences no longer have null values. On the basis of data analysis, it can reduce the imbalance of learning behavior and improve the reliability and completeness of data analysis. By analyzing the click rate of learners to online pages, we explore the behavior features, change trends and existing problems.

Based on the early warning analysis of unbalanced interactive learning behavior, the problems are mainly divided into two aspects: one is to test the significant impact between different interactive learning behaviors; the other is to test the significant impact between different interactive learning behaviors based on the data fusion of other online behaviors. The final assessment score of learners is taken as the observation variable. The test problems and relationships among different behaviors are shown in Figure 6.1. There are six test problems in the first aspect that are the pairwise relationships when other online behaviors are not integrated. There are also six test problems in the second aspect that are the pairwise relationships between the three types of learning behaviors after integrating other online behaviors. Relevant test problems are described as follows.

Q12: Generative learning behavior positively affects browsing learning behavior.

Q21: Browsing learning behavior positively affects generative learning behavior.

Q13: Generative learning behavior positively affects interactive and collaborative learning behavior.

Q31: Interactive and collaborative learning behavior positively affects generative learning behavior.

Q23: Browsing learning behavior positively affects interactive and collaborative learning behavior.

Q32: Interactive and collaborative learning behavior positively affects browsing learning behavior.

Q102: After integrating other online behaviors, generative learning behavior positively affects browsing learning behavior.

Q201: After integrating other online behaviors, browsing learning behavior positively affects generative learning behavior.

Q103: After integrating other online behaviors, generative learning behavior positively affects interactive and collaborative learning behavior.

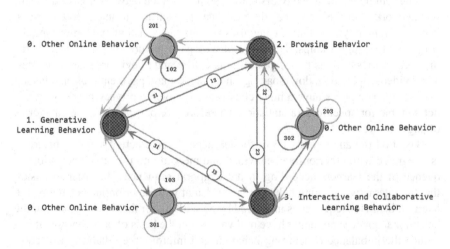

Figure 6.1 Key Relationships and Test Problems of Unbalanced Interactive Learning Behaviors

Q203: After integrating other online behaviors, browsing learning behavior positively affects generative learning behavior.

Q302: After integrating other online behaviors, interactive and collaborative learning behavior positively affects browsing learning behavior.

4   Method

In order to realize the early warning model of the fusion of interactive learning behavior and other online behaviors, overcome the data analysis obstacles caused by unbalanced learning data, and mine accurate risk learners, this study proposes a multi-type behavior sequence classification based on adversarial net (MT-BCSCAN) so that no risk information is required in the data training; there are no more restrictions on the requirements of the training set; as long as it contains the behavior samples of learners, it can meet the requirements. MT-BCSCAN uses non-risk learning behavior as the key target to test the risks in the learning process and form corresponding risk learners.

First, the online behavior sequences of learners are mined from the data or log of browsing learning behavior, generative learning behavior, interactive and collaborative learning behavior and other online behaviors, and the key features related to these four types of behaviors are defined. Second, LSTM is used to analyze and represent learners' vectors. Third, due to the analysis of learner behavior data and the learning process of GAN (Generative Adversarial Networks), it is very easy to have unbalanced training. It is necessary to improve the analysis process of GAN in combination with the features and relationships of multi-source data. At the same time, about the imbalance of data distribution, multiple encoders are trained by using the sparse data connected recurrent neural network. The improved GAN Discriminator is used to detect risk learners, and the training set size of the improved GAN is expanded to reduce noise interference.

The multi-source data training process of MT-BCSCAN is described in Figure 6.2, which mainly includes three parts: Multi-Source Behavior Feature Mining, Multi-Source Behavior Sequence Integration and Improved GAN. The relevant business mechanism is described as follows.

1   Multi-Source Behavior Feature Mining

   The processing of Multi-Source Behavior Feature Mining is based on four types of online behavior, namely browsing learning behavior, generative learning behavior, interactive and collaborative learning behavior as well as other online behaviors. The description of these online data is mainly realized with the help of key features and relationships. These features and relationships will also change in different learning periods. Therefore, the learning analysis process of behavioral data needs to calculate the temporal sequences.

   If the four kinds of behavior sequences are divided into sub-sequences with weeks as the temporal sequences, the online behavior of learners can be described as $X_I^L = (L_1, \cdots, L_t, \cdots, L_T)$, browsing learning behavior sequence is $X_I^B = (B_1, \cdots, B_t, \cdots, B_T)$, generative learning behavior sequence is $X_I^G = (G_1, \cdots, G_t, \cdots, G_T)$, interactive and collaborative learning behavior

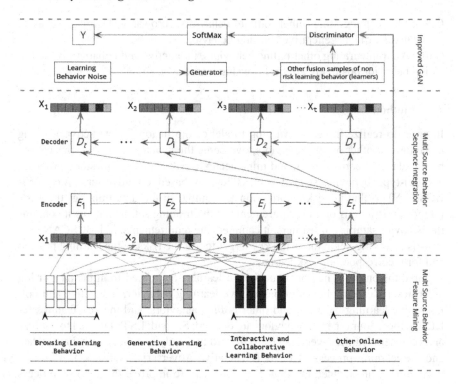

Figure 6.2 MT-BCSCAN for Multi-source Behavior Fusion of Learners

sequence is $X_l^{IC} = \left(IC_1, \cdots, IC_t, \cdots, IC_T \right)$ and other online behavior is $X_l^O = \left(O_1, \cdots, O_t, \cdots, O_T \right)$. The feature mining of each sub-sequence mainly includes the start time, end time, duration and click rate. Through the calculation of these different values, the learning enthusiasm, persistence and behavior change law are tested.

2 Multi-Source Behavior Sequence Integration

Multi-Source Behavior Sequence Integration is the middle layer of MT-BCSCAN. After sequence division and feature mining for the four types of behaviors, respectively, the four types of behavior features belonging to the same temporal sequence are merged, expressed as the online behavior feature vector of the learner *l*, and a complete feature sequence is constructed, namely $X_l = \left(x_1, \cdots, x_t, \cdots, x_T \right)$.

In the training process of MT-BCSCAN, only the features of non-risk learners are input into LSTM, and LSTM realizes the conversion of features, which includes encoding and decoding.

Encoder *E* calculates the implicit vector of the input features and encodes the learner's behavior sequences into the learner's description vector, $h_t^E = \text{LSTM}^E \left(x_t, h_{t-1}^E \right)$, x_t is the learner's feature vector of the *t*th week, h_t^E is the *t*th hidden vector of the encoder. The decoder *D* reconstructs the learner features based on the last hidden vector so that the reconstructed input value is infinitely close to the original input value, $h_t^D = \text{LSTM}^D\left(h_t^E, h_{t-1}^D\right)$, $X_t = f\left(h_t^D\right)$, h_t^D is the tth hidden vector of the encoder, $f(\cdot)$ is the iterative reasoning function of the neural network and is used to calculate the sequence output of the hidden vector in the decoding.

The encoder of LSTM can mine the relevant information of the learner's behavior sequence, and the last hidden vector h_t^E can reconstruct the learner's multi-source feature vector sequence.

3 Improved GAN

The vector formed by the four types of behavior features is used as the input of Improved GAN. Improved GAN is similar to common GAN, and also includes a Generator and a Discriminator. However, when processing the behavior samples of learners, the processing results of the improved GAN and common GAN are different. The Generator of common GAN gets samples close to non-risk learners. The Discriminator is used to distinguish the real samples that are relatively similar to the generated samples. The Generator of the Improved GAN calculates the density of the feature distribution. To generate complementary samples of low-density area of non-risk learners, the Discriminator can better distinguish between real samples and complementary samples. There is a significant difference between the Generator and the Discriminator.

The calculation principle of the Improved GAN Generator is described as follows: it is a feedforward neural network, the input value is a random vector z, the generated sample is defined as $\hat{v} = G(z)$, the feature distribution P_G obtained by the Generator is close to the complementary distribution P* of the in

put sample, P^* is defined as $P^*(\hat{v}) = \begin{cases} \dfrac{1}{\tau P_r(\hat{v})} & \text{if } P_r(\hat{v}) > \varepsilon \text{ and } \hat{v} \in L_v \\ C & f\ P_r(\hat{v}) \le \varepsilon \text{ and } \hat{v} \in L_v \end{cases}$, ε

is a threshold to define whether the generated samples are distributed in high-density areas, τ is a normalized term, C is a very small constant, L_v is a learner's description space and P_r is a true feature distribution of learners. To ensure P_G is closer to P^*, the Generator is fully trained to minimize the Kullback Leibler divergence. The objective function of the Generator is described as $OF_{KL\left(P_G\|P^*\right)} = -H(P_G) - E_{\hat{v}\sim P_G}\log P^*(\hat{v}) = -H(P_G) + E_{\hat{v}\sim P_G}\log P_r(\hat{v})$

$l\left[P_r(\hat{v}) > \varepsilon\right]$. H represents entropy, $l[\cdot]$ is the indicator function, the value of the function satisfying the condition is 1, and if not, it is 0.

The Discriminator of Improved GAN is described as follows: it is also a feedforward neural network, which takes the learner's feature vector v' and the description vector $\hat{v}$ of the generated sample as the input value, and the softmax function as the output layer. The Discriminator is used to distinguish the real non-risk behavior samples from the complementary samples generated by the Generator. The objective function of the Discriminator is described as:

$\max_D V(D) = E_{v\sim P_r}\left[\log D(v)\right] + E_{\hat{v}\sim P_G}\left[\log\left(1 - D(\hat{v})\right)\right] + E_{v\sim P_r}\left[D(v)\log D(v)\right]$.

The first two items of the objective function are used to distinguish input samples and generated samples, and the last item is entropy, which is used to motivate the Discriminator to complete the prediction of input samples with high confidence in the training stage, so as to significantly distinguish non-risk learners from risk ones.

5   Experiment

In order to test the performance of MT-BCSCAN, the data set of Section 3 is used to conduct sufficient experimental tests; meanwhile, a highly unbalanced subset is mined. In addition, during the preprocessing of the test set, the same continuous operation of the same learner in one second is reserved only once. All the behavior sequences of each learner are divided into different temporal intervals by week. The features in Table 6.1 are mined in each temporal interval, and the non-existent feature values are filled with 0.

For LSTM in MT-BCSCAN, the default hidden layer dimension is 120. For Improved GAN, the Discriminator contains two hidden layers with dimensions of 100 and 50, respectively. The Generator uses the hidden layer of the Discriminator with dimensions of 50 to receive noise, and includes the hidden layer with dimensions of 100. The output layer of the Generator is set to be consistent with the dimension represented by the learner. The iteration of Improved GAN is 5,000. When the probability that the predicted generated sample exceeds the set threshold, it can be proved that the sample is in the high-density area. The decision threshold of the high-density area is set according to the probability that the Discriminator predicts that all the real input samples are true, usually taking the median.

In order to better test the performance of MT-BCSCAN, several similar and relatively optimal frameworks are selected. The comparative frameworks are: (1) Nearest Neighbors (NN), which marks the test set according to the distance from the training set to the nearest neighbors and the average distance of these nearest neighbors. However, the verification set needs to be constructed and contains a certain number of high-risk learners. In this way, the detection threshold can be adjusted appropriately; (2) Support Vector Machine (SVM), which uses support vector machine to learn the decision hypersphere of positive data, and the data outside the hypersphere is regarded as outliers; (3) GAN, which is similar to the encoder of MT-BCSCAN, but adopts the common GAN. The training sets only contain non-risk interactive learning behavior data. In all non-risk data, 30% of the samples are randomly selected as the test set together with risk learners, and all the remaining data are used as the training set.

First, in order to test the performance of risk learners with different frameworks, the mean values of different running results of 30 experiments are calculated, and the test indicators are Precision, Recall, F1 and Accuracy, respectively. Through sufficient data analysis, the test results of different frameworks are obtained, as shown in Table 6.2. It can be seen that MT-BCSCAN can obtain better indicators. Improved GAN Discriminator is significantly better than others and can more accurately distinguish risk learners from non-risk ones.

Table 6.2 Comparison of Analysis Performance of Risk Learners

Technology Framework	Precision	Recall	F1 Value	Accuracy
NN	0.5709	0.4313	0.4814	0.5447
SVM	0.5780	0.4994	0.5290	0.5624
GAN	0,5911	0.6735	0.6294	0.5907
MT-BCSCAN	0.7516	0.7035	0.7185	0.7341

Note: The bold values represent the optimal results.

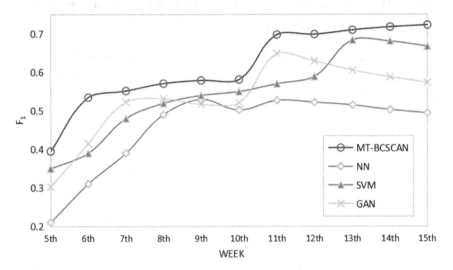

Figure 6.3 F1 for Different Frameworks

Second, in order to evaluate the performance of different frameworks for early warning of risk learners, the learning behavior feature vectors accumulated in different temporal sequence t are successively used as input, the corresponding learner representation vectors h_t^E are mined and the probability of risk learners is determined by Improved Gan Discriminator. The other three frameworks are also applied to the data set to predict the learning process from the 5th to 15th week, and F1 was obtained, as shown in Figure 6.3. Due to the improvement of GAN, MT-BCSCAN has better realized the adaptation of encoder, can solve the over fitting, and reduce the variance of prediction effect. With the passage of time, the predicted F1 shows an increasing trend. Especially in the 11th week and later, F1 reaches a relatively stable distribution, even equivalent to the final performance, that might drive the early warning of interactive learning behavior so that the whole learning period can have sufficient time to make timely intervention to risk learners in advance.

To further test the sensitivity of the super parameters in MT-BCSCAN, since MT-BCSCAN incorporates the encoder of LSTM, in the experiment, the dimensions of the hidden layer are set to 15, 35, 55, 75, 95, 115, 135 and 155, respectively, so as to compare the impact of different dimensions on the prediction performance of MT-BCSCAN. F1 and AUC are selected. After sufficient data training, the test results of these two indicators are obtained, as shown in Figures 6.4 and 6.5, respectively.

It can be seen from Figures 6.4 and 6.5 that the larger the coding dimension obtained by LSTM, the better the prediction performance of the Discriminator. If the dimension of the hidden layer is smaller, the coding dimension is smaller, too many learning behavior features will be lost, which will affect the differences between risk learners and non-risk ones, and reduce the prediction accuracy.

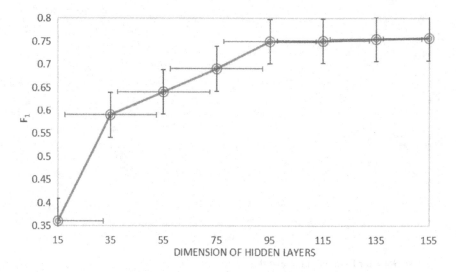

Figure 6.4 F1 of MT-BCSCAN

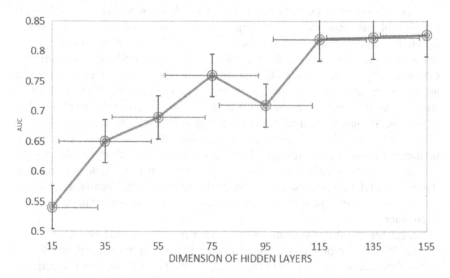

Figure 6.5 AUC of MT-BCSCAN

Since MT-BCSCAN adopts encoders with different structures, it can adaptively train multiple learner vectors with different dimensions and can more fully obtain important information. MT-BCSCAN can improve the prediction performance of classifiers. F1 in Figure 6.4 reaches a stable state when the dimension of the hidden layer reaches 95, and AUC in Figure 6.5 reaches a stable state when the dimension of the hidden layer reaches 115. In the subsequent analysis of learning behavior, the dimension of the hidden layer is set to 135; the experimental results will be in-depth discussion.

6   Result

Based on the experimental results when the hidden layer dimension of MT-BCSCAN is 115, we analyze the relevant test problems in Section 3 and draw corresponding conclusions. The analysis process is divided into two steps. The first step is to verify the relationships among the three types of interactive learning behavior that do not involve other online behaviors. The second step is to verify the relationships among the three types of interactive learning behavior after other online behaviors participate in the calculation.

The experimental analysis results of the first step are shown in Table 6.3. The analysis results of the six test problems show that interactive and cooperative learning behavior can significantly affect generative learning behavior and browsing learning behavior, and there is no significant relationship between other learning behaviors. Moreover, the iterative decisions of different hidden layers show an obvious discrete state; learners' relevant interactive learning behavior cannot mine typical impact features. It is also unable to mine the key relationships between features.

The second step realizes the fusion calculation of learners' other online behaviors and three types of interactive learning behavior. After the data training of MT-BCSCAN, the prediction and analysis results in Table 6.4 are obtained. It can be seen from Table 6.4 that after these six test problems are integrated into

Table 6.3 Test Results of Problems without Integrating Other Online Behaviors

Problem	Behavior Relationships	P Value	Results
Q12	Generative learning behavior→Browsing learning behavior	0.0784	Reject
Q21	Browsing learning behavior→Generative learning behavior	−0.216	Reject
Q13	Generative learning behavior→Interactive and collaborative learning behavior	0.245	Reject
Q31	Interactive and collaborative learning behavior→Generative learning behavior	0.019*	Accept
Q23	Browsing learning behavior→Interactive and collaborative learning behavior	−0.357	Reject
Q32	Interactive and collaborative learning behavior→Browsing learning behavior	0.044*	Accept

Note: *P<0.05.

Table 6.4 Results of Problems Integrating Other Online Behaviors

Problem	Behavior Relationships	P Value	Results
Q102	Generative learning behavior→Browsing learning behavior	0.0004***	Accept
Q201	Browsing learning behavior→Generative learning behavior	0.0011**	Accept
Q103	Generative learning behavior→Interactive and collaborative learning behavior	0.0038**	Accept
Q301	Interactive and collaborative learning behavior→Generative learning behavior	0.0001***	Accept
Q203	Browsing learning behavior→Interactive and collaborative learning behavior	0.0020**	Accept
Q302	Interactive and collaborative learning behavior→Browsing learning behavior	0.0007***	Accept

Note: ***P<0.001, **P<0.01.

the calculation of other online behaviors, generative learning behavior, browsing learning behavior as well as interactive and collaborative learning behavior have a significant positive impact, one learning behavior might enable another learning behavior. This is obviously different from Table 6.3, which also shows that there is a strong correlation between interactive learning behavior and other online behaviors, thus achieving a statistically significant prediction result.

Based on Table 6.4, the influential relationships between Q102 and Q201, Q103 and Q301, Q203 and q302 are drawn, as shown in Figures 6.6–6.8, respectively. The two different types of learning behaviors have formed a significant positive correlation, which indicates that after integrating the feature calculation of other online behaviors, the interactive learning behavior might have a close relationship with learning objectives as observation variables. One type of interactive learning behavior will drive the generation, tendency and interest of the others. Through data analysis, it is found that the three types of interactive learning behavior are consistent at the trigger times. However, the influential relationships formed by the two types of interactive learning behavior still have its own characteristics.

1 Generative learning behavior ↔ browsing learning behavior

As can be seen from Figure 6.6, in the construction of the influential relationships between generative learning behavior and browsing learning behavior, the features "G_content" "G_project" and "B_content" "B_project" have more important effects, learners have strong attention and interest in learning content and related training projects. At the same time, these features enable other similar features. Generative learning behavior and browsing learning behavior have a strong participation from the 3rd and 6th week, respectively. After calculation, the correlation of these two types of features forms a key temporal interval from the 6th to 18th week, which is the effective period of early warning intervention and temporal sequence tracking.

2 Generative learning behavior ↔ interactive and cooperative learning behavior

As can be seen from Figure 6.7, in the construction of influential topological relationships between generative learning behavior and interactive and

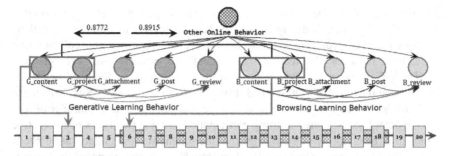

Figure 6.6 Influential Relationships Between Generative Learning Behavior and Browsing Learning Behavior

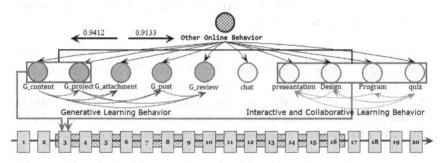

Figure 6.7 Influential Relationships Between Generative Learning Behavior and Interactive and Collaborative Behavior

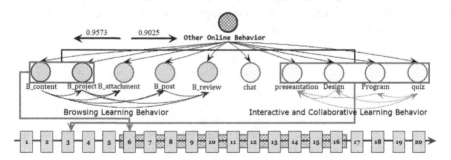

Figure 6.8 Influential Relationships Between Browsing Learning Behavior and Interactive and Collaboration Behavior

collaborative learning behavior, the features "G_content" "G_project" and "Presentation" "Design" "Program" "quiz" have more important effects, learners' needs for interaction and collaboration need strong attention and interest. At the same time, these features also drive others of the same type and generate a large number of data. The interactive and collaborative needs of the learning process can drive learners to learn earlier. The correlation process of these two types of features forms the key temporal interval in the 3rd and 16th week, which is the effective period for early warning intervention and temporal sequence tracking.

3   Browsing learning behavior ↔ interactive and cooperative learning behavior

As can be seen from Figure 6.8, in the construction of influential relationships between browsing learning behavior and interactive and collaborative learning behavior, the features "B_content" "B_project" and "Presentation" "Design" "Program" "Quiz" have more important effects; learners' needs for interaction and collaboration need strong attention and interest. Similarly, these features also drive others of the same type and generate a large number of feature data. Learners have a strong participation in these two types of interactive learning behavior, which indicates that the interactive and collaborative needs can stimulate learners to generate a large number of browsing needs for curriculum resources and related training projects. Through data analysis, the correlation process of these two types of features forms a key temporal interval in the 6th and 16th week, which is the effective period for early warning intervention and temporal sequence tracking.

In general, combined with the analysis results in Figures 6.6–6.8, the early warning model based on unbalanced interactive learning behavior is constructed, as shown in Figure 6.9. Through the correlation of the three types of interactive learning behavior, each type has a significant effect on the other two types and forms the relationships of mutual constraint and promotion. So the two temporal sequences of the early warning model are realized. One is temporal tracking, and the relevant temporal interval is in the 3rd to 18th week; during this continuous period, the learning platform needs to implement a timely learning behavior tracking process and realize a data analysis and feedback mechanism; The second is early warning intervention. The relevant temporal interval is in the 6th to 16th week. Effective intervention strategies are formulated in temporal tracking, and the effective learning behavior is guided and created.

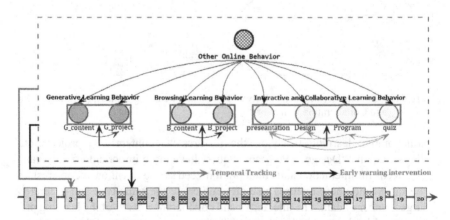

Figure 6.9 Early Warning Model Related to Three Types of Interactive Learning Behavior

7 Discussion

The learning behavior data generated by the online learning platform might be significant imbalance, the data scale is huge, but it does not improve the value of data analysis (Mangaroska et al., 2021b). In other words, the data is full of a large number of noise or meaningless outliers, and there are not many data with real analytical value. At the same time, it will also have an adverse impact on the prediction, early warning and intervention of learning behavior; it is difficult to truly reflect the significance of data-driven learning behavior. So we design MT-BCSCAN to achieve the effective analysis of unbalanced interactive learning behavior and obtain the key results of the experiment. Furthermore, the data analysis results are discussed, the early warning conditions of unbalanced learning behavior are analyzed and the decision application strategies of the early warning model are mined. It is mainly reflected in the following aspects:

1 Classification of effective interactive learning behavior

Interactive learning behavior is reflected by the data accumulation and association of many features. There are more differences because of different features, which are directly related to learning goals, trends and preferences. To mine the change rules and existing problems of interactive learning behavior from these different features, it is necessary to accurately analyze the relationships. For unbalanced data analysis, these features do not form significant relationships directly, but some features form a relatively similar distribution, and there will also be mutual correlation and restriction effects. Experiments show that classifying and analyzing learning behavior play an important role in improving the potential correlation. In addition, the analysis of learning behavior cannot be separated from the fusion of non-learning behavior data, which might be used to predict the change trend, but the premise is to design a method suitable for the interactive learning behavior.

Decision-making application strategy: the predictive analysis and early warning of interactive learning behavior cannot be separated from valuable data. When describing the features of interactive learning behavior, we should evaluate the possible learning behavior and possible changes in different temporal intervals. To realize the accurate application of data analysis results, we need to design applicable methods for the unbalanced feature relationships, reduce or avoid the imbalanced impact, and realize efficient mining and association of valuable data. At the same time, it is necessary to classify the features to enhance the calculation of other features.

2 Fusion of other behavioral data

The unbalanced interactive learning behavior is not only directly related to the relevant description features, learning methods and implementation strategies but also related to other features of the learners themselves such as the learning background, educational level, personal preference and personal understanding; these features are difficult to calculate significant impact in the huge learning behavior data, especially when learners are in an uncontrolled learning environment and the learning period has a certain range; the potential role of these data in learning description features cannot be accurately mined, and they are also easily limited and constrained by the limited analysis methods. Personalization is difficult to give full play, resulting in the inability to achieve data-driven behavior analysis and law tracking. However, the process of learners' participation in other online behaviors mainly comes from the subjective consciousness and self needs such as shopping, games and entertainment; these can show personalized preferences, which is easy to produce significance in the process of learners' participation in other online behaviors. The fusion of these data is used to discover the possible interest trends. The experimental results also show this conclusion.

Decision application strategy: the predictive analysis and early warning of interactive learning behavior are inseparable from multidimensional data, not just the calculation of relevant descriptive features. Therefore, the tracking process of interactive learning behavior should also track and collect other behavior data of learners so that the laws and relationships between these data can participate in the correlation analysis and prediction. This needs to improve the data compatibility of the online learning platform and locate the key features and effective data. After all, not all learner data has computational value, nor all other behaviors must have descriptive methods and models. It is necessary to start from the descriptive features to mine easily changed, intervening or even dispersing other behaviors. This is a good question for the learning platform.

3   Implementation of data-driven methods

With the increasing scale of learning behavior data, it poses many challenges to the traditional data analysis tools and statistical methods, and even can do nothing. After all, learning behavior data is different from other behaviors (such as trading behavior and social behavior). The data is generated by learners, who have ideas and habits, which are personalized and more collective. The discreteness, uncertainty and imbalance are obvious. Designing reliable analysis methods and value mining algorithms are important in learning analytics, and also pointed out a new direction for the research of educational technology. Mining data value from learning behavior and achieving effective prediction and decision are also the development direction of data technology. Based on a massive data set of interactive learning behavior, this study describes the problems and demonstrates the methods for the imbalance data. Experiments show that this method can improve the analysis accuracy, well realize the early warning interval positioning among the three types of learning behavior and provide data support for improving the decision intervention.

Decision application strategy: the predictive analysis and early warning of interactive learning behavior might achieve adaptability and autonomy under the support of key technologies that use the real-time data and historical data to predict benign learning behavior, potential learning behavior, implicit learning behavior or risk learning behavior, and build a reasonable and effective decision base and intervention rules; improved data technology can realize the adaptive feedback of corresponding decision and rules, so as to optimize the learning behavior and improve the learning effect. Therefore, while improving the key descriptive data and enriching their relationships, the learning platform should also set up effective predictive methods, so as to improve the utilization rate of data and realize the timeliness and feasibility of early warning.

8   Conclusion

The full application of online learning platform not only promotes the teaching objectives but also realizes the enthusiasm and autonomy of learners, which can provide flexible time allocation and place selection for the construction of learning behavior (Praharaj et al., 2021). The online learning process breaks away from the direct supervision and tracking mechanism of instructors in the traditional classroom and realizes learner-centered management and participation. The learners need to obtain the behavior transformation and knowledge understanding, and make data-driven predictive analysis and intervention feedback, so as to achieve reasonable and effective early warning. However, this is the ideal goal pursued by an online learning platform. In the actual online learning process, it is difficult to achieve the accurate analysis of massive learning behavior data. The huge amount of worthless data not only cannot provide key decision support but also interfere with the analysis effect of other key features. The learning behavior data are very easy to show significant imbalance and cannot play the real role.

About the massive unbalanced data generated in the online learning process, this study explores a technological framework applied to early warning of the interactive learning behavior. First, on the basis of analyzing the big data set generated by the online learning platform, three types of interactive learning behavior are mined, and other online behaviors of learners are introduced, and they participate in the feature calculation process, which realizes the unbalanced multi-source data fusion and further puts forward the related test problems. Second, according to the analysis requirements of unbalanced multi-source data, MT-BCSCAN supported by LSTM and Improved GAN is designed. Experiments show that MT-BCSCAN can effectively support the prediction of multi-source data fusion and ensure high data analysis performance. Third, based on the experimental analysis results, the conclusions of relevant test problems are obtained. The experiments show that after integrating other online behaviors of learners, the three types of learning behaviors form significant relationships, and the relevant early warning intervals are also trained to form a corresponding early warning model. Finally, three key decision strategies applied to online learning platform are discussed. The whole research process provides an analysis strategy for massive unbalanced learning behavior data. By using deep learning, it realizes the fusion of multi-source learning behavior data, improves the predictive quality and has important significance for early warning.

In the follow-up research, we will further refine the classification and fusion of interactive learning behavior, achieve the cost sensitivity analysis and adaptive prediction of unbalanced interactive learning behaviors, expand the calculation dimension of behavior data and provide more effective technical methods and decision suggestions for improving the early warning effect of interactive learning behavior.

References

Ameloot, E., Rotsaert, T., & Schellens, T. (2021). The supporting role of learning analytics for a blended learning environment: exploring students' perceptions and the impact on relatedness. *Journal of Computer Assisted Learning*. 38(1), 90–102. https://doi.org/10.1111/jcal.12593

Carter, M., & Egliston, B. (2021). What are the risks of virtual reality data? Learning analytics, algorithmic bias and a fantasy of perfect data. *New Media & Society*. 2021(3), 146144482110127. https://doi.org/10.1177/14614448211012794

Eberle, J., & Hobrecht, J. (2021). The lonely struggle with autonomy: a case study of first-year university students' experiences during emergency online teaching. *Computers in Human Behavior*. 121(3), 106804. https://doi.org/10.1016/j.chb.2021.106804

Geyer, P. D. (2021). Adjustment-seeking behavior: the role of political skill and self-efficacy in training students to be more actively engaged in their studies. *Active Learning in Higher Education*. 19, 1–13. https://doi.org/10.1177/1469787417721993

Mangaroska, K., Martinez-Maldonado, R., Vesin, B., & Gaevi, D. (2021a). Challenges and opportunities of multimodal data in human learning: the computer science students' perspective. *Journal of Computer Assisted Learning*. 37(4): 1030–1047. https://doi.org/10.1111/jcal.12542

Mangaroska, K., Vesin, B., Kostakos, V., Brusilovsky, P., & Giannakos, M. (2021b). Architecting analytics across multiple e-learning systems to enhance learning design. *IEEE Transactions on Learning Technologies*. 14(2), 173–188. https://doi.org/10.1109/TLT.2021.3072159

Mckenna, J. W., Brigham, F. J., Ciullo, S., Mason, L. H., & Judd, L. (2021). Persuasive quick-writing about text: intervention for students with learning disabilities. *Behavior Modification*. 45(1), 122–146. https://doi.org/10.1177/0145445519882894

Ouyang, F., Chen, S., & Li, X. (2021). Effect of three network visualizations on students' social-cognitive engagement in online discussions. *British Journal of Educational Technology*. 52(6), 2242–2262. https://doi.org/10.1111/bjet.13126

Praharaj, S., Scheffel, M., Drachsler, H., & Specht, M. M. (2021). Literature review on co-located collaboration modeling using multimodal learning analytics—can we go the whole nine yards? *IEEE Transactions on Learning Technologies*. 14(3), 367–385. https://doi.org/10.1109/TLT.2021.3097766

Razmerita, L., Kirchner, K., Kai, H., & Tan, C. W. (2020). Modeling collaborative intentions and behavior in digital environments: the case of a massive open online course (MOOC). *Academy of Management Learning and Education*. 19(4), 469–502. https://doi.org/10.5465/amle.2018.0056

Roldán, S. M., Marauri, J., Aubert, A., & Flecha, R. (2021). How inclusive interactive learning environments benefit students without special needs. *Frontiers in Psychology*. 12, 661427. https://doi.org/10.3389/fpsyg.2021.661427

Ruipérez-Valiente, J., Staubitz, T., Jenner, M., Halawa, S., Zhang, J., & Despujol, I. (2022). Large scale analytics of global and regional mooc providers: differences in learners' demographics, preferences, and perceptions. *Computers & Education*. 180, 104426. https://doi.org/10.1016/j.compedu.2021.104426

Sailer, M., Stadler, M., Schultz-Pernice, F., Franke, U., & Fischer, F. (2021). Technology-related teaching skills and attitudes: validation of a scenario-based self-assessment instrument for teachers. *Computers in Human Behavior*. 115, 106625. https://doi.org/10.1016/j.chb.2020.106625

Ugalde, L., Santiago-Garabieta, M., Villarejo-Carballido, B., & Puigvert, L. (2021). Impact of interactive learning environments on learning and cognitive development of children with special educational needs: a literature review. *Frontiers in Psychology.* 12, 674033. https://doi.org/10.3389/fpsyg.2021.674033

Xia, X. (2020a). Learning behavior mining and decision recommendation based on association rules in interactive learning environment. *Interactive Learning Environments.* 2020(8), 1–16. https://doi.org/10. 1080/10494820.2020.1799028

Xia, X. (2020b). Random field design and collaborative inference strategy for learning interaction activities. *Interactive Learning Environments.* 2020(12), 1–25. https://doi.org/ 10.1080/10494820.2020.1863236

Xia, X. (2021a). Interaction recognition and intervention based on context feature fusion of learning behaviors in interactive learning environments. *Interactive Learning Environments.* 2021(1): 1–19. https://doi.org/10.1080/10494820.2021.1871632

Xia, X. (2021b). Sparse learning strategy and key feature selection in interactive learning environment. *Interactive Learning Environments.* 2021(11), 1–25. https://doi.org/10. 1080/10494820.2021.1998913

Xia, X. (2021c). Decision application mechanism of regression analysis of multi-category learning behaviors in interactive learning environment. *Interactive Learning Environments.* 2021(4): 1–14. https://doi.org/10.1080/10494820.2021.1916767

Xia, X. (2022a). Diversion inference model of learning effectiveness supported by differential evolution strategy. *Computers and Education: Artificial Intelligence.* 3(1), 100071. https://doi.org/10.1016/j.caeai.2022.100071

Xia, X. (2022b). Application technology on collaborative training of interactive learning activities and tendency preference diversion. *SAGE Open.* 12(2), 1–15. https://doi. org/10.1177/21582440221093368

Xia, X., & Qi, W. (2022). Temporal tracking and early warning of multi semantic features of learning behavior. *Computers and Education: Artificial Intelligence.* 3(1), 100045. https://doi.org/10.1016/j.caeai.2021.100045

Yoon, S. W. (2021). Explosion of people analytics, machine learning, and human resource technologies: implications and applications for research. *Human Resource Development Quarterly.* 32(3), 243–250. https://doi.org/10.1002/hrdq.21456

7 Cost Sensitivity Analysis and Adaptive Prediction of Unbalanced Interactive Learning Behaviors

Abstract

Based on the early warning model and corresponding decisions achieved in Chapter 6, the following work is to design a cost sensitive analysis method of unbalanced interactive learning behaviors. The interactive learning behavior has obvious discreteness and autonomy, resulting in the problem of data imbalance, which poses a great obstacle to the research of interactive learning behavior that also cannot ensure the quality and reliability of learning analytics. However, it is almost difficult to obtain balanced data from the interactive learning process, especially in the online learning environment, which brings more difficulties to the direct application of traditional learning analytics and methods. Therefore, the analysis of unbalanced interactive learning behavior cannot rely on the existing means. It is necessary to design new applicable models and algorithms driven by data, so as to effectively reduce the interference caused by noise or outliers, and highlight the value and law contained in the data. So in this chapter, the multi-structures, multi-features and multi-relationships of interactive learning behavior are analyzed; then, an unbalanced interactive learning behavior analysis strategy is designed that integrates cost sensitive learning process and Bayesian optimal prediction theory. Through the comparison of multiple correlation methods, this novel method is suitable for the feature analysis of interactive learning behavior. The whole study realizes the value mining and law tracking, and achieves the reliable classification and adaptive prediction. Based on the study of this chapter, we might provide an effective analysis method of unbalanced interactive learning behavior, in order to enable the important conclusions of Chapter 8.

Keywords

Interactive Learning Behavior;
Unbalanced Data; Cost Sensitivity;
Bayesian Optimal Prediction

Theory; Sample Space; Learning
Analytics

DOI: 10.4324/9781003484905-7

1 Introduction

The interactive learning environment realizes the tracking and management of interactive learning behavior; it integrates multimedia technology, sharing technology and data technology, and also realizes the storage and scheduling of learning materials, content, data, documents and other resources (Eberle & Hobrecht, 2021; Sailer et al., 2021). In the interaction and cooperation, the various teaching modes and learning methods are implemented, and the learning objectives are completed (Mangaroska et al., 2021a). The construction of interactive learning behavior is inseparable from the technologies and tools, which makes the learning process break through the limitations of time and space (Xia, 2020a). Through the continuous expansion of platform services and interfaces (Praharaj et al., 2021) the interactive learning behavior is continuously improved. At the same time, it also increases the structural complexity, semantic complexity and correlation complexity. Because of the autonomy and discreteness of the learning process (Er et al., 2021), the massive interactive learning behavior data has a significant imbalance problem. It has become a hot and difficult issue of learning analytics.

The data balance mainly means that the proportion of various samples is relatively equal, and the cost of data misclassification is relatively balanced (Ouyang et al., 2021). However, in the actual interactive learning process, it is difficult to obtain balanced data, which will lead to the uncertainty (Xia, 2022a), and it is difficult to ensure the accuracy and reliability of data analysis and prediction (Li et al., 2021). Unbalanced problem has become an obstacle to effective data mining, prediction and recommendation. Traditional data mining algorithms usually make problem assumptions based on the balance data. The unbalanced learning problem is directly related to incomplete data, interference factors or data classes. Due to the particularity of interactive learning behavior, a small number of data classes only occupy a small share in the overall sample, which is likely to be mixed with a large amount of noise, resulting in great difficulty in data classification (Aguilar et al., 2021; Rebolledo-Mendez et al., 2021). Therefore, unbalanced interactive learning behavior requires new models and algorithms to effectively learn effective information and value (Xia, 2020a).

There are two general trends in the research of unbalanced data: one is to design applicable methods for the multidimensional and sparse problems, driven by specific data (Song et al., 2021; Xia & Qi, 2022); or, using domain knowledge and technical means to mine the undiscovered laws and risks, so as to provide basis for decision and prediction; second, the research objective changes from ideal standard data to general unbalanced data. This analysis process requires statistical models and explores effective theories and technologies (Jovanovi et al., 2021). Based on the large data set of interactive learning behavior, this study integrates the two analysis trends of unbalanced data, puts forward a cost sensitive learning method, comprehensively analyzes the features, structures and relationships, and puts forward the relevant test problems. Then, we demonstrate the logical structures and algorithms of the data description model, and effectively test the robustness and reliability. On this basis, the value mining and law tracking of data set are realized.

2   Related Work

The unbalanced data of interactive learning behavior is mainly divided into internal imbalance and external imbalance. The internal imbalance is mainly the natural state of the interactive learning process (Ruipérez-Valiente et al., 2022), which is affected by the data diversity; External imbalance is mainly affected by variable factors such as time and storage mode (Ameloot et al., 2021). For the unbalanced data, these two situations need to be comprehensively considered, in order to generate a classifier with high accuracy on a few data classes that will not seriously damage the accuracy of most data classes (Silvola et al., 2021). The imbalance affects that the traditional evaluation criteria (such as global accuracy or error rate) cannot provide sufficient information (Zelenkov & Volodarskiy, 2021); it is necessary to give more evaluation metrics to interactive learning behavior such as ROC (Receiver Operating Characteristics Curve), Precision-recall Curve and Cost Curve.

The solution of unbalanced data depends on the breakthrough and innovation of data analytics (Mckenna et al., 2021). After sorting out relevant references, the research in this field mainly focuses on three aspects.

1 Data-based analysis method. This aspect mainly refers to the data resampling technology, including undersampling, oversampling and mixed sampling. In order to improve the imbalance, oversampling and undersampling adopt different methods, respectively, to achieve the balanced sample categories (Razmerita et al., 2020). Oversampling increases the number of positive samples by increasing the synthetic samples, and undersampling matches the positive samples by removing the negative samples (Ihm et al., 2021). The two sampling methods have their own advantages and disadvantages, which can be applied to different application requirements, but they are also prone to over fitting.

2 Integration method. Because the integration method can combine a variety of algorithms and models, it has significant advantages in dealing with unbalanced data. The algorithm design, domain correlation, model correlation and model selection will enable the practical application (Geyer, 2021). Based on statistical analysis and optimization theory, the integration method has become one of the important data mining methods (Roldán et al., 2021). By integrating relatively mature theories, it ensures the development of integrated learning methods (Jang & Yoon, 2020). However, the technical requirements for unbalanced data are high. If the integration of mature methods cannot be completed effectively, the application of this method is still inefficient.

3 Model selection. For the unbalanced data in different fields, a variety of different models and measurement strategies have been produced. The integration method is usually combined with model selection. In order to complete the integration of methods, many models need to be weighed and compromised. While selecting the evaluation methods, the mode and weight should also be selected (Wong et al., 2020). This method can achieve more efficient selection in the case of less data features, but for the model identification of massive

data or multi-category features, it needs sufficient, reliable and accurate weight operation and performance comparison, and the amount of operation is huge.

The essence of data mining is to simulate the understanding process of human knowledge. The data analytics is to show the potential or hidden laws and knowledge, rather than the creation process of new knowledge and new laws, in order to understand and apply data more deeply (Zhao et al., 2020). For the existing methods, unless they are well integrated with the data, it is impossible to judge which algorithm is more applicable, and it is difficult to realize the overall calculation and analysis (Xia, 2021b). Therefore, in order to improve the efficiency and effectiveness of the above three research aspects, we need to process the data imbalance problem and minimize the global misclassification cost. About the imbalance of interactive learning behavior, the complexity and feature diversity of massive data, this study proposes a cost sensitive learning analysis strategy.

3   Data Processing and Problem Description

This study obtains the whole data of an online learning platform for four years. The platform is an autonomous learning system provided to learners by an open university, including the systematic learning contents of three majors, all of which belong to STEM. Learners complete the assessment after one period of autonomous learning. The learning period is directly related to the professional training needs. The period mainly includes 12 months, 18 months and 24 months, respectively. The learning period is divided into different sub-stages. The assessment time of each learning content is unified. When failing the assessment, the learner is needed to relearn this content. Therefore, the assessment time of every learning content is relatively fixed. After all the learning contents of a major pass the assessment, the learner will be certified. Relevant data are shown in Table 7.1.

Table 7.1 Data Description

Major	Corresponding Contents	Sub-periods	Period Range
M1	Four courses // C11, C12 in the first sub-period; C13, C14 in the second sub-period	Two sub-periods	12 months
M2	Five courses // C21, C22 in the first sub-period; C23, C24 in the second sub-period; C25 in the third sub-period	Three sub-periods	18 months
M3	Nine course // C31, C32, C33 in the first sub-period; C34, C35, C36 in the second sub-period; C37, C38 in the third sub-period; C39 in the fourth sub-period	Four sub-periods	24 months

Note: Every sub-period includes six months.

In Table 7.1, M1 involves four learning contents, M2 involves five learning contents and M3 involves nine learning contents. Each learning content needs to be assessed. It can be seen that M3 has the most assessment needs. These learning contents are distributed in different sub-stages; there is an inevitable relationship between these learning contents. There is a parallel relationship between the learning contents in the same sub-stage of one major. The learning contents in the early sub-stage are the basis of the later sub-stage; learners participate in one content and should complete the assessment of precursor content and pass the assessment. If the learner fails to pass the assessment, the subsequent learning process is locked and cannot be activated. In this way, in different sub-stages, a learner may produce multiple learning processes in one learning content. We take the major and learning content as clues, analyze and count the relevant interactive learning behavior and learners, as shown in Table 7.2.

Table 7.2 includes two types of data. One is the number of learners who have passed the assessment, which is mainly divided into four categories; learners form repeated behaviors of the same learning content. As can be seen from Table 7.2, the largest number of learners passes the assessment for the first time. The more times, the fewer learners. M1 can set four learning contents in one year, so in the data of four years, each learning content of M1 generates four periods, and will also have the opportunity to participate in the assessment for 1–4 times. Five learning contents of M2 and nine learning contents of M3 are distributed in two years; each learning content produces learning behavior of two learning periods. For the same

Table 7.2 Data Scale

Learning Contents	Pass the Assessment*				Record Item**
	First	Second	Third	Fourth	
C11	13,566	3,019	1,336	407	14,450,120
C12	11,902	2,881	993	234	12,117,008
C13	9,944	3,215	417	225	8,914,221
C14	10,553	2,903	1,104	790	9,500,377
C21	27,004	4,184	–	–	34,663,209
C22	28,153	4,792	–	–	36,290,335
C23	25,544	3,285	–	–	30,127,408
C24	28,359	2,303	–	–	29,347,899
C25	26,641	3,811	–	–	31,004,118
C31	34,025	2,107	–	–	31,885,237
C32	33,996	1,936	–	–	25,442,184
C33	37,218	2,035	–	–	30,006,010
C34	35,902	1,937	–	–	22,432,195
C35	24,118	2,101	–	–	21,504,223
C36	27,334	2,054	–	–	20,313,207
C37	29,482	1,553	–	–	20,004,149
C38	22,150	1,391	–	–	15,432,911
C39	19,988	1,475	–	–	10,983,162

Note: *Number of learners who pass the assessment at different times.
**Number of learning behavior record items of different learning contents.

Table 7.3 Related Indicators of Learning Behavior

Activity	Standard Deviation	Variance	Kurtosis	Skewness	Confidence (95.0%)
Data plus	101.25	2,419.33	17.92	4.64	2.62
Data pane	44.13	5,007.16	19.37	10.42	4.39
Upload	19.06	756.11	13.9	2.97	2.02
Download	23.94	1,206.73	12.93	13.05	4.09
Forum	693.43	480,842.46	40.03	5.47	33.51
Glossary	47.54	2,260.15	245.28	13.58	2.3
Shared page	309.95	96,071.14	54.68	5.54	14.98
Collaborate	28.67	822.15	11.06	2.87	1.39
Content	113.90	12,973.35	10.19	2.43	5.5
Wiki	2.13	4.54	461.62	19.45	0.1
Quiz	14.55	211.84	165.43	8.53	0.7
Resource	137.07	18,788.94	1,160.09	31.39	6.62
Questionnaire	136.61	18,663.33	6.32	2.12	6.6
Url	30.82	949.58	284.13	12.04	1.49
Video	3.10	5.47	46.89	13.55	0.17

learning content of M2 and M3, there are two assessments in the data set. The interactive learning behavior remains in the form of record items.

For different learner participation modes, the learning behavior is defined as a continuous change in relevant features (Oppermann et al., 2021); the effective click rate is defined as the statistics. The data statistical results are shown in Table 7.3. The whole data involves 15 features. From the standard deviation, variance, kurtosis and skewness in Table 7.3, it can be seen that the traces of each feature form great differences, and the learning behavior has strong discreteness (Xia, 2020a). There is an obvious imbalance problem. Especially for learners who have taken part in the assessment for many times, the change of their learning behavior is of great significance. For the learning behavior of each learning content, especially for the learners who have participated in the same learning content for many times, it is necessary to first solve the imbalance, and then achieve sufficient data training that will be further tested in the experiment.

Combined with the data distribution and relevant indicators in Tables 7.1–7.3, the relevant influencing factors and possible relationships are designed to construct relevant test problems. As shown in Figure 7.1, the relevant problems are divided into four series; each series is divided into several sub-problems, and the test objectives of sub-problems are different, there are four series, which are described as follows.

About the first series, the corresponding questions of interactive learning behavior and different assessment times are serialized as:

Q11: the key interactive learning behaviors and correlations that pass the first assessment of M1, involving four learning contents;

Q12: the key interactive learning behaviors and correlations that pass the second assessment of M1, involving four learning contents;

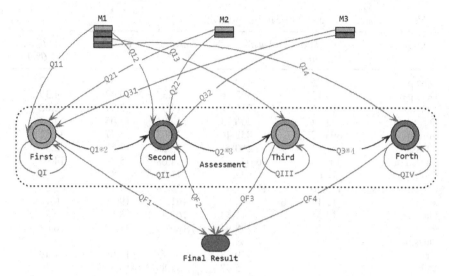

Figure 7.1 Test Problems and Relationships Related to Interactive Learning Behavior

Q13: the key interactive learning behaviors and correlations that pass the third assessment of M1, involving four learning contents;

Q14: the key interactive learning behaviors and correlations that pass the fourth assessment of M1, involving four learning contents;

Q21: the key interactive learning behaviors and correlations that pass the first assessment of M2, involving five learning contents;

Q22: the key interactive learning behaviors and correlations that pass the second assessment of M2, involving five learning contents;

Q31: the key interactive learning behaviors and correlations that pass the first assessment of M3, involving nine learning contents;

Q32: the key interactive learning behaviors and correlations that pass the second assessment of M3, involving nine learning contents;

About the second series, the corresponding questions of different assessment times are serialized as:

Q1→2: the change sequence of interactive learning behavior that fails the first assessment but passes for the second time, involving three majors;

Q2→3: the change sequence of interactive learning behavior that fails the second assessment but passes for the third time, involving one major;

Q3→4: the change sequence of interactive learning behavior that fails the third assessment but passes for the fourth time, involving one major;

About the third series, the corresponding questions of key interactive learning behaviors and correlations that pass the assessment for different times are serialized as:

QI: the commonness and difference of key learning behaviors that pass the first assessment, involving three majors;

QII: the commonness and difference of key learning behaviors that pass the second assessment, involving three majors;

QIII: the commonness and difference of key learning behaviors that pass the third assessment, involving one major;

QIV: the commonness and difference of key learning behaviors that pass the fourth assessment, involving one major;

About the fourth series, the passing the assessment is defined as the observation variable, the corresponding questions of different assessment times and assessment results are serialized as:

QF1: the significance of the assessment results from the first assessment, involving three majors;

QF2: the significance of the assessment results from the second assessment, involving three majors;

QF3: the significance of the assessment results from the third assessment, involving one major;

QF4: the significance of the assessment results from the fourth assessment, involving one major.

4　Method

Cost sensitive learning methods mainly include three categories: data space weighting, cost sensitive learning classification and Bayesian risk theory. The goal is to assign samples to the data class with the least risk. The first category converts the costs into sample weights. The weighted training samples are used in the standard learning algorithms, which is a data level method, and the algorithm is not modified. The second category and the third category are algorithm level. The original algorithms are modified to adapt to cost sensitive learning. These two categories are more suitable for unbalanced data of interactive learning behavior. This study designs an applicable cost sensitive learning method.

The analysis process needs to change the classification algorithms to make it have cost sensitive recognition. The cost of misclassification of positive classes is higher than that of negative classes. In the process of data classification, the number of high-cost errors and the total cost of misclassification are the smallest. However, changing the existing classification algorithm makes it cost sensitive, and the effect is not obvious. Therefore, for the multi-structures, multi-features and multi-relationships of interactive learning behavior, it is not feasible to change the original classification algorithms. We add a key logical analysis process to convert the original classification algorithms into cost sensitive. The interactive learning behavior is analyzed, and the cost sensitive analysis process is described as Algorithm CSA.

Algorithm CSA

Step 1. The interactive learning behavior is randomly divided into training set and test set according to an appropriate proportion;

Step 2. Sample the training set for many times to generate multiple data models;

Step 3. For the generated data model, analyze the probability that the test samples are classified into each model;

Step 4. Calculate all the misclassification costs of the test samples, and get the data class according to the minimum cost.

Step 5. Implement the cost sensitive learning for interactive learning behavior, and the analysis process will call Algorithm CSL.

Algorithm CSL

Step 1. Spatial weighting of data is processed. The distribution of data set is trained according to the misclassification cost correction. The modified data distribution is biased to high-cost categories by Translation Theorem. Matching with the normal space without considering the cost factors, the data space $X \times Y \times C$ is defined as the cost space, X represents the input space, Y represents the output space and C represents the cost. If the sample distribution of the cost space is D, the distribution model of the normal

space is expressed as $\hat{D}(X,Y) \equiv \dfrac{C}{E_{X,Y,C \sim D}[c]} D(X,Y,C)$, $E_{X,Y,C \sim D}[C]$

is the expectation of the cost. According to Translation Theorem, the classifier that obtains the optimal error rate will also ensure the minimum classifier. When updating the sample weight of the integration cost, the distribution D is selected. The construction process of interactive learning behavior random subspace will call Algorithm RSP.

Step 2. The experiment is needed to use the decision tree for cost induction, build an effective strategy to adapt to the minimized misclassification cost, select the optimal data distribution of the split data and determine whether the sub-tree is pruned.

Step 3. Bayesian optimal prediction theory is used to assign the sample to the class with the least risk, assign the category label that minimizes the classification cost to the leaf node.

Algorithm RSP

Step 1. N is set as the number of training sample, F is set as the feature number of training data, N and F are initialized;

Step 2. $d(d < F)$ is selected as input variable of each classifier, for different classifiers, d can have different values;

Step 3. L classifiers are selected to be integrated;

Step 4. Each classifier creates a vector set by selecting d features from F features without resetting and training the classifier;

Step 5. In order to classify a new sample, the outputs of L classifiers are connected through majority voting or a posteriori probability.

Step 2 of CSL realizes the fusion of cost sensitive learning process and decision tree. For the construction of decision tree, this study adopts one improved random forest integration method. A fixed probability distribution is used to generate random vectors, the random forest is improved by means of the bagging process of decision tree and N samples are randomly taken from the original training set.

The same uniform probability is also used in the whole model construction and bagging to generate self-help samples, composed of multiple classifiers, and the sample category is predicted based on the output of each classifier. In this way, the random forest is transformed into a set of decision trees. The random subspace classifiers can be composed of linear classifier, support vector machine and other types of classifiers.

Step 3 of CSL realizes the integration of cost sensitive learning process and Bayesian optimal prediction theory. This study realizes the classification of samples based on MetaCost method. Multiple samples are taken in the training set to generate multiple models; then we obtain the probability $P(i \mid x)$ that each sample belongs to some category and calculate the expected cost $R(j \mid x) = \sum_{i}^{I} P(i \mid x) \text{cost}(i, j)$ of each sample in the training set belonging to each category; $\text{cost}(i, j)$ represents the cost matrix of the training set, and modify the label of the data classes according to the minimum expected cost. Further, the modified data set is trained to obtain a new model.

Bayesian optimal prediction theory means that the sample space of interactive learning behavior is divided into I sub-domains, and the category i is the prediction of the minimum expected cost obtained in the sub-domain i. If the cost of sample i is higher than other misclassification categories, a part of the sample space is in the category i that does not belong to the sub-domain i; it will be reclassified at the least expected cost.

5 Experiment

The experimental process is to realize the classification of data sets, and the comparative test adopts the ten-fold cross validation. On the one hand, it compares the different performances of traditional classifiers and cost sensitive analysis algorithms, and plays the role of cost sensitive learning process in realizing data balance; on the other hand, the performances are compared to verify the feasibility and reliability of the classifiers and algorithms, and the optimal sample space and classification strategy are selected; Furthermore, the interactive learning behavior features are analyzed based on the sample space; considering the feature weights, the influence on interactive learning behavior is analyzed. The algorithms involved in the whole experiment are implemented in Python 3.8. The experimental scheme is mainly divided into two steps.

Step 1. The classifier algorithms suitable for interactive learning behavior are compared with CSA. Experiments show the classifiers that can be applied to interactive learning behavior, including Naive Bayes, Bayesian Network and C4.5 Decision Tree, Random Tree, Random Forest, K-Nearest Neighborhood (KNN), Logistic Regression and BP Neural Network. Multi-level classification is implemented, and the four performance indicators of Accuracy, Mean Absolute Error (MAE), F1 and AUC (Area Under curve) of each algorithm are recorded and

Table 7.4 Performance Indicators of Comparison Algorithms

Algorithm	Accuracy	MAE	F1	AUC
Naive Bayes	0.3201	0.1993	0.324	0.544
Bayesian network	0.4115	0.1748	0.417	0.625
C4.5 decision tree	0.5255	0.1457	0.531	0.687
Random tree	0.4552	0.1603	0.459	0.650
Random forest	0.4404	0.1688	0.399	0.634
KNN	0.3229	0.1992	0.303	0.547
Logistic regression	0.4590	0.1707	0.450	0.645
BP neural network	0.5929	0.1122	0.556	0.711
CSA	0.5929	0.1053	0.616	0.759

Note: The bold values represent the optimal results.

compared. The greater the Accuracy, F1 and AUC, the better. The smaller the MAE, the better.

Step 2. We compare different sample spaces, take the information gain and symmetric uncertainty as the feature measurement criteria, generate the corresponding feature importance ranking and intercept the feature subset according to 25%, 50% and 75% cut. Each feature subset calls Step 1, respectively. Finally, the evaluation indicators of different sample spaces are averaged.

About Step 1 of the experiment, the relevant algorithms are, respectively, applied to the sample space of interactive learning behavior. After sufficient and multi-level iterative data analysis and calculation, the performance indicators in Table 7.4 are obtained. It can be seen from Table 7.4 that Accuracy, BP Neural Network and CSA have achieved large values, but for F1 and AUC, CSA is obviously better than BP Neural Network, which is the maximum value. For MAE, CSA is relatively small. On the whole, the sample space analysis of CSA is relatively optimal.

About Step 2 of the experiment, the data set is feature filtered, and six feature subsets of sample space are formed. The information gain of Figures 7.2–7.4 and the symmetric uncertainty of Figures 7.5–7.7 are obtained. Each figure shows the cost sensitive classification of different algorithms.

Through the experimental analysis of these two steps, the following conclusions can be drawn.

1 The distribution trend of the four performance indicators of the classification is basically the same. The features with high accuracy also have high F1 and AUC, while MAE is small, and no great difference is found. CSA also meets this law, and compared with other comparison methods, CSA achieves better performances.
2 No matter which feature analysis method, the classification of the feature subset after processing the imbalance problem is better than the original sample space. There are obvious irrelevant or redundant features in the original data set. The solved imbalance problem can effectively improve the separability of data

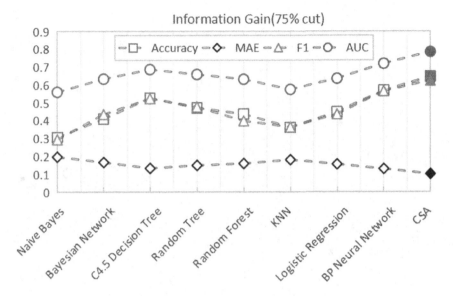

Figure 7.2 Information Gain (75% Cut)

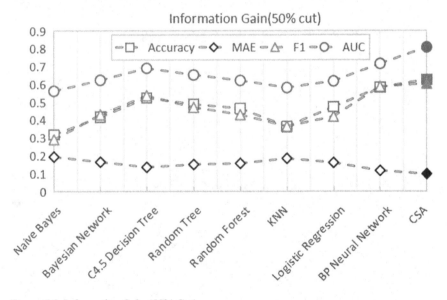

Figure 7.3 Information Gain (50% Cut)

space and improve the classification effect. At the same time, the feature subset obtained by 50% cut is better than 75% and 25% cut, and the generated feature subset might distinguish categories well.

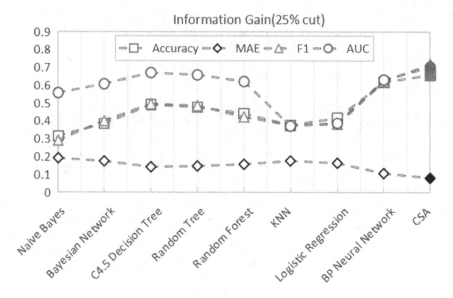

Figure 7.4 Information Gain (25% Cut)

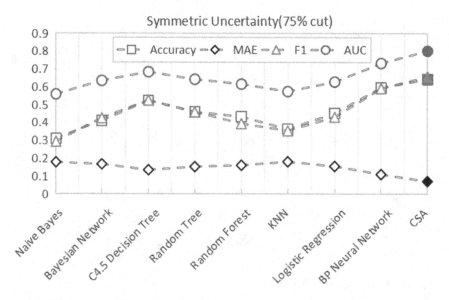

Figure 7.5 Symmetric Uncertainty (75% Cut)

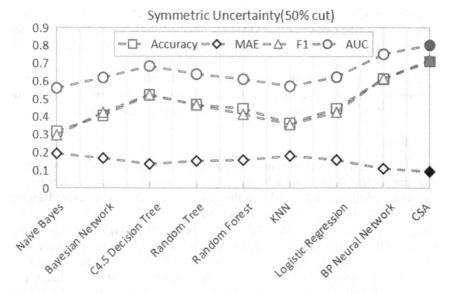

Figure 7.6 Symmetric Uncertainty (50% Cut)

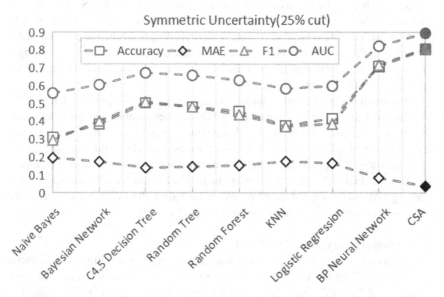

Figure 7.7 Symmetric Uncertainty (25% Cut)

3 About Accuracy, F1 and AUC in Figures 7.2–7.7, CSA is better than the other eight methods. At the same time, the MAE of CSA is relatively small. Whether it is information gain or balancing uncertainty, CSA is more stable, efficient and reliable.

The whole experiment shows that the cost analysis method of unbalanced interactive learning behavior is feasible, and the data analysis results are based on the accuracy and integrity of the original data, which has better references and significance.

6   Result

Based on the experimental results of unbalanced interactive learning behavior by Algorithm CSA, the features of sample space are mined and sorted according to the symmetrical uncertainty rule. In the first step, considering different learning contents, learners may produce different behaviors, and divide the data set into different subsets according to Table 7.2. In the second step, the Algorithm CSA is applied to different data subsets to implement sufficient data training and prediction. The third step is to select the top five features with the largest weight. Through the analysis and prediction of the experimental results, we can explore the change law of learning behavior in the same major. Furthermore, it tests the relevant problems for interactive learning behavior.

As for the weight of feature selection in the second step, two factors need to be considered: one is the large participation of learners in a feature, and the algorithm can be used to sort the features according to the descending order. Second, there is a large correlation between features and others, forming a "feature pair". Similarly, the relationships between features are sorted according to the descending order. Considering the two-level ranking, when the order of a feature in the two ranking is inconsistent, its selection preference shall be determined based on the higher order, so as to select the top five features.

After completing the cost sensitive iterative analysis of Algorithm CSA on the unbalanced learning behavior, as well as the sufficient feature weight calculation, taking the assessment results as the observation variables, the first five features of each data subset and the strong correlation are analyzed. Based on this, the feasibility of subsequent or potential interactive learning behavior is predicted. The results are shown in Figure 7.8. As can be seen, the five key features corresponding to each learning content have great overlap, mainly including the following six cases that form two categories of feature clusters with great weight.

I   The first category of feature cluster

This category mainly constructs learning behavior around three key features. As the enabling force of learning behavior, "video" is strongly related to "content" and "forum". Based on different learning contents, it is also related to other features of great weight. It is mainly divided into three aspects.

1   video→(content, forum)+(collaborate, download). This aspect involves four learning contents, C11, C12, C13 and C21, and involves M1 and M2. The first three learning contents are relearned every year, and C21 is relearned every two years, but there is a very obvious regularity.

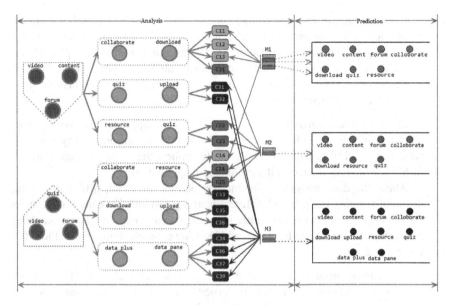

Figure 7.8 Analysis and Prediction of Unbalanced Interactive Learning Behavior

2 video→(content, forum)+(quiz, upload). This aspect only involves two learning contents of M3, C31 and C32. Based on the key features, the learning process is accompanied by frequent periodic tests and homework submission. The two learning contents are implemented in two interactive learning processes in four years, and the tendency and attention of learning behavior are basically the same.

3 video→(content, forum)+(resource+quiz). This aspect only involves two learning contents of M2, C22 and C23. Based on the key features, learners have a high demand for related resources of learning content, and more frequent tests are integrated into the learning process. The learning content has relatively basic and principled characteristics.

II The second category of feature cluster

This aspect also constructs learning behavior around three key features, which is similar to the first category of feature clusters; "quiz" and "forum" are driven by the "video" of learning content, forming a strong correlation among the three, and strengthening the participation of collaboration and testing in the learning process. At the same time, based on different learning contents, two other features with large weight are associated, which are mainly divided into three aspects.

1 video→(quiz,forum)+(collaborate,resource). This aspect involves four learning contents: C14 of M1, C24 and C25 of M2 and C33 of M3. On the basis of the key features, the learning behavior is toward the needs of cooperation and resources, the relevant contents need the cooperation of experimental and practical projects, as well as guiding learners to find and solve problems independently.

2   video→(quiz,forum)+(download,upload). This aspect mainly involves two learning contents of M3, C35 and C38. Based on the key features, the learning process is accompanied by a large number of data "upload" and "download", mainly reflected in the relevant auxiliary materials and the participation of relevant training projects. Data requirements and task submission are completed through the learning platform.

video→(quiz,forum)+(data plus,data pane). This aspect mainly involves four learning contents of M3, C34, C36, C37 and C39. Based on the key features, "data plus" and "data pane" have been fully applied; the application and practice of M3 are directly related to the training and application.

About the data analysis of interactive learning behavior, different majors, different learning periods and different learning contents have great overlap in the features; there are certain similarities between learning objectives, teaching methods, assessment needs, majors and learning contents. It mainly includes the following aspects.

1   Learning behavior is mainly driven by "video", which is the main expression of learning content. In the process of viewing "video", learners realize the participation and association between "video" and other features.
2   Learning behavior has obvious interactive features. In Figure 7.8, features such as "collaborate" and "forum" have been fully involved and associated; the learning content needs to realize the full cooperation and communication.
3   Learning behavior needs periodic tests as timely incentive and test measures. In the process of feature analysis, "quiz" is a typical feature of learning behavior.
4   Learning behavior requires resources related to learning contents. Whether these resources are directly related, auxiliary or data support, they will have relevant participation and correlation.

The similarities in these four aspects are applicable not only to beginners of a learning content but also to secondary and tertiary learners. For the learning assessment objectives of a major, the five key features and relationships shown in Figure 7.8 are universal, and are necessary conditions for learners to pass the assessment. This conclusion is very important; through the prediction of the feasible learning behavior features, the key features of the three majors are obtained, which are as follows.

M1→(video, content, forum, collaborate, download, quiz, resource)
M2→(video, content, forum, collaborate, download, resource, quiz)
M3→(video, content, forum, collaborate, download, upload, resource, quiz, data plus, data pane)

About the prediction results of key features in different majors, M1 and M2 have strong similarities, learning methods, assessment methods and teaching methods. Compared with M1 and M2, M3 has three key features: "upload", "data plus" and "data pane". The learning behavior generated by some learning contents is also obviously consistent with M1 and M2. It can be seen that M3, M1 and M2 have strong interoperability, especially in the same learning period; the potential recommendation and guidance between the contents of different majors can mine the learners with potential interest and improve the participation and awareness of interdisciplinary.

Based on the above analysis results, the data and relationships are further trained for the test problems proposed in the third section. Taking each major as the classification condition, the visual learning content, pass times, key features and correlation are obtained in Figures 7.9–7.11, respectively.

I For the first series of test problems, about the correlation between interactive learning behavior and different assessment times, the correlation analysis results are as follows.

Figures 7.9–7.11 show the relationships of key features of interactive learning behavior. Through the full cost analysis of unbalanced data, it is found that the interactive learning behavior is not affected by the times of the assessment; Q11, Q12, Q13 and Q14 form an interactive learning behavior with the same key feature trend and relationships, which is also applicable to Q21 and Q22, Q31 and Q32. However, the correlation of different assessment times has changed. At the same time, no matter which learning content, the interactive learning behavior of the second assessment is generally higher than the first, but the interactive learning behavior of the third and fourth assessment begins to decrease, which is directly related to the reduction of learner scale.

II For the second series, about the correlation between different assessment times, the analysis results are as follows.

For Q1→2, the interactive learning behavior that fails the assessment for the first time but passes for the second time is the most complex, involving M1, M2 and M3. It can be seen from Figures 7.9–7.11 that the key features and correlation of interactive learning behavior have not changed; For Q2→3 and Q3→4, only M1 is involved. The learners who need to participate in the third

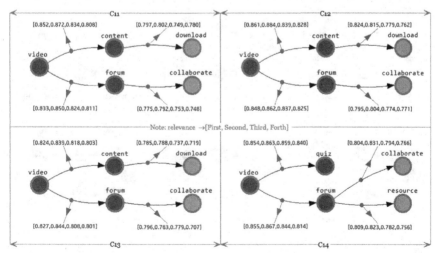

Figure 7.9 Test Results of M1 Related Problems

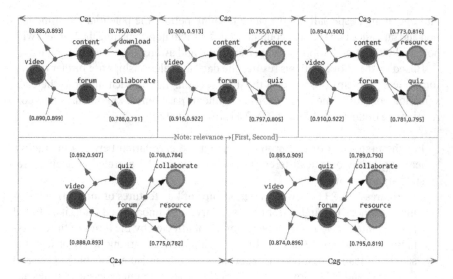

Figure 7.10 Test Results of M2 Related Problems

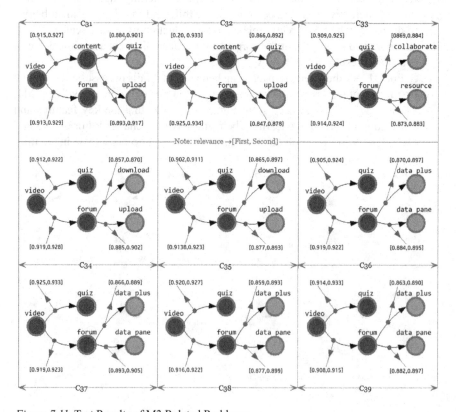

Figure 7.11 Test Results of M3 Related Problems

or fourth assessment are greatly reduced; the interactive learning behavior has not changed significantly.

III For the third series, about the key interactive learning behaviors that have passed the assessment for different times and their correlation, the correlation analysis results are as follows.

Taking the assessment results ("Pass") as the observation variables, combined with the analysis of the first series and the second series, the interactive learning behaviors involved in QI, QII, QIII and QIV have strong commonalities in key features. Figures 7.9–7.11 have shown the relevant features; the significant learning behavior features form more stable and effective learning methods. For learners who fail the assessment, the participation of these features is relatively discrete and does not form stability.

IV For the fourth series, about the significance test of different assessment times and assessment results, the correlation analysis results are as follows.

Taking the assessment results ("Pass") as the observation variables, the data set of each learning content is viewed as the sample; the significance test is achieved on the data related to QF1, QF2, QF3 and QF4, and the results are shown in Table 7.5. According to the p-value, it can be seen that the interactive learning behavior for the first assessment has different significance, while the second time is significantly stronger than that the first one and the interactive learning behavior has no significance for the third or fourth time.

Table 7.5 Significance Test of Different Assessment Times and Assessment Results

Major	Content	Assessment (Pass)			
		P(First)	P(Second)	P(Third)	P(Fourth)
M1	C11	0.0174*	0.0032**	0.0595	0.0844
	C12	0.0191*	0.0055	0.0633	0.1415
	C13	0.0266*	0.0029**	0.0502	0.2052
	C14	0.0310*	0.0094**	0.0681	0.5471
	C15	0.0114*	0.0037**	0.0573	0.0996
M2	C21	0.0051**	0.0003***	–	–
	C22	0.0047**	0.0008***	–	–
	C23	0.0035**	0.0006***	–	–
	C24	0.0100*	0.0009***	–	–
	C25	0.0061**	0.0001***	–	–
M3	C31	0.0403*	0.0002***	–	–
	C32	0.0311*	0.0004***	–	–
	C33	0.0098**	0.0001***	–	–
	C34	0.0022**	0.0000***	–	–
	C35	0.0053**	0.0000***	–	–
	C36	0.0001***	0.0000***	–	–
	C37	0.0004***	0.0000***	–	–
	C38	0.0004***	0.0000***	–	–
	C39	0.0007***	0.0000***	–	–

Note: $*0.01 < P \leq 0.05$, $**0.001 < P \leq 0.01$, $***P \leq 0.001$.

Therefore, for learners who fail to pass the assessment in the first time, it is more possible to produce effective interactive learning behavior in the second time, and the recognition of passing the assessment is stronger.

7   Discussion

Through the cost sensitivity analysis of unbalanced interactive learning behavior, it is found that there are significant regularity and collectivity, and it is also proved that the necessary conditions of effective learning process are obtained, so as to deduce the basic learning methods and trends; it is of great significance to improve the participation effect of benign interactive learning behavior (Tian et al., 2021). Combined with the above data analysis and problem testing, it is concluded that interactive learning behavior has the following characteristics.

1   The interactive learning behavior of the same learning content is consistent
    In order to pass the assessment, learners may participate in the learning process of the same learning content for many times. Data analysis shows that for learners who pass the learning assessment, there is consistency in the key features of interactive learning behavior; learning behavior about the same learning content tends to be relatively stable, although the features may be different. Therefore, the interactive learning behavior of the same learning content can be predicted according to historical data (Xia, 2021a), and the conclusions can also be recommended to learners to guide them to build appropriate interactive learning behavior in advance.
2   The second assessment of the same learning content is more significant
    The unbalanced interactive learning behavior in this study involves the data tracking and analysis of 18 learning contents. The data analysis shows that for learners who fail to pass the assessment for the first time, the correlation between the key features of learning behavior is stronger, and the significance of assessment results is stronger in the second time. The passing rate of learners is relatively high. This conclusion is universal. Therefore, for learners who participate in a certain learning content for the second time, the learning platforms or lecturers should strengthen the early construction of effective and benign learning behavior (Xia, 2021c), strengthen the tracking and supervision of the learning process and improve the passing rate.
3   The interactive learning behaviors of different learning contents are similar
    The interactive learning behaviors formed by different learning contents are similar in some key features. This conclusion can be found from Figures 7.8–7.11. The data analysis shows that the learning methods and reinforcement methods are similar. Of course, there may be the correlation between these learning contents, and the formed interactive learning behavior has further demonstrated its feasibility (Huang et al., 2021). Therefore, different learning contents can provide basis for learners' interest guidance and recommendation direction.

4 The interactive learning behavior between different majors is similar

According to the prediction results of interactive learning behavior of M1, M2 and M3, it is found that the key features of M1 and M2 are consistent, and M3 expands more interactive features. At the same time, the three majors have formed similar interactive learning behaviors among some learning contents. Data analysis shows that the learning objectives of the three majors about a certain content are the same such as practical and applied training, deepening of key principles and knowledge (Valle et al. 2021); it makes these majors have certain potential mobility and relevance (Müller & Mildenberger, 2021); we can learn from the interactive learning behavior of relevant majors, in order to improve the learning initiative and participation.

5 Effective interactive learning behavior is a necessary condition for passing the assessment

This study involves the iterative problem of multiple learning processes; learners do not necessarily pass the assessment at one time. In the process of participating in the same learning content for many times, they form a relatively stable, reliable and applicable interactive learning behavior (Hew et al., 2021). It also proves that the significance of interactive learning behavior is the strongest when participating in the assessment for the second time. The interactive learning behavior formed by the learners who pass the assessment is effective. Therefore, by analyzing the historical data and constructing an effective learning behavior, it will drive learners to build reasonable learning methods and help to improve the learning effects.

These conclusions are based on the cost sensitive analysis of unbalanced interactive learning behavior, but there is no effective method in the original data, which seriously affects the analysis and application of data (Carter & Egliston, 2021), and is also the key problem hindering the data tracking and analysis (Mangaroska et al. 2021b). There are still more challenges in the classification accuracy and decision reliability of learning behavior.

8   Conclusion

Interactive learning behavior has obvious discreteness and autonomy, resulting in the problem of data imbalance, which poses a great obstacle to the research of interactive learning behavior that also cannot ensure the quality and reliability of learning analytics (Xia., 2022b). However, it is almost difficult to obtain balanced data from the interactive learning process, especially in the online learning environment, which brings more difficulties to the direct application of traditional learning analytics and methods (Ugalde et al. 2021). Therefore, the analysis of unbalanced interactive learning behavior cannot rely on the existing means. It is necessary to design new applicable models and algorithms driven by data, so as to effectively reduce the interference caused by noise or outliers, and highlight the value and law of interactive learning behavior (Xia., 2020b).

In this study, the complete data sets of interactive learning behavior are obtained about the analysis trends of imbalance in data science; a cost sensitive analysis method of interactive learning behavior is proposed. According to the characteristics of multi-structures, multi-features and multi-relationships of interactive learning behavior, the test problem of data analysis is designed. Based on this method, the analysis strategy integrating cost sensitive learning process and Bayesian optimal prediction theory is designed. Combined with the MetaCost method, the accurate classification and prediction of sample space are realized. The comparative experiments of several related methods show that this method is suitable for the interactive learning behavior; it can obtain more reliable and accurate descriptive indicators and ensure the robustness and effectiveness of data analysis results. Further, we summarize the analysis results of interactive learning behavior, deduce the demonstration conclusions of relevant test problems, as well as the laws and characteristics, which can provide help for the improvement, tracking and analysis of interactive learning behavior.

On the one hand, this study creatively designs an effective analysis method of unbalanced interactive learning behavior. On the other hand, it reaches an important conclusion from data mining. In the follow-up research work, the relevant models and algorithms will be further deepened and improved, in order to achieve the cost sensitivity analysis and adaptive prediction of unbalanced interactive learning behaviors, and find more practical value and suggestions.

References

Aguilar, S. J., Karabenick, S. A., Teasley, S. D., & Baek, C. (2021). Associations between learning analytics dashboard exposure and motivation and self-regulated learning. *Computers & Education.* 162, 104085. https://doi.org/10.1016/j.compedu.2020.104085

Ameloot, E., Rotsaert, T., & Schellens, T. (2021). The supporting role of learning analytics for a blended learning environment: exploring students' perceptions and the impact on relatedness. *Journal of Computer Assisted Learning.* 38(1), 90–102. https://doi.org/10.1111/jcal.12593

Carter, M., & Egliston, B. (2021). What are the risks of virtual reality data? Learning analytics, algorithmic bias and a fantasy of perfect data. *New Media & Society.* 2021(3), 146144482110127. https://doi.org/10.1177/14614448211012794

Eberle, J., & Hobrecht, J. (2021). The lonely struggle with autonomy: a case study of first-year university students' experiences during emergency online teaching. *Computers in Human Behavior.* 121(3). https://doi.org/10.1016/j.chb.2021.106804

Er, E., Dimitriadis, Y., & Gašević, D. (2021). Collaborative peer feedback and learning analytics: theory-oriented design for supporting class-wide interventions. *Assessment & Evaluation in Higher Education.* 46(2), 169–190. http://doi.org/10.1080/02602938.2020.1764490

Geyer, P. D. (2021). Adjustment-seeking behavior: the role of political skill and self-efficacy in training students to be more actively engaged in their studies. *Active Learning in Higher Education.* 19, 1–13. https://doi.org/10.1177/1469787417721993

Hew, K. F., Bai, S., Dawson, P., & Lo, C. K. (2021). Meta-analyses of flipped classroom studies: a review of methodology. *Educational Research Review.* 33(1), 100393. https://doi.org/10.1016/j.edurev.2021.100393

Huang, H. L., Hwang, G. J., & Chen, P. Y. (2021). An integrated concept mapping and image recognition approach to improving students' scientific inquiry course performance. *British Journal of Educational Technology*. 53(3), 706–727. https://doi.org/10.1111/bjet.13177

Ihm, S.-Y., Park, S.-H., & Park, Y.-H. (2021). UB-H: an unbalanced-hierarchical layer binary-wise construction method for high-dimensional data. *Computing*. 105(8). https://doi.org/10.1007/s00607-020-00871-0

Jang, J., & Yoon, S. (2020). Feature concentration for supervised and semisupervised learning with unbalanced datasets in visual inspection. *IEEE Transactions on Industrial Electronics*. 68(8), 7620–7630. https://doi.org/10.1109/TIE.2020.3003622

Jovanovi, J., Saqr, M., Joksimovi, S., & Gaevi, D. (2021). Students matter the most in learning analytics: the effects of internal and instructional conditions in predicting academic success. *Computers & Education*. 172(1), 104251. https://doi.org/10.1016/j.compedu.2021.104251

Li, H., Majumdar, R., Chen, M., & Ogata, H. (2021). Goal-oriented active learning (goal) system to promote reading engagement, self-directed learning behavior, and motivation in extensive reading. *Computers & Education*. 171(2), 104239. https://doi.org/10.1016/j.compedu.2021.104239

Mangaroska, K., Martinez-Maldonado, R., Vesin, B., & Gaevi, D. (2021a). Challenges and opportunities of multimodal data in human learning: the computer science students' perspective. *Journal of Computer Assisted Learning*. 37(4), 1030–1047. https://doi.org/10.1111/jcal.12542

Mangaroska, K., Vesin, B., Kostakos, V., Brusilovsky, P., & Giannakos, M. (2021b). Architecting analytics across multiple e-learning systems to enhance learning design. *IEEE Transactions on Learning Technologies*. 14(2), 173–188. https://doi.org/10.1109/TLT.2021.3072159

Mckenna, J. W., Brigham, F. J., Ciullo, S., Mason, L. H., & Judd, L. (2021). Persuasive quick-writing about text: intervention for students with learning disabilities. *Behavior Modification*. 45(1), 122–146. https://doi.org/10.1177/0145445519882894

Müller, C., & Mildenberger, T. (2021). Facilitating flexible learning by replacing classroom time with an online learning environment: a systematic review of blended learning in higher education. *Educational Research Review*. 34(1). https://doi.org/10.1016/j.edurev.2021.100394

Oppermann, E., Vinni-Laakso, J., Juuti, K., Loukomies, A., & Salmela-Aro, K. (2021). Elementary school students' motivational profiles across Finnish language, mathematics and science: longitudinal trajectories, gender differences and stem aspirations. *Contemporary Educational Psychology*. 64(1), 101927. https://doi.org/10.1016/j.cedpsych.2020.101927

Ouyang, F., Chen, S., & Li, X. (2021). Effect of three network visualizations on students' social-cognitive engagement in online discussions. *British Journal of Educational Technology*. 52(6), 2242–2262. https://doi.org/10.1111/bjet.13126

Praharaj, S., Scheffel, M., Drachsler, H., & Specht, M. M. (2021). Literature review on co-located collaboration modeling using multimodal learning analytics—can we go the whole nine yards? *IEEE Transactions on Learning Technologies*. 14(3), 367–385. https://doi.org/10.1109/TLT.2021.3097766

Razmerita, L., Kirchner, K., Kai, H., & Tan, C. W. (2020). Modeling collaborative intentions and behavior in digital environments: the case of a massive open online course (MOOC). *Academy of Management Learning and Education*. 19(4), 469–502. https://doi.org/10.5465/amle.2018.0056

Rebolledo-Mendez, G., Huerta-Pacheco, N. S., Baker, R. S., & Boulay, B. D. (2021). Meta-affective behaviour within an intelligent tutoring system for mathematics. *International Journal of Artificial Intelligence in Education*. 32, 1–22.

Roldán, S. M., Marauri, J., Aubert, A., & Flecha, R. (2021). How inclusive interactive learning environments benefit students without special needs. *Frontiers in Psychology*. 12, 661427. https://doi.org/10.3389/fpsyg.2021.661427

Ruipérez-Valiente, J., Staubitz, T., Jenner, M., Halawa, S., Zhang, J., & Despujol, I.(2022). Large scale analytics of global and regional MOOC providers: differences in learners' demographics, preferences, and perceptions. *Computers & Education*. 180, 104426. https://doi.org/10.1016/j.compedu.2021.104426

Sailer, M., Stadler, M., Schultz-Pernice, F., Franke, U., & Fischer, F. (2021). Technology-related teaching skills and attitudes: validation of a scenario-based self-assessment instrument for teachers. *Computers in Human Behavior*. 115, 106625. https://doi.org/10.1016/j.chb.2020.106625

Silvola, A., Nykki, P., Kaveri, A., & Muukkonen, H. (2021). Expectations for supporting student engagement with learning analytics: an academic path perspective. *Computers & Education*. 168(12), 104192. https://doi.org/10.1016/j.compedu.2021.104192

Song, D., Hong, H., & Oh, E. Y. (2021). Applying computational analysis of novice learners' computer programming patterns to reveal self-regulated learning, computational thinking, and learning performance. *Computers in Human Behavior*. 120(6), 106746. https://doi.org/10.1016/j.chb.2021.106746

Tian, J., Koh, J. H. L., Ren, C., & Wang, Y. (2021). Understanding higher education students' developing perceptions of geocapabilities through the creation of story maps with geographical information systems. *British Journal of Educational Technology*. 53(4), 1–19. https://doi.org/10.1111/bjet.13176

Ugalde, L., Santiago-Garabieta, M., Villarejo-Carballido, B., & Puigvert, L. (2021). Impact of interactive learning environments on learning and cognitive development of children with special educational needs: a literature review. *Frontiers in Psychology*. 12, 674033. https://doi.org/10.3389/fpsyg.2021.674033

Valle, N., Antonenko, P., Valle, D., Dawson, K., & Baiser, B. (2021). The influence of task-value scaffolding in a predictive learning analytics dashboard on learners' statistics anxiety, motivation, and performance. *Computers & Education*. 173(1), 104288. https://doi.org/10.1016/j.compedu.2021.104288

Wong, S. W., Lin, J. Y., Yang, Y., Zhu, H., Chen, R. S., & Zhu, L. (2020). Cavity balanced and unbalanced diplexer based on triple-mode resonator. *IEEE Transactions on Industrial Electronics*. 67(6), 4969–4979. https://doi.org/10.1109/TIE.2019.2928253

Xia, X. (2020a). Learning behavior mining and decision recommendation based on association rules in interactive learning environment. *Interactive Learning Environments*. 2020(8), 1–16. https://doi.org/10.1080/10494820.2020.1799028

Xia, X. (2020b). Random field design and collaborative inference strategy for learning interaction activities. *Interactive Learning Environments*. 2020(12), 1–25. https://doi.org/10.1080/10494820.2020.1863236

Xia, X. (2021a). Interaction recognition and intervention based on context feature fusion of learning behaviors in interactive learning environments. *Interactive Learning Environments*. 2021(1), 1–19. https://doi.org/10.1080/10494820.2021.1871632

Xia, X. (2021b). Sparse learning strategy and key feature selection in interactive learning environment. *Interactive Learning Environments*. 2021(11), 1–25. https://doi.org/10.1080/10494820.2021.1998913

Xia, X. (2021c). Decision application mechanism of regression analysis of multi-category learning behaviors in interactive learning environment. *Interactive Learning Environments*. 2021(4), 1–14. https://doi.org/10.1080/10494820.2021.1916767

Xia, X. (2022a). Diversion inference model of learning effectiveness supported by differential evolution strategy. *Computers and Education: Artificial Intelligence*. 3(1), 100071. https://doi.org/10.1016/j.caeai.2022.100071

Xia, X. (2022b). Application technology on collaborative training of interactive learning activities and tendency preference diversion. *SAGE Open*. 12(2), 1–15. https://doi.org/10.1177/21582440221093368

Xia, X., & Qi, W. (2022). Temporal tracking and early warning of multi semantic features of learning behavior. *Computers and Education: Artificial Intelligence*. 3(1), 100045. https://doi.org/10.1016/j.caeai.2021.100045

Zelenkov, Y., & Volodarskiy, N. (2021). Bankruptcy prediction on the base of the unbalanced data using multi-objective selection of classifiers. *Expert Systems with Applications*. 185(15), 115559. https://doi.org/10.1016/j.eswa.2021.115559

Zhao, J., Jin, J., Chen, S., Zhang, R., Yu, B., & Liu, Q. (2020). A weighted hybrid ensemble method for classifying imbalanced data. *Knowledge-Based Systems*. 201–202(1), 106083. https://doi.org/10.1016/j.knosys.2020.106083

8 Diagnostic Analysis Framework and Early Warning Mechanism of Forgettable Learning Behaviors

Abstract

Based on the conclusions of Chapter 7, namely the application of precipitation prediction model in the early warning of learning behaviors, the following work is to analyze the early warning of forgettable learning behaviors. This chapter designs a diagnostic analysis framework for forgettable learning behaviors, constructs a set of matching data segmentation rules and designs an adaptive data segment aggregation method. The feasibility and reliability of the technical framework are verified by sufficient comparative experiments. Furthermore, the topological relationships of forgettable learning behavior are visually built, and the potential problems, laws and corresponding early warning strategies are discussed. The whole research process is a key attempt of applying intelligent decision technology to the diagnostic analysis of massive learning behavior, which can provide effective theoretical basis and feasible technical support for the forgettable learning behavior, and has strong practical significance. On the one hand, this chapter implements and demonstrates the feasibility of early warning for forgetting learning behaviors, and on the other hand, the early warning diagnosis framework is a comprehensive research of all the work of Chapters 2–7.

Keywords

Interactive Learning Environment; Forgettable Learning Behavior; Data Segment; Diagnostic Learning Analytics; Early Warning; Deep Learning

1 Introduction

Through the integration of sharing technology and online technology, interactive learning environment provides learners and instructors with important facilities for online learning process and resource management (Carter & Egliston, 2021; Xia, 2022a); it has relatively complete learning resources, collaborative tools and communication methods, and can provide a relatively timely and efficient learning experience. In order to achieve a certain learning objective, the behavior in

DOI: 10.4324/9781003484905-8

the learning process in a continuous period is called learning behavior that includes many features, attributes and factors, as well as constraints and related tasks (Hasenbein et al., 2022; Ruiz-Calleja et al., 2021). Due to the full application of online learning mode, learning time and space are no longer the key factors for the construction of learning behavior. Without the supervision of face-to-face teaching, online learning behavior shows more autonomy and randomness of learners, resulting in a large number of discrete data (Valle et al., 2021a; Xia, 2021a; Xia, 2022b). The learning behavior of every learner forms a continuous process of resources, interaction and cooperation, but a large number of invalid data are left, which creates many obstacles to describe learning behavior. However, completely clearing such data as noise may affect the relationship description or correlation analysis (Dolmark et al., 2021). This will also involve potential learning behavior, which is mixed in the explicit data, which we call forgettable learning behavior.

The forgettable learning behavior might have different computing needs; there are three main applications: (1) if the assessment results are used as observation variables, the forgettable learning behavior can be used to analyze the learning effectiveness, the influencing factors of learning behavior changes and the relationship with learners' interests and trends (Xia, 2021b); (2) If timely early warning strategies and decision intervention are adopted for learning process, it is necessary to mine effective learning behavior and clean up meaningless forgettable learning behavior, so as to find out the key early warning and decision intervention (Xia & Qi, 2022); (3) in the diagnostic analysis of learning behavior, it is necessary to accurately locate the forgettable learning behavior with private information, highlight the key descriptive and semantic features, and mine corresponding laws (Xia, 2021c). To achieve early warning and intervention of learning behavior, it is also necessary to integrate these three applications to fully clean and calculate the forgettable learning behavior (Ameloot et al., 2021; Li et al., 2021). So the application of forgettable learning behavior still needs to be deeply designed and demonstrated.

The massive data of learning behavior generated by an interactive learning environment are viewed as the research target; we analyze the early warning needs, define the features of forgettable learning behavior and put forward the testable problems required for the early warning strategy in learning process. Then, the diagnostic analysis framework is constructed, and the training set is defined as a data segment set to test the diagnostic recognition of forgettable learning behavior, verify the feasibility and reliability of the framework, and draw the analysis conclusion of testable problems. According to the results of data analysis, we further demonstrate the early warning strategy that might provide more feasible technical support and conclusion for the interactive learning environment (Silvola et al., 2021).

2   Related Work

Forgettable learning is a method to delete samples that can be forgotten from the data set. This method has good analysis effect for small-scale data sets (Lee, 2021), but the forgettable learning process for massive data is very complex and will pay a large computational cost (Dietrich et al., 2021). Forgettable learning has been applied to the training and testing of massive data, and has produced relevant research conclusions. For example, the training set is randomly divided into several disjoint data segments, and the forgettable learning sub-model and aggregation sub-model are trained based on each data segment, in order to obtain the final prediction result. When we need to forget some data samples, we only need to retrain the corresponding sub-model.

The forgettable learning has been partially applied in the interest recommendation of some information systems. It is mainly integrated into the business framework, such as mapping users and items to the potential factor space, and realizing the classification of effective features and invalid features through the feedback of potential interests. The invalid features become forgettable behavior (Zeeshan et al., 2021). In order to better recommend the effective behavior, some researchers have improved the forgettable learning methods. For example, non-sampling method defines the observed data as forgettable samples to meet the needs of non-sampling data analysis (Low et al., 2021); An adaptive non-sampling loss method is constructed to realize the unity of efficiency and accuracy (Roozbahani et al., 2021), or improve the sampling strategy to optimize the forgettable learning analysis model (Peng, 2021).

Due to deep learning, the neural network to improve forgettable learning has been explored. The neural collaborative filtering mode is adopted to realize the decomposition of forgettable learning matrix and the construction of feedforward neural network that adapts to different forgettable learning scenarios. Recently, the application of deep learning in forgettable learning process has become a trend (Ikram & Farooq, 2022), and has been partially effectively applied, such as attention mechanism, convolutional neural network and recursive neural network, which promote and optimize forgettable learning methods at different levels, so as to eliminate nonlinear problems, and expand the reliability of relevant activation function and feature transformation.

For the massive research on learning behavior, there is also forgettable learning behavior; the selection or application has not been effectively designed and demonstrated. Because the learning behavior data is continuous based on the learning process and learning period, randomly dividing the data into segments may affect the relevance of the learning behavior, and it is easy to misjudge the forgettable learning behavior. The existing forgettable learning methods assign a static weight to each sub-model. Some studies realize the weight distribution by the learning process, but the scale of data analysis is limited. When predicting the interaction and cooperation of learning behavior, the weight can-not be adaptive.

About the problems of forgettable learning method, we will propose a new and efficient diagnostic analysis framework. While maintaining efficient feature training, we will realize the accurate recognition of forgettable learning behavior, which is different from the traditional data clustering. The framework also divides the training set into a series of data segments, but considers the calculation indexes between segments, in order to achieve the balance of data segments so that the unbalanced data segments will not affect data analysis. The design of the whole method is mainly divided into the following three aspects:

1   A forgettable analysis method applied to massive learning behavior data is proposed to realize a relatively general framework and improve the efficiency of forgettable analysis;
2   The adaptive segmentation rules are constructed in the massive learning behavior data, and an aggregation method between segments is designed according to the rules to further optimize the robustness and reliability;
3   The sufficient experiments and comparisons in the real massive learning behavior data set are carried out, the topology of forgettable learning behavior is formed and the early warning strategies are discussed.

3   Data Processing and Problem Description

The learning behavior features and the potential relationships constitute the basic structure of learning behavior (Xia, 2020a). This study selects the desensitization learning behavior data set of an online interactive learning environment with a scale of 1.6PB and nearly 20 million learning behavior records; then it focuses on the design and application of forgettable learning methods, analyzes and classifies the features of learning behavior in the data set, and puts forward the relevant test problems. The learning behavior is defined as a set of features and their relationships; the values and relationships of learning behavior features will be updated with the changes of learners' interaction and cooperation. The analysis of forgettable learning behavior is an important step to discover the risk of learning process.

The learning behavior features are used to describe the interaction and cooperation among learners, instructors and platforms, as well as the related conditions or constraint attributes to realize the learning process (Gan et al., 2021). With the help of features, the related resources and interaction modes are related. This study divides learning behavior features into five types: page view, content retrieval, collaborative interaction, Q&A discussion and test. Among them, page view is the web page access caused by learning interaction process. The link anchor will be associated with more features, resulting in "page", "homepage" and "subpage" related to learning content. Content retrieval is initiated by learners, and resources are obtained according to the search mechanism or download mechanism. Collaborative interaction is to realize the interaction and cooperation among learners and instructors in order to complete the group task. Q&A discussion is an effective supplement to the learning process. The process of submitting questions and answering feedback is realized by platform communication tools and third-party support tools. Test is to test learning effectiveness with the help of different methods. The data set selected in this study involves a total of 20 features, mainly static and dynamic features, as shown in Figure 8.1. "datapane", "folder", "glossary", "wiki" and "dataplus", as shared static features, are used to promote the association and application of dynamic features in the learning process.

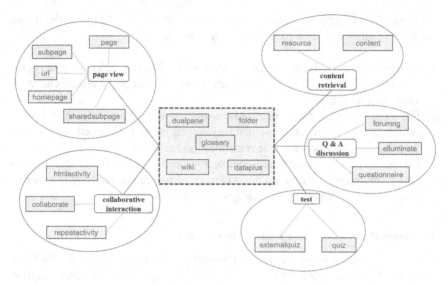

Figure 8.1 Features and Relationships

Learning effectiveness is the result of the assessment. The test has two basic methods: external test and platform test. The external test consists of two parts: TA (Tutor Assessment) with the direct participation of the instructor and FE (Final Exam). The platform test is reflected in the online review and marked as CA (Computer Assessment). If the final score of learners exceeds 60, they will pass the learning assessment.

Test is affected by the other four types of learning behavior, and the relevant features are interrelated. Positive learning behavior will lead to active page view, content retrieval, collaborative interaction and Q&A discussion. In the interactive process of page view and content retrieval, it also enhances the participation frequency of collaborative interaction and Q&A discussion. There are also impacts between the two features. For example, the positive learning effect also brings benign guidance to the learning interaction. Combined with the selection of forgettable learning behavior and early warning needs, this study puts forward relevant test problems, as shown in Table 8.1.

The test problems and its relationships are shown in Figure 8.2. Features or relationships do not have the impact on the constitute forgettable learning behavior. The forgettable learning behavior caused by the limited influence between features is rarely involved in the existing references, but this aspect may have different influence (even significant influence), which is an important basis for the accurate early warning. This study tests the impact between test and learning effectiveness, mines the forgettable features and relationships between different types of learning behavior, constructs the relationships of forgettable learning behavior and ensures the sufficiency and necessity of the problem testing.

Table 8.1 Relevant Test Problems

I: Test Problems	II: Test Problems	III: Test Problems
$H_{1\to2}$: page view will not affect content retrieval	$H_{1\to5}$: page view has forgettable learning behavior, which will not affect their test behavior	$H_{5\to le}$: test has forgettable learning behavior, which will not affect their test behavior
$H_{1\to3}$: page view will not affect collaborative interaction		
$H_{1\to4}$: page view will not affect Q&A discussion		
$H_{2\to1}$: content retrieval will not affect page view	$H_{2\to5}$: content retrieval has forgettable learning behavior, which will not affect their test behavior	
$H_{2\to3}$: content retrieval will not affect collaborative interaction		
$H_{2\to4}$: content retrieval will not affect Q&A discussion		
$H_{3\to1}$: collaborative interaction will not affect page view	$H_{3\to5}$: collaborative interaction has forgettable learning behavior, which will not affect their test behavior	
$H_{3\to2}$: collaborative interaction will not affect content retrieval		
$H_{3\to4}$: collaborative interaction will not affect Q&A discussion		
$H_{4\to1}$: Q&A discussion will not affect page view	$H_{4\to5}$: Q&A discussion has forgettable learning behavior, which will not affect their test behavior	
$H_{4\to2}$: Q&A discussion will not affect content retrieval		
$H_{4\to3}$: Q&A discussion will not affect collaborative interaction		

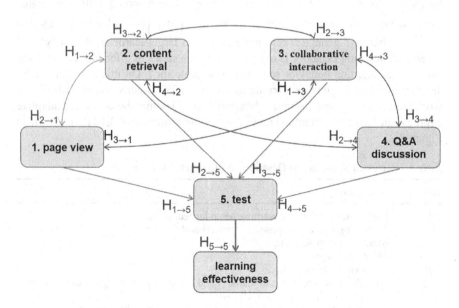

Figure 8.2 Test Problems of Forgettable Learning Behavior and Relationships

4   Method

Approximate forgettable learning is a method based on a statistical analysis method. The principle is to relax the demand for accurate deletion. As long as the data constraints of the statistical model are met, it must be remembered (essentially data clustering meets certain conditions), and others are forgettable data. A gradient updating method is usually used to quickly eliminate the influence of samples. Compared with precise forgettable learning, approximate forgetting learning is more effective and efficient, but it is not suitable for the processing of non-convex models, such as deep neural network, which are unfavorable for the mining of potential learning behavior and early warning recommendation.

The principle of precise forgettable learning is to completely delete the data that needs to be forgotten from the learning model. In order to speed up the accurate learning speed, the cross-validation method of support vector machine or the naive Bayesian method is used to quickly delete the forgettable data, on the premise that the data is orderly. At the same time, if new forgettable data is generated, forgettable learning can be effectively realized.

This study integrates the approximate forgetting and accurate forgetting. In the forgettable data analysis of learning behavior, two principles will be met: (1) design the method of dividing the learning behavior features, and ensure the relative integrity of interactive and collaborative information; (2) an adaptive clustering method is designed to improve the quality of all learning behavior analysis.

Table 8.2 shows the relevant symbols and descriptions. The learner set and feature set are represented as L and F respectively. The mapping matrix generated by learners and features is expressed as M, $M = \left[m_{l,f} \right] \in \left[0,1 \right]$, which is used to describe whether l generates relevant F. Given a target learner l, the analysis of forgettable learning behavior is to provide l with a series of effective features, and the retained learning behavior sequence is suitable for l. On this basis, an analysis framework of forgettable learning behavior (LFTF) is constructed. This framework includes two parts: balanced data partition of learning behavior and adaptive aggregation based on attention mechanism. The structure of LFTF is shown in Figure 8.3.

Table 8.2 Relevant Symbols and Descriptions of Forgettable Learning

Symbol	Description
L,F	L is learner set, F is the learning behavior feature set.
M	A mapping matrix composed of learners and feature
K	Number of data segments
$Slice_i$	The ith data segment
sMi	Submodel of training $Slice_i$
$\bar{p}_l, \bar{q}_f$	The relevant embeddings of learner l and feature f pretraining are used for data segment division, respectively
$p_l^i q_f^i$	Relevant embeddings of learner l and feature f learned through sMi
$p_l q_f$	Relevant embeddings after clustering by learner l and feature f

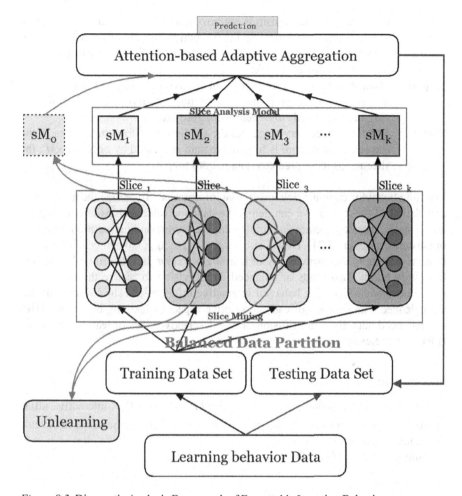

Figure 8.3 Diagnostic Analysis Framework of Forgettable Learning Behavior

The analysis framework of LFTF is mainly divided into five steps:

Step 1: divide the learning behavior data into training set and test set, divide the training set and test set into balanced data, retain the data relationships and convert the training set and test set into slice set;

Step 2: realize the mapping of data to segments, and use sM_i train every Slice$_i$. The implementation mechanism of all M_i is the same, and multiple d can be used to realize the parallel training, so as to improve the training efficiency and obtain the prediction model. If canceling the training process of the training set slice, goto Step 4; otherwise, iterate Step 2 until all slices of the training set have completed the training;

Step 3: use the prediction model to predict the test set and analyze each slice. In the prediction process, the adaptive clustering strategy combined with attention mechanism is optimized, and the best weight of different sM_i is selected. If canceling the prediction process of the test set slice, goto Step 3. Otherwise, iterate step 3 until all slices of the test set complete the prediction, break;

Step 4: when it is necessary to cancel the analysis of forgettable data in the training set, and even if there is forgettable data processed by only one sM_i, the slice needs to be retrained, goto Step 3;

Step 5: when it is necessary to cancel the prediction of forgettable data in the test set, even if there is forgettable data processed by only one sM_i, the slice needs to be predicted again, goto Step 4.

Learning behavior contains rich interactive information. To realize the mining and calculation of these data, we can define the data and relationships of learning behavior as a network structure and implement the corresponding partition detection or clustering (Geyer, 2021). However, it might lead to high imbalance of data partition. According to the particularity of learning behavior data, based on Figure 8.1, this study adopts two kinds of balanced data division to realize the analysis of two dimensions of learning behavior interactive information. The two dimensions are balanced data division of each descriptive aspect of learning behavior (ABP) and balanced data division of fusion of five descriptive sides of learning behavior (FBP). The relevant algorithms are as follows.

Algorithm ABP

Initialization: the embeddings of learners $\overline{P} = \left\{ \overline{P_1}, \overline{P_2}, \cdots, \overline{P_m} \right\}$, interactive information of learning behavior Y, the max number K of data segment, the max scale T of each data segment.

Output: $Slice = \left\{ Slice_1, Slice_2, \cdots, Slice_K \right\}$

PROCESS:

1 Select K anchors randomly from L, $A = \left\{ a_1, a_2, \cdots, a_K \right\}$
2 While end condition of data balance segmentation is not satisfied do
3 For each a_i in A do
4 For each l in L do

5 Calculate the distance of a_i and l, $\mathrm{dist}\left(a_i, l \right) = \left\| \overline{P_{a_i}} - \overline{P_l} \right\| = \sqrt{\left(\sum_{j=1}^{n} \overline{P_{a_i, j}} - \overline{P_{l, j}} \right)^2}$

6 End for
7 End for
8 Sort $\mathrm{dist}\left(a_i, l \right)$ in ascending order, then get $\mathrm{dist}_{\mathrm{order}}\left(a_i, l \right)$
9 Empty $Slice$
10 For $\mathrm{dist}_{\mathrm{order}}\left(a_i, l \right)$ do

11 If $|Slice_i| < T$ and l is not allocated

12 Then $Slice_i \leftarrow Slice_i \bigcup Y_l$

13 End if

14 End for

15 Update A by $a_i = \dfrac{\sum_{j \in sSlice_i} \overline{P_j}}{|Slice_i|}$

16 End while

17 Return *Slice*

Algorithm FBP

Initialization: the embeddings of learners $\overline{P} = \left\{ \overline{P_1}, \ \overline{P_2}, \ \cdots, \ \overline{P_m} \right\}$, interactive information of learning behavior Y, the max number K of data segment, the max scale T of each data segment.

    Output: $Slice = \left\{ Slice_1, \ Slice_2, \ \cdots, \ Slice_K \right\}$

PROCESS:

18 Select K anchors randomly from Y, $A = \left\{ a_1, a_2, \cdots, a_K \right\}$

19 While end condition of data balance segmentation is not satisfied do

20 For each a_i in A do

21 For each y_{mn} in Y do

22 Calculate the distance of a_i and y_{mn},

$$\text{dist}\left(a_i, y_{mn} \right) = \left\| \overline{P_i} - \overline{P_m} \right\|_2 \times \left\| \overline{q_i} - \overline{q_n} \right\|_2 = \sqrt{\left(\sum_{j=1}^{n} \overline{P_{i,j}} - \overline{P_{m,j}} \right)^2} \times \sqrt{\left(\sum_{j=1}^{n} \overline{q_{i,j}} - \overline{q_{n,j}} \right)^2}$$

23 End for

24 End for

25 Sort $\text{dist}\left(a_i, y_{mn} \right)$ in ascending order, get $\text{dist}_{\text{order}}\left(a_i, y_{mn} \right)$

26 Empty *Slice*

27 For $\text{dist}_{\text{order}}\left(a_i, y_{mn} \right)$ do

28 If $|Slice_i| < T$ and y_{mn} is not allocated

29 Then $Slice_i \leftarrow Slice_i \bigcup Y_{mn}$

30 End if

31 End for

32 Update A by $a_i = \left(\dfrac{\sum_{j \in sSlice_i} \overline{P_j}}{|Slice_i|}, \dfrac{\sum_{j \in sSlice_i} \overline{q_j}}{|Slice_i|} \right)$

33 End while

34 Return Slice

After the balanced data segmentation of ABP and FBP, the adaptive aggregation based on attention mechanism is implemented, which is the basis of forgettable learning behavior prediction. sM_i will be used to train each $slice_i$. Considering that learning behavior includes five types of learner behavior features, different sub-models may need to be embedded in different data spaces. Therefore, all learners and learning behavior features need to be transformed into the same presentation space first, and sM_i is used to obtain P^i and Q^i, and the transformation model is described as $P^i_{Tr} = W^i P^i + b^i$ and $Q^i_{Tr} = W^i Q^i + b^i$, where $W^i \in R^{d \times d}$ is a transformation matrix that P^i and Q^i map to the presentation space, $b^i \in R^d$ is a deviation vector and d represents the scale of the embeddings.

The calculation formula of aggregate embeddings is described as: $P = \sum_{i=1}^{K} \alpha_i P^i_{Tr}$,

$Q = \sum_{i=1}^{K} \beta_i Q^i_{Tr}$, α_i and β_i are the weight parameters of attention mechanism, which is used to aggregate the embeddings of learners and features, α_i and β_i are defined as $\alpha^*_i = h_1^T \sigma \left(W_1 P^i_{Tr} + b_1 \right)$, $\alpha_i = \dfrac{\exp\left(\alpha^*_i\right)}{\sum_{j=1}^{K} \exp\left(\alpha^*_j\right)}$, $\beta^*_i = h_2^T \sigma \left(W_2 P^i_{Tr} + b_2 \right)$ and

$\beta_i = \dfrac{\exp\left(\beta^*_i\right)}{\sum_{j=1}^{K} \exp\left(\beta^*_j\right)}$. $W_1 \in R^{k \times d}$, $b_1 \in R^k$ and $h_1 \in R^k$ are the parameters of attention mechanism, and k is the analysis dimension of attention, σ is a nonlinear activation function. Attention weight is normalized by softmax function. Adaptive aggregation method of data segments based on attention mechanism $\min_\Theta \mathcal{L}(P, Q, Y) + \lambda \|\Theta\|_2^2$ assigns weights to different sub-models and realizes self-optimization, where $\mathcal{L}$ is the loss function and Θ is a parameter of attention mechanism.

The interactive information Y can also request to cancel the training process. When receiving the request to cancel learning, the data segment may be retrained. The diagnostic analysis framework proposed in this study only needs a few iterative training processes to learn the relatively optimal attention score, so as to improve the efficiency of forgetting learning behavior analysis.

5   Experiment

The experimental process of LFTF will analyze learning behavior data set and carry out sufficient experiments. The experiment is mainly divided into three steps.

Step 1:   prediction test of forgettable learning behavior data segments.

Because two kinds of balanced data partition methods are adopted, the LFTF framework mainly realizes ABP and FBP. Therefore, the first step of the experiment is to test the prediction effect of balanced data partition and set the recommended sorting lengths of forgettable learning behavior to $n = 10, 20, 30$ and 50, respectively, The random balanced data division method is used as the test baseline of the comparative experiment.

In order to cooperate with the experimental analysis process of Random, ABP and FBP, we select three relatively optimal recommended algorithms to test the prediction effect. They are: (1) BPR, which is a commonly used recommendation model, uses Bayesian personalized sorting function to optimize matrix decomposition and realize data recommendation; (2) WMF, the algorithm is a non-sampling recommendation model, which regards all missing interactive information as forgettable content and uniformly weights them; (3) LightGCN, this is the most advanced graphic neural network model. It simplifies the design of GNN (graph neural network). Random, ABP and FBP are fused into the three recommendation algorithms, respectively, so as to determine the most suitable recommendation algorithm for balanced data division. Recall with different recommended sorting length is selected as the test index. All programs implement executable code through Python 3.8.

After experiments, the predicted Recall values of different recommendation sorting lengths of learning behavior are shown in Figure 8.4. It can be seen that

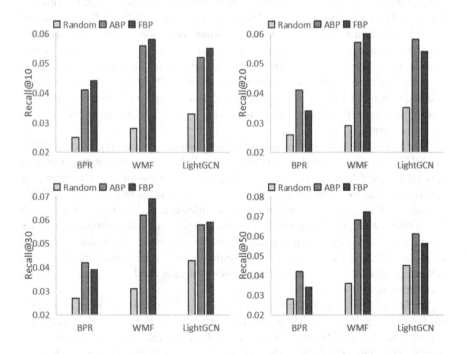

Figure 8.4 Predicted Recall of Different Recommended Sorting Lengths of Learning Behavior

when Random, ABP and FBP fuse different recommendation algorithms, Recall of Random algorithm has always been at a low value. The data balanced division of ABP and FBP can help the recommendation algorithms achieve a high Recall; the fusion of ABP, FBP and WAF is the most efficient and stable.

Step 2:   Test the influence of the number of data segments.

The number of data segments might have an impact on the algorithm performances. When Recall is set the performance index, it is still needed to set the recommended sorting lengths of forgettable learning behavior to $N = 10, 20, 30$ and 50, respectively. Similarly, BPR, WMF and LightGCN are selected as the comparison algorithms to average the analysis time of forgettable learning behavior. The experimental results are shown in Figure 8.5. The bar chart shows the learning behavior prediction Recall of LFTF framework integrating different recommendation algorithms, and the line chart shows the analysis time of forgettable learning behavior. As can be seen from Figure 8.5, when the number of segments increases, the predicted Recall shows a downward trend, and the average forgetting time will also decrease. However, the average time of LFTF framework fusing WMF is the least affected by the number of data segments, and maintains a low value.

Step 3:   comparative experiment of LFTF.

We randomly select 80% of the learning behavior data to construct the training set, and take the rest as the test set, and then randomly select 10% of the training set as the verification set. For each learner's learning behavior, the evaluation process will sort the non-positive interactive information in the training set. Select two evaluation indexes here, Recall@N and NDCG@N. Recall@N is used to measure Recall of LFTF for forgettable learning behavior; NDCG@N (Normalized Discounted Cumulative Gain) is a ranking index describing the position perception of learning behavior features, which is used to assign high scores to the features of higher positions.

Based on Step 1 and Step 2, it is found that the learning behavior prediction effect of LFTF is the best. Therefore, combined with WMF, three similar and relatively optimal forgettable analysis algorithms are selected to complete the comparative experiment. The three algorithms are: (1) Retrain: this is the most basic forgettable learning method that can delete revoked samples and generate new models; (2) SISA: this is a relatively efficient forgettable learning method. It randomly divides the training set into corresponding data segments, aggregates the training results of all sub models and then completes the prediction; (3) GraphEraser: this is also an advanced forgettable learning method, which is mainly used for forgettable analysis of graphic data.

We first evaluate the performances of different algorithms in forgettable learning behavior analysis, set the number of data segments to 50, and after sufficient experiments, Recall@N and NDCG@N are shown in Table 8.3. For different forgettable learning methods, with the increase of N, Recall@N and NDCG@N show an upward trend, and LFTF has achieved the highest indexes in different sorting lengths. LFTF is effective for the analysis of forgettable learning behavior and can obtain more accurate and reliable results.

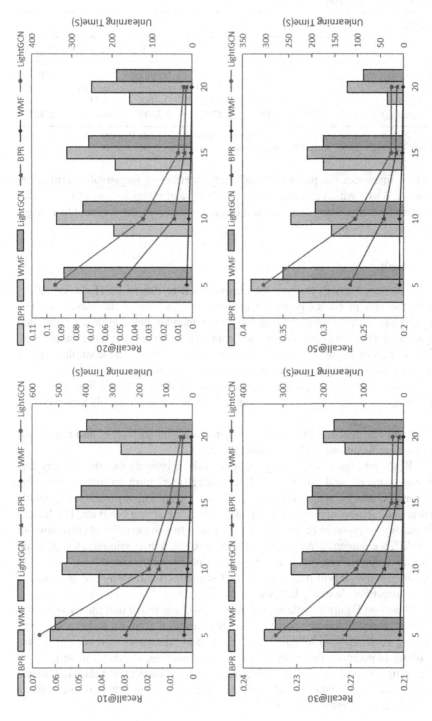

Figure 8.5 Predicted Recall and Average Forgetting Time Affected by the Number of Data Segments

Table 8.3 Recall@N and NDCG@N

Algorithm	Recall			NDCG		
	$N = 10$	$N = 30$	$N = 50$	$N = 10$	$N = 30$	$N = 50$
Retrain	0.2216	0.2527	0.3066	0.3903	0.3994	0.4272
SISA	0.1518	0.2235	0.3808	0.2562	0.2636	0.3032
GraphEraser	0.1341	0.1874	0.2903	0.2415	0.2473	0.2519
UnlearningLFTF	**0.2005***	**0.3119***	**0.4742***	**0.3803***	**0.3793***	**0.4217***

Note: * indicates that the test of pairwise comparison between LFTF and Retrain, SISA, GraphEraser, $P=0.05$. The bold values represent the optimal results.

LFTF integrates the prediction and analysis effect of forgettable learning behavior of WMF, which can ensure the reliability and completeness of data analysis. Therefore, this study analyzes and discusses based on the forgettable analysis results.

6   Result

In this section, we will analyze the experimental results of LFTF fusion WMF, verify the test problems proposed in Table 8.1, as shown in Table 8.4. The "conclusion=reject" proves that the forgettable learning behavior has a significant impact on the learning effectiveness and obtains the implicit data and relationships. This provides an important basis for the study of learners who have similar explicit learning behavior but have different learning effectiveness.

Based on Table 8.4, the key experimental conclusions obtained from the analysis of forgettable learning behavior mainly include the following six aspects:

1 Content retrieval and Q&A discussion interact with each other and easily produce significant forgettable learning behavior.

   Based on Figure 8.1, through data analysis, it is found that the two key features "content" and "resource" of content retrieval form an indirect two-way strong correlation with "forumng" and "wiki", resulting in potential forgettable data and relationships, which are finally used for learning behavior. The feature topology is shown in Figure 8.6. It can be seen that in the indirect correlation of "wiki", the guidance from content retrieval to Q&A discussion has a significant negative correlation; on the contrary, it is a positive correlation.

2 Content retrieval will positively affect test methods and easily produce significant forgettable learning behavior.

   Based on Figure 8.1, through data analysis, it is found that the two key features "content" and "resource" of content retrieval form an indirect one-way strong correlation with "quiz" with the help of "datapane" and "dataplus", resulting in potential forgettable data and relationships, which ultimately act on learning behavior, as shown in Figure 8.7; in the indirect correlation between "datapane" and "dataplus", the orientation from content retrieval to test has a significant positive correlation.

Table 8.4 Significance Test Results

Problem Hypothesis	P Value	Conclusion
$H_{1 \to 2}$, $H_{2 \to 1}$: page view↔content retrieval	±0.455	Accept
$H_{3 \to 4}$, $H_{4 \to 3}$: collaborative interaction↔Q&A discussion	±0.078	Accept
$H_{3 \to 1}$, $H_{1 \to 3}$: collaborative interaction↔page view	±0.101	Accept
$H_{2 \to 4}$, $H_{4 \to 2}$: content retrieval↔Q&A discussion	±0.032	Reject
$H_{3 \to 2}$, $H_{2 \to 3}$: collaborative interaction↔content retrieval	±0.411	Accept
$H_{1 \to 4}$, $H_{4 \to 1}$: page view↔Q&A discussion	±0.715	Accept
$H_{2 \to 5}$: test←content retrieval	0.042	Reject
$H_{3 \to 5}$: test←collaborative interaction	−0.018	Reject
$H_{4 \to 5}$: test←Q&A discussion	0.031	Reject
$H_{1 \to 5}$: test←page view	0.044	Reject
$H_{5 \to 5}$: Learning effectiveness←test	0.012	Reject

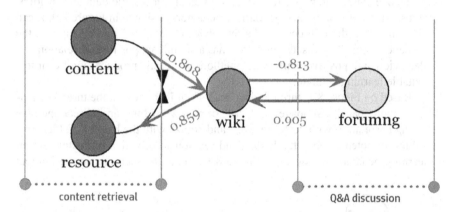

Figure 8.6 Forgettable Learning Behavior Feature Topology of $H_{2 \to 4}$ and $H_{4 \to 2}$

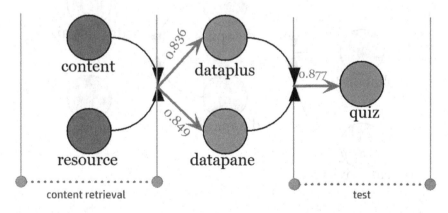

Figure 8.7 Forgettable Learning Behavior Feature Topology of $H_{2 \to 5}$

3 Collaborative interaction will negatively affect the test methods and easily produce significant forgettable learning behavior.

Based on Figure 8.1, through data analysis, it is found that the three key features "collaborate", "htmlactivity" and "repeatability" of collaborative interaction form an indirect one-way strong correlation with "externalquiz" and "quiz" with the help of "datapane" and "dataplus", resulting in potential forgettable data and relationships, which ultimately act on learning behavior, as shown in Figure 8.8. It can be seen that in the indirect correlation between "datapane" and "dataplus", the guidance from collaborative interaction to test has a significant positive correlation.

4 Q&A discussion will negatively affect the test methods and easily produce significant forgettable learning behavior.

Based on Figure 8.1, through data analysis, it is found that the two key features "forumng" and "questionnaire" of Q&A discussion form an indirect one-way strong correlation with "externalquiz" and "quiz" with the help of "datapane" and "dataplus", resulting in potential forgettable data and relationships, which ultimately act on learning behavior, as shown in Figure 8.9. It can be seen that in the indirect correlation between "datapane" and "dataplus", the guidance from Q&A discussion to test has a significant positive correlation.

5 Page view will positively affect test methods and easily produce significant forgettable learning behavior.

Based on Figure 8.1, through data analysis, it is found that the three key features "homepage", "subpage" and "url" of page view form an indirect one-way strong correlation with "externalquiz" and "quiz" with the help of "folder", resulting in potential forgettable data and relationships, which ultimately act on learning behavior, as shown in Figure 8.10. It can be seen that in the indirect

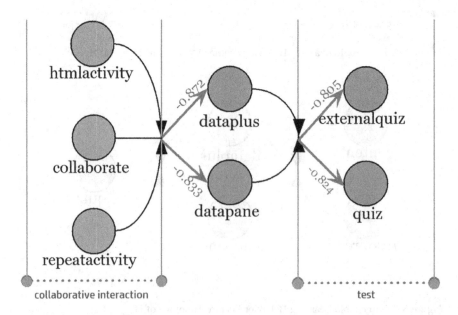

Figure 8.8 Forgettable Learning Behavior Feature Topology of $H_{3\rightarrow5}$

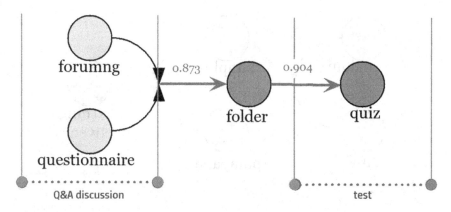

Figure 8.9 Forgettable Learning Behavior Feature Topology of $\mathbf{H}_{4\to5}$

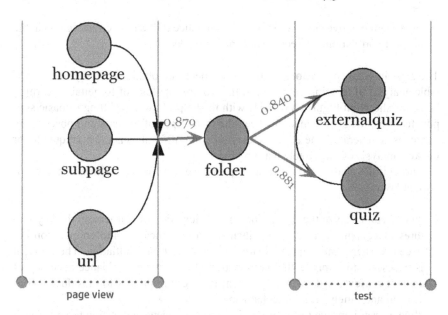

Figure 8.10 Forgettable Learning Behavior Feature Topology of $\mathbf{H}_{1\to5}$

correlation of "folder", the guidance from page view to test has a significant positive correlation.

6 Test methods will positively affect the learning effectiveness and easily produce significant forgettable learning behavior.

Based on Figure 8.1, through data analysis, it is found that the two key features "externalquiz" and "quiz" have indirect one-way strong correlation with the learning effectiveness with the help of "datapane" and "dataplus", resulting in potential forgettable data and relationships. The test method and the generated data will significantly affect the learning effectiveness and ultimately affect the learning behavior, as shown in Figure 8.11. As can be seen, test has a

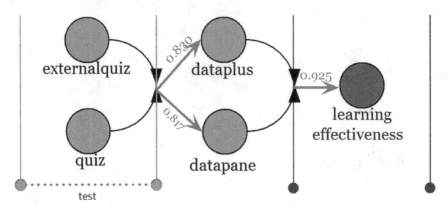

Figure 8.11 Forgettable Learning Behavior Feature Topology of $\mathbf{H}_{5 \to le}$

significant positive correlation with the guidance of learning effectiveness in the indirect correlation between "datapane" and "dataplus".

The experimental conclusions of these six aspects are obtained through the forgettable analysis of learning behavior. In the feature topology of forgettable learning behavior shown in Figures 8.6–8.11, with the help of the scheduling of basic support features, the significance between different types of features and observation variables is generated; the effective classification of features is the prerequisite for the key analysis of forgettable learning behavior.

Through the analysis of these six aspects, we can find the following three important laws:

1 "wiki" can catalyze the discussion and participation of learners on the key features of content retrieval, strengthen the communication and cooperation between learners, and improve learners' enthusiasm and initiative. Therefore, it is necessary to improve the participation efficiency and guidance accuracy of content retrieval and Q&A discussion; it is very important to introduce a convenient and timely search mechanism.
2 "folder" can improve Q&A discussion and page view, and enable the efficiency and effect of online testing. Data analysis shows that learners use "forunmg" more frequently. "folder" realizes the effective classification and display of platform resources, has a good role in resource navigation, can provide timely help for Q&A discussion and indirectly highlights the importance of Q&A discussion to quiz.
3 "datapane" and "dataplus" are data resources directly related to the learning content, which have a strong correlation with the related online test and learning effectiveness. It can better drive learners about the relevance of content retrieval and collaborative interaction to the online test method, and can achieve better learning results.

"wiki", "folder", "datapane" and "dataplus" are used as basic supporting features, and are used to significantly reveal the data and relationships of forgettable learning behavior, which improves the quality and effect of diagnostic analysis. It is of great significance to study the key problems that explicit learning behavior has no obvious differences but has obvious learning effects.

7 Discussion

The interactive learning environment provides learners with a more autonomous and personalized learning platform. With the accumulation of time, a large amount of learning behavior data has been formed. The early warning and intervention in the learning process is the key business to realize the self-feedback of the interactive learning environment (Xia, 2020b). The early warning is an intervention measure implemented at an appropriate time, so as to optimize learning behavior and improve learning effect (Koko et al., 2021). However, some of these data are explicit and some are implicit. These implicit data are also generated by learners in the learning process. The data are usually distributed in a discrete and sparse state, forming potential relationships (Mangaroska et al., 2021). Therefore, the analysis of learning behavior should not only consider the description and demonstration of explicit data but also integrate the potential impact and constraints brought by implicit data. After all, approximate explicit learning behavior does not necessarily bring approximate learning effectiveness, which shows that the forgettable learning behavior described by implicit data plays an important role.

Forgettable learning behavior might hide risks in the learning process, which is part of the key basis for the early warning strategies. Combined with the data processing, this section discusses the division of content retrieval, page view, collaborative interaction, Q&A discussion, test and key supporting features, and puts forward feasible early warning strategies.

7.1 Content Retrieval

Content retrieval often produces a large amount of participation data in the learning process. There are strong similarities in the participation tendency and enthusiasm of learners, but it is not easy to have an obvious impact on the features of other types, nor can it reflect different learning objectives, assessment needs and course nature. Obviously, it is not enough to describe learning behavior only with the explicit data of content retrieval. Through data analysis, we find that "content" and "resource" can produce a large amount of participation data, and it is also very easy to have a strong association with search engines or knowledge bases, which indirectly affects the features of other types. The formed feature topology relationship will significantly affect the learning effect.

Early warning strategy: the personalization of the relevant features of content retrieval is not obvious. Therefore, it can not only stay at the level of knowledge base. Learners need to build an adaptive association and independent recommendation mechanism between these features, realize content association with learning tasks at different stages, implement timely tracking and data analysis of learning behavior, transform the early warning strategy into content recommendation and feedback, and complete the mapping of content retrieval with relevant features such as search engine, Q&A and test, so as to realize the adaptive classification of relevant content, and form a learner-centered personalized knowledge base and interest guidance scheme.

7.2   Page View

Page view is mainly the business realized by the data page and scheduling link provided by the interactive learning environment. It is the basic organizational facility to realize online learning. The relevant features are not the direct description elements of learning behavior, but the key components to realize the association, transfer or scheduling. The data retained by page view is another description of learning behavior, or reflect the changes of learners' participation in the learning process, but in a large number of learning behavior research references, the relevant features of page view are not considered; this part is easily forgotten "learning behavior". Therefore, the full analysis of learning behavior needs to consider the calculation of these features. Through the data analysis, it is found that the three key features of page view will significantly affect the test in the associated scheduling of "folder".

Early warning strategy: the relevant features of page view are the key business of online technology supporting the learning process. At the same time, it is also different from the presentation and feedback means of traditional education mode. How to ensure that the interactive learning environment provides more convenient and effective learning support and forms benign learning behavior? The learning behavior needs to give full play to the advantages of page view such as real-time feedback and friendliness of data view. Then, it is necessary to timely collect the usage habits and participation needs for page view, adjust the relevant features, organizational structure and application mode, and improve the immersion and adaptability of the learning process.

7.3   Collaborative Interaction

Collaborative interaction is the relevant feature type in the learning process; the interactive learning environment provides technical support, collects the data traces generated in the learning process through the relevant features, and has also become a more active form of learning behavior. Such features are directly driven by learning tasks and learning contents, but the setting of existing collaborative interaction is relatively fixed. Some features do not produce data at all, and some features cannot meet the learning needs, unable to provide effective support for the learning process. Although there are many data generated, the value is not obvious, so it is easy to be forgotten. Therefore, different learning courses produce different groups and participation, and learners' awareness of this feature is also different.

Early warning strategy: the features of collaborative interaction have a strong demand for the training of online projects. Many science and engineering R&D projects are no longer completed by one learner, but are the common task of a group. Of course, some research projects in humanities and social sciences have gradually realized online modes that require collaborative interaction to provide more appropriate features to track more sufficient learning behavior data. In addition, these features have obvious correlation needs with project related data features. In the assessment contents of many courses, project has been regarded as an important part. In this way, in the tracking of the learning process, it is necessary to provide appropriate collaborative interaction features for appropriate projects, provide independent early warning mechanisms for instructors, learners and relevant data resources, timely feedback relevant needs, adjust the ways of cooperation and interaction, and even directly customize the collaborative interaction features related to tests and learning effectiveness.

7.4   Q&A Discussion

Q&A discussion is a feature type provided by the learning platform. "forumng", "questionnaire" and others are generally initiated by learners or instructors, and others feedback relevant answers. This has been actively participated by learners near the stage of assessment. In order to improve the efficiency of Q&A, it also needs timely answers from instructors or learning platforms. In fact, this aspect has not received enough attention, many questions have not been answered and some survey contents have not received the active cooperation of relevant learners or instructors. The data is incomplete or even cannot reflect the key problems, and has become extremely easy to forgettable learning behavior. In the whole learning process, the learning problems should be fed back in time through Q&A discussion, and the required answers should also be effectively replied within the tolerance time.

Early warning strategy: for the early warning of Q&A discussion, the key measure is to improve the timeliness of problem initiation and response. Data analysis shows that Q&A discussion has a strong indirect relationship with "quiz" through "folder". Therefore, Q&A discussion needs to realize the aggregation and retrieval of learning resources, design relevant intelligent prediction mechanism, analyze the potential semantic information, so as to remind the problem-related instructors and improve the completion rate and accuracy of Q&A.

7.5   Test

With the full development of online learning process, standardized online testing has become the routine setting of interactive learning environment. Data analysis shows that test will still have a strong enabling effect on learning enthusiasm and participation, and it is an important force for the above four types of features. Many types of features have a significant direct or indirect relationship with test, and test will also have an impact on the learning effectiveness. For a period before and after the test, learning enthusiasm obviously has a high degree of investment, and also has a high demand for the resources, interaction, cooperation and Q&A. The data distribution in this regard is a manifestation of learning behavior, but it is easy to become a forgettable part. Therefore, it is necessary to deploy appropriate test links for the learning process, which is directly related to the learning content and learning objectives.

Early warning strategy: test is a common means to implement early warning. The effective application of test can find the problems existing in the learning process or learning behavior. Different learning contents are distributed in different stages of the whole learning process. Different learning contents contain different knowledge. Different knowledge corresponds to different learning duration and comprehensibility, which affect the test time and content. Therefore, the early warning strategy should fully consider these factors, set targeted test methods for different courses, different knowledge and learners, and design test contents with relatively strong flexibility and relevance. In this regard, the long-term data tracking is required, and make relatively realistic decisions.

7.6   Key Support Features

In this study, five features such as "folder", "dataplus", "datapane", "wiki" and "glossary" are set as key support features that are obtained through sufficient data analysis. These features are related to other types of features, but they do not generate a large amount of participation and attention, indicating that they are more suitable as scheduling links. Through data analysis, it is found that these features have significance after they are associated with other types of features. Therefore, the data generated by these features cannot be defined as "forgettable learning behavior" because of their low participation, which will affect the results of learning behavior analysis.

Early warning strategy: when tracking the learning process, we can't ignore the correlation of these low participation features, analyze the relationship between these features and others, and mine the possible potential learning behavior, so as to give full play to the forgettable data and improve the accuracy of early warning. Therefore, the data support of early warning strategy should not ignore the relationships between different features. The resulting forgettable learning behavior should become the key basis for the early warning strategy.

8   Conclusion

The research on forgettable learning behavior is an effective way to improve the early warning of interactive learning environment, but this aspect has always been a blank in learning analytics (Valle et al., 2021b). About the massive learning behavior data, this study integrates the prediction and recommendation mechanism, and designs a diagnostic analysis framework applied to forgettable learning behavior. Therefore, the relevant test problems are proposed, and the adaptive data segmentation rules are constructed. Through sufficient comparative experiments and data analysis, the feasibility and reliability of this framework are verified. On the premise of ensuring better performance indexes, it can achieve efficient prediction and mining of forgettable learning behavior. Based on the learning behavior analysis, the topological relationships of forgettable learning behavior are visualized. The potential problems and rules of forgettable learning behavior are further discussed, and the corresponding early warning strategies are designed. The whole research process is an in-depth demonstration in the analysis of massive learning behavior, which can provide theoretical basis, comparable results and technical support for the subsequent research and application, and has strong practical significance.

In the follow-up research work, the results of this study will be further optimized. For example, the social features of learners will be introduced to make more detailed processing and correlation, so as to improve the universality and robustness of the diagnostic analysis framework, effectively improve the performance indexes and expand the results of data analysis.

References

Ameloot, E., Rotsaert, T., & Schellens, T. (2021). The supporting role of learning analytics for a blended learning environment: exploring students' perceptions and the impact on relatedness. *Journal of Computer Assisted Learning*. 38(1), 90–102. https://doi.org/10.1111/jcal.12593

Carter, M., & Egliston, B. (2021). What are the risks of virtual reality data? Learning analytics, algorithmic bias and a fantasy of perfect data. *New Media & Society*. 2021(3), 146144482110127. https://doi.org/10.1177/14614448211012794

Dietrich, J., Greiner, F., Weber-Liel, D., Berweger, B., Kmpfe, N., & Kracke, B. (2021). Does an individualized learning design improve university student online learning? A randomized field experiment. *Computers in Human Behavior*. 122(9), 106819. https://doi.org/10.1016/j.chb.2021.106819

Dolmark, T., Sohaib, O., Beydoun, G., & Wu, K. (2021). The effect of individual's technological belief and usage on their absorptive capacity towards their learning behaviour in learning environment. *Sustainability*. 13(2), 1–17. https://doi.org/10.3390/su13020718

Gan, Z., An, Z., & Liu, F. (2021). Teacher feedback practices, student feedback motivation, and feedback behavior: how are they associated with learning outcomes? *Frontiers in Psychology*. 12(6), 1–14. https://doi.org/10.3389/fpsyg.2021.697045

Geyer, P. D. (2021). Adjustment-seeking behavior: the role of political skill and self-efficacy in training students to be more actively engaged in their studies. *Active Learning in Higher Education*. 2021(6), 1–13. https://doi.org/10.1177/1469787417721993

Hasenbein, L., Stark, P., Trautwein, U., Queiroz, A. C. M., Bailenson, J., Hahn, J.-U., & Göllner, R. (2022). Learning with simulated virtual classmates: effects of social-related configurations on students' visual attention and learning experiences in an immersive virtual reality classroom. *Computers in Human Behavior*. 133(8), 107282. https://doi.org/10.1016/j.chb.2022.107282

Ikram, F., & Farooq, H. (2022). Multimedia recommendation system for video game based on high-level visual semantic features. *Scientific Programming*. 2022. https://doi.org/10.1155/2022/6084363

Koko, M., Akapnar, G., & Hasnine, M. N. (2021). Unfolding students' online assignment submission behavioral patterns using temporal learning analytics. *Educational Technology & Society*. 24(1), 223–235. https://www.researchgate.net/publication/348936534

Lee, A. (2021). Determining quality and distribution of ideas in online classroom talk using learning analytics and machine learning. *Educational Technology & Society*. 24(1), 236–249. https://www.researchgate.net/publication/348957829

Li, H., Majumdar, R., Chen, M., & Ogata, H. (2021). Goal-oriented active learning (goal) system to promote reading engagement, self-directed learning behavior, and motivation in extensive reading. *Computers & Education*. 171(2), 104239. https://doi.org/10.1016/j.compedu.2021.104239

Low, M. P., Cham, T. H., Chang, Y. S., & Lim, X. J. (2021). Advancing on weighted pls-sem in examining the trust-based recommendation system in pioneering product promotion effectiveness. *Quality & Quantity*. 2021(4), 1–30. https://doi.org/10.1007/s11135-021-01147-1

Mangaroska, K., Vesin, B., Kostakos, V., Brusilovsky, P., & Giannakos, M. (2021). Architecting analytics across multiple e-learning systems to enhance learning design. *IEEE Transactions on Learning Technologies*. 14(2), 173–188. https://doi.org/10.1109/TLT.2021.3072159

Peng, B. (2021). Research and implementation of electronic commerce intelligent recommendation system based on the fuzzy rough set and improved cellular algorithm. *Mathematical Problems in Engineering*. 2021(1), 1–8. https://doi.org/10.1155/2021/6671219

Roozbahani, Z., Rezaeenour, J., Katanforoush, A., & Bidgoly, A. J. (2021). Personalization of the collaborator recommendation system in multi-layer scientific social networks: a case study of ResearchGate. *Expert Systems*. 2021(11), 1–18. https://doi.org/10.1111/exsy.12932

Ruiz-Calleja, A., Prieto, L., Ley, T., Rodriguez-Triana, M. J., & Dennerlein, S. (2021). Learning analytics for professional and workplace learning: a literature review. *IEEE Transactions on Learning Technologies*. 14(3), 353–366. https://doi.org/10.1109/TLT.2021.3092219

Silvola, A., Nykki, P., Kaveri, A., & Muukkonen, H. (2021). Expectations for supporting student engagement with learning analytics: an academic path perspective. *Computers & Education*. 168(12), 104192. https://doi.org/10.1016/j.compedu.2021.104192

Valle, N., Antonenko, P., Valle, D., Dawson, K., & Baiser, B. (2021a). The influence of task-value scaffolding in a predictive learning analytics dashboard on learners' statistics anxiety, motivation, and performance. *Computers & Education*. 173(1), 104288. https://doi.org/10.1016/j.compedu.2021.104288

Valle, N., Antonenko, P., Dawson, K., & Huggins-Manley, A. C. (2021b). Staying on target: a systematic literature review on learner-facing learning analytics dashboards. *British Journal of Educational Technology*. 5(2), 1724–1748. https://doi.org/10.1111/bjet.13089

Xia, X. (2020a). Learning behavior mining and decision recommendation based on association rules in interactive learning environment. *Interactive Learning Environments*. 2020(8), 1–16. https://doi.org/10. 1080/10494820.2020.1799028

Xia, X. (2020b). Random field design and collaborative inference strategy for learning interaction activities. *Interactive Learning Environments*. 2020(12), 1–25. https://doi.org/10.1080/10494820.2020.1863236

Xia, X. (2021a). Interaction recognition and intervention based on context feature fusion of learning behaviors in interactive learning environments. *Interactive Learning Environments*. 2021(1), 1–19. https://doi.org/10.1080/10494820.2021.1871632

Xia, X. (2021b). Sparse learning strategy and key feature selection in interactive learning environment. *Interactive Learning Environments*. 2021(11), 1–25. https://doi.org/10.108 0/10494820.2021.1998913

Xia, X. (2021c). Decision application mechanism of regression analysis of multi-category learning behaviors in interactive learning environment. *Interactive Learning Environments*. 2021(4), 1–14. https://doi.org/10.1080/10494820.2021.1916767

Xia, X. (2022a). Diversion inference model of learning effectiveness supported by differential evolution strategy. *Computers and Education: Artificial Intelligence.* 3(1), 100071. https://doi.org/10.1016/j.caeai.2022.100071

Xia, X. (2022b). Application technology on collaborative training of interactive learning activities and tendency preference diversion. *SAGE Open.* 12(2), 1–15. https://doi.org/10.1177/21582440221093368

Xia, X., & Qi, W. (2022). Temporal tracking and early warning of multi semantic features of learning behavior. *Computers and Education: Artificial Intelligence.* 3(1), 100045. https://doi.org/10.1016/j.caeai.2021.100045

Zeeshan, Z., Ain, Q. U., Bhatti, U. A., Memon, W. H., & Shoukat, M. U. (2021). Feature-based multi-criteria recommendation system using a weighted approach with ranking correlation. *Intelligent Data Analysis.* 25(4), 1013–1029. https://doi.org/10.3233/IDA-205388

9   Conclusion

Abstract

The early warning mechanisms driven by educational big data is not only an important direction in the field of learning behavior research but also a challenge for the application of learning analysis in dynamic learning process. For the three key problems in the early warning of interactive learning "learning pattern recognition", "early warning model design" and "behavior pattern optimization", this book takes the learning behaviors as the research object, mines the continuous temporal series of interactive process, and designs seven associated early warning mechanisms for online learning behaviors and provided corresponding implementation strategies, ultimately forming a diagnostic analysis framework. The entire book can provide assistance and suggestions for the research and application of early warning mechanisms driven by educational big data, as well as corresponding models and methods for the analysis and argumentation of related issues. This is an important achievement that learning analytics and educational big data jointly serve the entire process of online learning behaviors and has important practical significance and implementation value.

Traveling with big data is an inevitable direction for educational development. Online and shared technologies promote the convenience and real-time nature of online learning processes, as well as the completeness and continuity of online learning behaviors, making it possible for educational big data-driven online learning processes. The interaction and collaboration between learners and learning platforms, learners and instructors, and instructors and learning platforms generate a massive amount of data in the online learning process. The learning behavior that integrates multidimensional elements of the learning periods and online learning process has significant dynamism, heterogeneity, complexity and uncertainty. At the same time, these data may have different structures, types, and relationships in different learning periods. There may also be potential connections and constraints between different learning periods, which can be defined as the characteristics and attributes of online learning behaviors. Mining and calculating online learning process data, analyzing and demonstrating learning behaviors, and evaluating explicit and implicit learning patterns and problems can provide a basis for dynamic tracking and early warning in the online learning process.

DOI: 10.4324/9781003484905-9

Due to the strong autonomy of learners in participating in online learning processes, as well as the constraints of evaluation criteria and requirements for learning objectives, learning behaviors will exhibit a certain degree of self-awareness, passivity and volatility within a certain temporal sequences. A continuous temporal sequence can be divided into multiple stages with transitivity and correlation. The study of the continuity of learning behaviors requires analyzing and recording the behavior patterns of different stages, identifying potential early risks of learning behaviors, facilitating learning platforms or instructors to provide early warning appropriately, implementing targeted intervention measures and optimizing the learning process, thereby improving learner assessment results.

There are multiple identification dimensions for the explicit or implicit risks in the online learning process. The usual approach includes three types: first, developing evaluation criteria for benign learning behaviors, defining each learner as a decision object and detecting problems in the temporal sequences of the online learning process. This approach is suitable for tracking the behavior of small-scale learners. The second approach is to identify the characteristics and factors that describe learning behaviors, identify problems and adjust strategies based on data distribution trends. This approach is suitable for situations where the temporal sequences of learning process are short. The third approach is to treat the learning process as a complete behavioral process, divide it into stages according to the temporal sequences, and demonstrate the influencing factors and process topology of the learning behaviors. This approach is used to analyze the stage relationships of the complete learning behaviors. These three approaches are interrelated. However, based on educational big data, dynamic temporal tracking and early warning of online learning processes need to consider the group and individual characteristics of learners, and effectively highlight the phased and temporal characteristics of the learning process with the support of massive data. To achieve the integration and supplementation of these three approaches, it is necessary to construct a self-organizing and self-adjusting strategy and early warning mechanism.

There are differences in different temporal sequences and corresponding learning behaviors in the online learning process, and there are still great opportunities and challenges to achieve educational data-driven early warning, which is extremely difficult. The existing academic achievements have not systematically conducted in-depth research on the series of models and methods related to early warning of online learning behaviors. Many literature points out the importance of early warning, but how to achieve self-organization, self-feedback, and self-decision of early warning through data technology or intelligent technology has not yet formed effective application and practical direct results.

The research content of this book will trace the online learning process, explore key factors that affect learning effectiveness, implement early warning strategies for tracking the entire learning process and predicting potential patterns, design educational big data-driven models and algorithms for the particularity and complexity of the online learning process, and construct dynamic temporal sequence tracking strategies and then achieve the early warning mechanisms at different levels of the online learning behaviors.

We have made the following three specific contributions in this book.

1 Academic Innovativeness

   This book focuses on the in-depth design and optimization of learning analytics in the context of big data for studying online learning behaviors. It primarily emphasizes early warning of risky learning behavior and adaptive interventions. The research results exhibit significant academic innovation by integrating relevant theories from natural sciences and social sciences. This integration is beneficial for improving data generation, transmission, monitoring, and feedback in online learning behavior. Therefore, the research topic holds strong practical significance.

2 Academic Perspective Innovativeness

   The research questions addressed in this book have innovative academic viewpoints. Early warning mechanisms are critical issues for achieving dynamic optimization in online learning behavior. However, there is a scarcity of systematic academic achievements globally in this area. Most existing results are based on specific cases and small samples, directly applying and locally adapting existing methods. They have not yet carried out substantial and effective implementation work to explore key learning patterns. This limits the construction, improvement and collaboration of educational big data-driven constructive learning behaviors. Hence, the research topic exhibits a proactive spirit of innovation.

3 Interdisciplinary Integration and Methodological Innovativeness

   The research content and research plan of this book aim to achieve the organic integration of multidisciplinary theories, methods, technologies, and demands. The research approach demonstrates the innovativeness of interdisciplinary thinking and research methods by coordinating diverse disciplinary concepts and ideas. This book designs and provides applicable methods, models, algorithms, and solutions. As a result, the research topic has promising prospects for practical applications and provides a theoretical foundation and application framework for improving online interactive learning environments and innovating learning models.

The highlights of this book are reflected in the following two aspects:

1 Based on a large dataset of online learning behaviors, this book aims to construct scientifically sound models, deep learning methods and predictive analysis algorithms to meet the design requirements of early warning mechanisms at different levels. From the perspective of technological innovation and methodology construction, it horizontally explores the dynamic nature, reliability, adaptability and precision of warnings and decision interventions for online learning behaviors.

2 Building upon a progressively early warning mechanisms of online learning behaviors, this book optimizes the self-tuning ability and dynamic supervisory of online learning behaviors. It vertically explores the value of early warning and

decision feedback for complete learning processes involving multiple features, relationships, structures, requirements and temporal sequences, from both theoretical deepening and practical applications.

This book aims to design and construct the early warming mechanisms based on the dynamic temporal tracking technology for online learning behaviors driven by educational big data. So we fully analyze and calculate the multidimensional features, attributes and influencing factors of the online learning process, to achieve the dynamic temporal sequence tracking technologies; we construct the early warning mechanisms, accurately capture key risk points at different levels of the online learning process, shorten the time for early warning optimization and improve the accuracy and timeliness of decision feedback.

Index

Note: **Bold** page numbers refer to tables and *italic* page numbers refer to figures.

Printed in the United States
by Baker & Taylor Publisher Services